Praise for

OPPENHEIM
TOY PORTFOLIO

If thoughts of holiday shopping have you fretting about what to buy for the little ones, help is on the way... the Oppenheim Toy Portfolio is just out... recognizing the year's best new toys.

—*USA Today*

...cuts through the confusion and offers the consumer sound information about what's good—and not so good.

—*Associated Press*

Sane comprehensive survey... absolutely worth the price.

—*Miami Herald*

Put away the aspirin, because there's a new book... that should make your toy buying decisions smart and easy.

—*Houston Post*

Definite parental appeal.

—*Booklist*

The authors of the Oppenheim Toy Portfolio have yet again answered the call of parents who are tired of guessing which are the best toys and products for children—they've published a book.

—*New York Family*

The Oppenheim Toy Portfolio tells parents which are the best and dumbest toys.

—*Business Week*

OPPENHEIM
TOY PORTFOLIO

2000 Edition

The Best Toys, Books, Videos,
Music & Software For Kids

Joanne Oppenheim
and Stephanie Oppenheim
with **James Oppenheim,** *Technology Editor*

Illustrations by **Joan Auclair**

With thanks to our family and the many other families who helped us test for the best.

—Joanne, Stephanie, & James

Designed by Joan Auclair

ISBN: 0-9664823-2-8

Contents

Introduction

Dear Readers:

It's hard to count the number of people who have asked us, **"What about the box?"** You know, "Why is it that my kid seems to like the box more than the toy?" While there is a stage when the box often holds as much interest as the toy... if this is an on-going problem, you've come to the right place!

In this seventh annual edition you'll find the results of another year's search for quality products. Given the overwhelming number of new toys, books, videos, music, and software introduced each year, it's harder than ever to know what products have real value. Few parents have the budget or time to sift through the duds and turn up those memorable products that will entertain, engage, and fit their child's developing needs. That's what we do for you.

To make **shopping quick and easy,** you will find our lists of this year's award-winning and top-rated products in the opening pages of this book. In addition to our Platinum Award Winners list, you'll find lists of outstanding products for group play, parent-child interactions, office quiet time, as well as top-rated science, educational, and gender-free products.

You'll find full descriptions of these as well as other excellent new products along with shopping information in the age-appropriate chapters of the book. As always, we've included Blue Chip classics, since we believe it would be a shame for kids to miss such products just because they weren't invented yesterday. In fact, we have compiled our **Millennium Toy List**—toys we believe will continue well into the next century.

Children's products have a short shelf life. Once again, far too many of our favorites are gone. For example, the Fisher-Price classic vacuum cleaner we all grew up with has been discontinued. (Does this signal a decline in the cleanliness of America?) In fact, over 60% of this year's book is entirely new—responding to the thousands of new choices introduced this year (6,000 new toys alone).

While we tested plenty of products that just didn't work or live up to our expectations, in the end we were delighted with the range of wonderful choices available to consumers this year.

What are the trends for 2000?

- **At the Cross-roads in Toyland.** The proliferation of high tech toys seems appropriate as we enter a new millennium. However, there is almost an equal emphasis on old-fashioned play—card games, board games, backyard games—all family centered. There are many new, but traditional games that our testers truly enjoyed. It's not an either/or situation. Kids need a mix of both types of play.

- **Danger! Will Robinson, Danger!** Inspired perhaps by the millennium, there are robots everywhere. Robot dolls for babies, robots that will bring you a cold drink, and even robots that you build that are voice activated! This year's Lego Mindstorms robots come with computers on board. For a generation of parents that grew up with Lost in Space and the Jetsons, these products provide a little delayed wish fulfillment!

- **Amazing Construction Sets.** We were thrilled with the variety of new building materials this year. The inventor of the Hoberman sphere that opens and closes has created a build-your-own-set—we had a hard time putting it down. Plastic ball runs for toddlers as well as school age kids got high marks from our testers as did Lego's Episode I Star Wars. We look forward to testing the robot kits that were not ready to test at press time. We will post the results on our website.

- **Music, Please.** There are more interesting music toys this year. We found everything from Neurosmith's high-tech Music Blocks to Boomerangs's low-tech plastic tubes that are played by whacking something (even your head). With all of the research on the importance of music to development, putting more emphasis on music is worth noting!

- **Broader Roles to Choose.** We got a kick out of Barbie in her Women's Soccer League Uniform. She's also piloting a plane this year, but it's not just Barbie who's taking a more pro-active role. American Girls dolls have clothes for karate, baseball, soccer, and gymnastics class—their ballerina days are but a memory! Nor have the boys been forgotten. We often hear from parents that it's hard to find dolls for boys. This year there are great choices—everything from huggable Groovy Boys to Corolle's anatomically correct drink-and-wet kind!

- **Swamped.** Last year's bugs have made room for reptiles, amphibians, and fish. We counted at least four fish bowl toys, board games featuring the Rainbow Fish, electronic fishing games, and lots of reptile puppets. While not all made our list, we were particularly fond of the 30th Anniversary Edition of Kermit the Frog who sings, hums, and eats an occasional fly.

- **Pleasing Puzzles.** For all age groups there are new puzzles that are graphically interesting. While there are still lots of splintery puzzles in the market place, several new collections have smoothed out the edges, so to speak.

- **The Magic Number.** Manufacturers keep finding new ways of getting down to the magic price of $19.99. On the whole, this means you'll find more choices for less, but you may also find that you need to do more assembling of the simplest toys. On the other end of the spectrum, we found more super-special high-ticket items.

- **Historic Fiction & Sports Stories for Both Genders.** In the past historic fiction was largely directed to girls and books about sports were directed to boys. This year we found more choices in both categories for both genders.

On the down side...

- **Grossness is Back.** We had commented on a kinder and gentler toyland, but get ready—grossness is making a comeback. Remember Gooie Louie, the nose-picking game? He now does this with the benefit of electronic sounds. Bubba now swims and passes gas under water. Both obviously appeal to the higher taste level of our children!

- **A Plastic Natureland.** There were an overabundant number of nature-themed toys this year—ironically, most done in plastic. Crib toys that simulate ocean waves, a babbling brook, or splashing fish (however they sound). The whole good Earth message doesn't quite ring true to us in plastic and electronic chips. Here's an idea—take your kids outside.

- **Pink Re-visited.** There's definitely a resurgence of pink in toyland—more toy kitchens, playhouses, and dollhouses are returning to gender specific color coding. Manufacturers at toy fair told us that's what their market research indicates moms want. We think it's still a chicken/egg issue. If you can't find anything but a pink or black trike, that's what you buy. We continue to applaud companies that make products that will appeal to both boys and girls (see our Gender-Free Top-Rated Products list). For a society that talks about shared parenting, nurturing, and household responsibilities, it seems that we moved beyond this type of "girls only" role play a long time ago.

- **Whistles & Bells.** It was hard not to hear and see the biggest trend of the year. Electronics have been added to almost everything from rattles with electronic music to high-tech building sets. Even classic push toys and garages now have lots of sound and there's even a key chain with a security alarm sound to open Little Tike's Cozy Coupe. While many of the sounds are novel, some are intrusive and are so literal that there is little room for "kid-inspired" sound effects.

- **For Crying Out Loud.** We think the volume level of toys has more to do with the increase of try-me packages that have to be loud enough to be heard in a busy store setting. As a result, many toys with sound didn't make it on our list—because in a home setting they were just too LOUD. We also rejected many classic baby and toddler toys that have been updated with electronic chips (even with volume control) because the quality of the music/sound was intrusive. Your best bet is to listen before you buy and remember that you're going to hear it again and again. You may be surprised that by law toys can be louder than a power drill! With the help of The League for the Hard of Hearing, a nonprofit group that has brought attention to the issue of toys and hearing loss, we continue to monitor this issue. For now, their best advice is to avoid toys that have persistent loud noise or sudden extreme bursts of noise. We have included more information in our Safety Guidelines section.

- **Dirty Toys.** We mean real dirt here. Check all toys before you give them to your kids. We were astounded by the number of toys that came out the boxes with human hair and visible smudges of dirt. Yuck!

- **Computer Consolidation.** Most children's software manufacturers have been bought this year by toy companies. As a result the same old games have been cloned for a variety of licensed-driven packages. Once the dust settles, we hope there will be a return to the creativity that once flourished in the children's software.

- **Tethered Toys.** Last year we noted the pervasiveness of remote control toys. This year, there are more products that are actually tethered. While some of these products made our Platinum Award list, this was kind of like going back a step in technology.

- **Millennium Everything.** As you can imagine there are plenty of millennium editions of games and toys. Most will be more interesting to collectors than to kids.

A little bit of both... or a Mixed Bag

- **Do You Have a License?** Even tradition-bound companies like Lego and Little Tikes have joined the licensing bandwagon with properties such as Winnie the Pooh and Star Wars. Blue's Clues has been joined by Maisy and Kipper, two new storybook players that have made their way to television and toyland. We don't take an absolutist position on licensed goods—it's important to look beneath the license to evaluate the play value. Some work and actually pull kids into important types of play, while others are really just merchandise—more souvenirs of a show rather than quality playthings. This is a trend we are watching with some concern. It would be a shame if companies that have consistently produced quality open-ended classics were consumed by character-licensed play agendas in order to compete and survive in today's "entertainment-driven" market. Kids need the building blocks for spinning their own story lines.

- **Pokemon.** This latest craze to sweep the school-age set is hard to miss. Cartoons, a full-length movie, videos, trading cards, dolls, CD, and Gameboy cartridges all play into the show's theme song "gotta get 'em all"—referring to the main objective of the game to capture all 150 Pokemon, which means "pocket monsters." While we're not giving out any awards here, we recognize that much of the Pokemon phenomenon is an age-typical social/collector's thing.

Owning a piece of the "in" toy is a way of belonging. As with all electronic games, be forewarned—you'll need to monitor the time kids spend plugged in and tuned out. As to the cards—Ka-ching! Ka-ching! Kids yen (make that dollars) to have them all—this too shall pass.

- **Age labels continue to be extremely misleading.** Once again, we continue to take issue with the misleading ages we find on many products that push the age range as broadly as possible to reach the largest audience. Small wonder that parents often bring home products that kids can't handle. Bottom line: there is nothing wrong with your child. A word of caution: toys marked "not for children under 3" signal that there are small parts. We urge you to follow this guideline, but that is just one aspect of what makes a product age-appropriate. Craft or building kits that are too complicated under-mine a child's sense of confidence. We've tried to put more realistic age guides in our reviews where we differ from the manufacturer's suggested range.

- **Books as merchandise.** We saw more movie and TV tie-ins for all age-groups. While the familiarity of the stories or characters can be a plus for reluctant readers, we were often disappointed that the quality of the books did not measure up.

- **What's in a name?** Make no assumptions. As always, we find that a company can make both gems and duds in the same year. A brand name does not guarantee that a toy will work, or that the rules will make sense, or that all the pieces will be in the package. We also found that you can't just assume that all books, videos, or software in a series will be equally good. We look at each, one by one, since series tend to be uneven.

- **Slim pickin's for your VCR.** We wonder, who's in charge of videos for kids? The "Perils of Pauline" mentality (à la a Bruce Willis action film) has been repackaged for very young children. For example, why did the animated version of "The King & I" need a sea monster to rock the boat as Anna begins her journey to Siam? In "Mighty Joe Young" the mother is shot to death (ten feet from her child) within the first five minutes of the film. And who dreamed up a Madeline story in which she is abducted, forced into a sweat shop, and threatened with having to make lace from her own hair? This goes beyond safe scare. Maybe we're over-protective, but is this the best we can do to "entertain" our kids? Our advice is to screen before you buy and have a seat next to your child—you may be surprised by what they're watching.

We're often asked why don't we write about all the products that don't work. The fact is that there isn't room. We do tend to write more negative reviews in our newsletter and on our website. In this book we want to share the good news and there is also plenty of that this year. We'd like to thank all of the families that contribute to this book.

As always, we welcome your feedback on the selections. You can write, or visit our Website: www.toyportfolio.com. For new readers, you'll find our review process and criteria for our award program below.

Happy playing!

Joanne Stephanie Amy

How We Select the Best

We shop for children year-round—only we get to do what most parents wish they could do before they buy. We open the toys, run the videos, read the books, play the music, and boot up the software. We get to compare all the toys that may look remarkably similar but often turn out to be quite different. For example, we put the toy trains together and find out which ones don't stay on the tracks.

How We're Different

The Oppenheim Toy Portfolio was founded in 1989 as the only independent consumer review of children's media. Unlike most other groups that rate products, we do not charge entry fees or accept ads from manufacturers. When you see our award seals on products, you can be assured that they are "award-winning" because they were selected by a noted expert in child development, children's literature, and education, and then rated by the most objective panel of judges—kids.

The Real Experts Speak: Kids and Their Families

To get a meaningful sampling, we deal with families from all walks of life. We have testers in the city and in the country, in diapers and in blue jeans, in school clothes and in tutus. They have parents who are teachers, secretaries, lawyers, doctors, writers, engineers, doormen, software programmers, editors, psychologists, librarians, engineers, business people, architects, family therapists, musicians, artists, nurses, and early childhood educators. In some instances we have tested products in preschool and after-school settings where we can get feedback from groups of children. Since all new products tend to have novelty appeal, we ask our testers to live with a product for a while before assessing it. Among other things, we always ask—would you recommend it to others?

Criteria We Use for Choosing Quality Products

• What is this product designed to do and how well does it do it?

• What can the child do with the product? Does it invite

active doing and thinking or simply passive watching?

- Is it safe and well-designed, and can it withstand the unexpected?

- Does it "fit" the developmental needs, interests, and typical skills of the children for whom it was designed?

- What message does it convey? Toys as well as books and videos can say a great deal about values parents are trying to convey. For example, does the product reflect old sexual stereotypes that limit children's views of themselves and others?

- What will a child learn from this product? Is it a "smart" product that will engage the child's mind or simply a novelty with limited play value?

- Is it entertaining? No product makes our list if kids find it boring, no matter how "good" or "educational" it claims to be.

- Is the age label correct? Is the product so easy that it will be boring or so challenging that it will be frustrating?

Rating System

Outstanding products, selected by our testers, are awarded one of four honors:

Oppenheim Toy Portfolio Platinum Award— These represent the most innovative, engaging new products of the year. See the 2000 Platinum Award List.

Oppenheim Toy Portfolio Gold Seal Award— Given to outstanding new products that enhance the lives of children. All products selected for this book have received a Gold Seal Award unless they are marked "Mixed Emotions." Those products that receive a Gold Seal during the year are nominated for the year-end top Platinum Award List.

Oppenheim Toy Portfolio Blue Chip Classic Award—Reserved for classic products that should not be missed just because they weren't invented yesterday.

Oppenheim Toy Portfolio SNAP Award—Our Special Needs Adaptable Product Award is given to products that can be used by or easily adapted for children with special needs. All products reviewed in that chapter are recommended; the most outstanding are SNAP Award winners.

Using This Book

Each section begins with a play profile that tells you what to expect during each developmental stage and what "basic gear" will enhance learning and play. We also give you suggestions for best gifts for your budget and, perhaps most importantly, a stage-by-stage list of toys to avoid.

Because we know how busy people are these days, our reviews are purposely short and provide information on how to get your hands on the product.

A word about prices: Our award-winning products are not all high-ticket items. We have selected the very best products in toy supermarkets, as well as those that you will find in specialty stores, museum shops, and quality catalogs. We have listed the suggested retail prices, but they will vary tremendously depending on where you shop.

Telephone numbers: Where available, we have given a customer service number in case you have difficulty locating the product in your area. For some educational products, you'll find a catalog number for ordering.

Child's Play—More Than Fun!

For children, playing is more than a fun way to fill the day. It's through play that children learn and develop all sorts of important physical, intellectual, and social skills. Like musicians, children use well-chosen toys, books, and music to orchestrate their play. As they grow and develop, so does their need for more complex playthings that challenge and enhance their learning. Toys and stories with the right developmental fit help create a marvelous harmony for learning and fun. **The Oppenheim Toy Portfolio** is a resource book you can use to make that kind of mix.

OPPENHEIM TOY PORTFOLIO PLATINUM TOY AWARDS 2000

INFANTS

Baby Bed Bugs Mobile (North American Bear) *p. 3*

Kick Start Gym (Playskool) *p. 8*

Tolo Gramophone Music Box (Small World) *p. 9*

Rainbow Sports Balls (Gund) *p. 22*

Earlyears Soft Busy Blocks (International Playthings) *p. 15*

TODDLERS

Ambi Teddy Copter* (Learning Curve)/**Little People Adventure Airlines*** (Fisher-Price) *p. 51*

Music Blocks (Neurosmith) *p. 59*

Bigger Family Shuttle Bus Ride-On (Step 2) *p. 35*

Tomy Ball Party Connecting Bridge (International Playthings) *p. 43*

Groovy Boys (Manhattan Toy) *p. 49*

Animal Stackables (Little Tikes) *p. 46*

PRESCHOOLERS

Pretend & Play Teaching Telephone (Learning Resources) *p. 71*

School Bus* (Play-hut)/**My Playhouse*** (Alex) *p. 70, 101*

Duplo Brick Mixer (LEGO Systems) *p. 85*

Walk'n'Wag Baby Pluto* (Mattel)/**Magic Talking Kermit*** (Fisher-Price) *p. 74, 75*

Sonny the Seal (Milton Bradley) *p. 86*

Crayola Magic Modeling Critter Kit (Crayola) *p. 106*

*indicates a tie in the category

OPPENHEIM TOY PORTFOLIO PLATINUM TOY AWARDS 2000

EARLY SCHOOL YEARS

Construction/Vehicles

Expandagon Hoberman Kit (Hoberman) *p. 122*

Naboo Fighter (LEGO Systems) *p. 123*

Oogly Googly Motorized Gear Set (Learning Resources) *p. 153*

X-V Racers Scorcher Chamber Stunt Set (Mattel) *p. 118*

All Terrain Trekker (K'nex) *p. 124*

Crafts

Stone Sculpture Clock (Curiosity Kits) *p. 143*

Musical Jewelry Box Activity Kit (Alex) *p. 141*

Hand Painted Ceramic Treat Jar (Creativity for Kids) *p. 137*

Dolls

Madeline Doll & Dollcase (Eden) *p. 157*

Soccer Barbie* (Mattel)/**American Girls Sports Collection*** (Pleasant Co.) *p. 116*

Games

I Scream (Moran) *p. 128*

Ice Blocks (Gamewright) *p. 126*

Millennium Monopoly (Hasbro) *p. 126*

Laser Tennis (Tiger) *p. 126*

Equipment

Polaroid Cameras (Polaroid) *p. 157*

Air Cushion Hockey (Hedstrom) *p. 148*

Build-a-Bank (Magnif) *p. 152*

*indicates a tie in a category

OPPENHEIM TOY PORTFOLIO PLATINUM BOOK AWARDS 2000

INFANTS AND TODDLERS

Baby Story (Chimeric) *p. 162*

Peek-A-Boo Baby (Bolam, Price, Stern, Sloan) *p. 161*

Knock at the Door (Chorao, Dutton) *p. 163*

Guess Who's On the Farm (Russell, Candlewick) *p. 164*

Arnold (Inkpen, Harcourt Brace) *p. 164*

Five Little Kittens (Jewell/Sayles, Clarion) *p. 166*

Sleepytime Rhyme (Charlip, Greenwillow) *p. 168*

PRESCHOOLERS

The Best Place (Meddaugh, Houghton Mifflin) *p. 170*

Copy Me, Copycub (Edwards/Winter, HarperCollins) *p. 173*

Don't Make Me Laugh (Stevenson, Farrar, Straus) *p. 171*

Leola and the Honeybears (Rosales, Scholastic) *p. 171*

Look-Alikes Jr. (Steiner, Little Brown) *p. 174*

Snow Bear (George/Minor, Hyperion) *p. 171*

The Very Clumsy Click Beetle (Carle, Philomel) *p. 176*

What! Cried Granny (Lum/Johnson, Dial) *p. 173*

EARLY SCHOOL YEARS

Harry Potter series (Rowling, Scholastic) *p. 196*

Hitty, Her First Hundred Years (Field/Wells/Jeffers, Simon & Schuster) *p. 177*

Koi and the Kola Nuts (Aardema/Cepeda, Atheneum) *p. 181*

Horace and Morris but Mostly Dolores (Howe/Walrod, Atheneum) *p. 180*

Swine Lake (Marshall/Sendak, HarperCollins) *p. 178*

OPPENHEIM TOY PORTFOLIO PLATINUM BOOK AWARDS 2000

historic fiction

Amelia and Eleanor Go for a Ride (Ryan/Selznick, Scholastic) *p. 187*

If a Bus Could Talk (Ringgold, Simon & Schuster) *p. 188*

Rushmore (Curlee, Scholastic) *p. 188*

Tea with Milk (Say, Houghton Mifflin) *p. 179*

non-fiction

Bedtime! (Swain/Smith, Holiday) *p. 187*

The Emperor's Egg (Jenkins/Chapman, Candlewick) *p. 184*

Ice Bear and Little Fox (London/San Souci, Dutton) *p. 185*

How Are You Peeling? (Freymann/Elffers, Scholastic) *p. 199*

OPPENHEIM TOY PORTFOLIO PLATINUM VIDEO AWARDS 2000

PRESCHOOLERS

Blue's Clues Rhythm and Blue (Paramount) *p. 216*

Count with Maisy (Universal) *p. 220*

Kipper (Hallmark) *p. 220*

Little Bear Summertime Tales (Paramount) *p. 221*

Madeline at the Ballet (Sony) *p. 221*

EARLY SCHOOL YEARS

Air Bud Golden Receiver (Disney) *p. 226*

Behind the Scenes series (First Run Features) *p. 219, p. 231*

Charlotte's Web (Paramount) *p. 226*

Franklin Goes to School (Polygram) *p. 235*

The Making of Zoom (WGBH) *p. 234*

Math Curse (Reading Rainbow/GPN) *p. 233*

Mulan (Disney) *p. 228*

OPPENHEIM TOY PORTFOLIO PLATINUM AUDIO AWARDS 2000

Sweet Dreams of Home (Magnolia Music/Lyric Partners) p. 244

Color Me Singing (Susan Salidor) p. 243

On the Good Ship Lollipop (Music for Little People) p. 244

Singin' In the Bathtub (Sony) p. 244

My Front Porch (David Alpert, D&A Records) p. 245

Never Grow Up (Flying Fish/Rounder Records) p. 246

Really Rosie (Sony) p. 249

The Power of Classical Music (Twin Sisters) p. 250

Tarzan Read & Sing Along (Disney) p. 254

Love from Your Friend, Hannah (Listening Library) p. 254

OPPENHEIM TOY PORTFOLIO PLATINUM SOFTWARE AWARDS 2000

Encarta Africana (Microsoft) p. 268

JamCam 2 (K B Gear) p. 275

IntelPlay QX3 Digital Microscope (Mattel) p. 265

Pokemon Pinball (Nintendo) p. 280

Magic Artist 2 (Disney) p. 274

Lego Mindstorms Droid Developer Kit (LEGO Systems) p. 261

Roller Coaster Tycoon (Hasbro) p. 270

Due to the late release dates of children's software, the complete Oppenheim Toy Portfolio Platinum Software Awards 2000 List will be posted on our website, www.toyportfolio.com.

OPPENHEIM TOY PORTFOLIO SPECIAL NEEDS ADAPTABLE PRODUCT AWARDS 2000

MILLENNIUM TOY LIST

WHAT TOYS DO YOU REMEMBER BEST? Are they still around? What toys will kids still be playing with in the 21st century? We have chosen some of the best known and best loved toys. These are toys kids have played with in the 20th century and that we think will keep on going well into the 21st century. Did we miss your favorite? Let us know (www.toyportfolio.com); we'll be updating the list throughout the year.

Barbie	Lincoln Logs
Candyland	Play-Doh
Corn Popper	Radio Flyer Red Wagon
Crayolas	
Frisbee	Scrabble
G.I. Joe	Slinky
Hula Hoops	Teddy Bear
Legos	Tonka Trucks
Lite Brite	Wooden Blocks
Matchbox & Hot Wheels	Wooden & Electric Trains
Monopoly	Yo-Yo

TOP-RATED GROUP TOYS 2000

Kids are by nature social beings, and enjoy few things more than being with other kids. Still, learning to share and play together can be rough going. We kept an eye out this year for toys that work especially well with groups of kids. For kids who are still at the "it's mine" stage, the key is to find toys with enough multiple pieces to go around. We also looked for products that lend themselves to cooperative play—whether it's a board game or activity kit that more than one child can enjoy together or simply side by side. We often talk these days about interactive toys, but here are some wonderful products for interactive kids.

Barnyard Boogie Woogie Game
  (International Playthings) *p. 87*

Boomwhackers Tuned Percussion Tubes
  (Whacky Music) *p. 255*

Classic Lego Bucket (LEGO Systems) *p. 112*

I Scream (M.J. Moran) *p. 128*

Crayola Magic Modeling Critter Kit (Crayola) *p. 106*

Puppet Stages (Alex/Creative Ed. of Canada) *p. 78, 113*

Rokenbok Expandable RC Building System
  (Rokenbok) *p. 118*

School Bus (Play-hut) *p. 70*

Sonny the Seal (Milton Bradley) *p. 86*

Unit Wooden Blocks (Various makers) *p. 83*

Whether your kids are getting top grades or the other kind, there are playful ways you can help. Here are some of our highlighted favorites that give school skills a boost without having to break out the flashcards.

Alphabet & Phonics

Phonics Writing Desk (Leap Frog) *p. 135*
Alphapatterns Puzzle (Small World) *p. 90*

Storytelling & Language

Three Pigs Puzzle (Small World) *p. 90*
FELTKids Playhouse Playmat (Learning Curve) *p. 78*
Illustory Kit (Chimeric) *p. 138*
Easel & art supplies *p. 137*
Puppet & puppet stages *p. 76, 113*

Prewriting/Fine Motor Skills

Lacing & Tracing Dinosaurs (Lauri) *p. 90*
Lacing Animals (Alex) *p. 144*
Lite Brite Star Wars (Hasbro) *p. 125*
Peg Bead Kits (Hama/Perler) *p. 143*
Sewing Kits (Quincrafts, Curiosity Kits) *p. 144*
Duplo & Lego (LEGO Systems) *p. 44–45, 85, 115, 122–23*

Math Skills

Peppino the Clown (Ravensburger) *p. 129*
Pie in the Sky (Learning Resources) *p. 129*
Rhombo Continuo (U.S. Games) *p. 129*
Twist & Shout Addition (Leap Frog) *p. 131*
Unifix Cubes (Didax) *p. 130*
Unit Wooden Blocks (Various makers) *p. 83*

TOP-RATED OFFICE TOYS 2000

Whether your office is in a complex or in a corner of your home, when kids come to visit, having a few quiet toys can make the time more enjoyable for everyone. Besides a pack of crayons and paper, here are some top choices:

Toddlers and Preschoolers

Duplo School Bus (LEGO Systems) *p. 45*

Home Sweet Home Doll House (Fisher-Price) *p. 57*

Magna Doodle (Fisher-Price) *p. 103*

Mr. Potato Head Silly Suitcase (Playskool) *p. 109*

Early School Years

Block-N-Roll (Taurus) *p. 121*

Classic Lego Bucket (LEGO Systems) *p. 112*

Crayola White Board Drawing Set (Crayola) *p. 156*

Electronic Hand-Held Yahtzee (Milton Bradley) *p. 156*

Expandagon Hoberman Kit (Hoberman) *p. 122*

Flip-Top Doodler (Fisher-Price) *p. 156*

Gameboy Pokemon Pinball (Nintendo) *p. 280*

Markers to Go (Alex) *p. 157*

Railroad Rush Hour (Binary Arts) *p. 134*

Gears Set (Learning Resources) *p. 153*

Tape Player with volume lock & headphones *p. 256*

While it's important for kids to know how to play independently, games and cooperative projects provide the raw materials for interactions that can be rewarding for adult and child. Without taking over, adults can help kids get started and be there as "consultants," giving kids strategies for working in an orderly fashion. Making time to do such things together gives you a chance to play and experiment together—a chance to solve problems, think creatively, and even have fun learning together.

Here are some of our favorites:

Hand Painted Ceramic Treat Jar
   (Creativity for Kids) *p. 137*

Hanging Bird Feeder & Birdhouse Kits
   (TWC of America) *p. 153*

Lego Mission System Control (LEGO Systems) *p. 123*

Puppets & Puppet Stage (various makers) *p. 76, 113*

Rokenbok Expandable RC Building System
   (Rokenbok) *p. 118*

Rolit (Pressman) *p. 127*

Soap Scapes (Curiosity Kits) *p. 142*

Stick Around (Great American Trading Co.) *p. 127*

Wild Rumpus Card Game (Briarpatch) *p. 129*

Yummy Chocolates (Curiosity Kits) *p. 142*

TOP-RATED GENDER FREE PRODUCTS **2000**

Many of the toys, books, and videos you bring home may have a built-in Gender Agenda™—products that reinforce stereotypes and shape your child's self-image. It often begins innocently in the nursery with pastel color coding, but quickly moves on to a glut of products with themes of hairplay for girls and gunplay for boys. The gender issue is not just one that is important to girls. The overly aggressive and violent-themed toys and video games directed at boys are even more alarming to us than the dating games or lavendar blocks that come with blueprints for a shopping mall.

Can you avoid all gender-specific toys? Probably not. These are often the products kids want the most, not only because they are heavily promoted on TV, but also because children tend to sort the world out in the simple and absolute terms of right or wrong, hard or easy, boy or girl. There are, however, positive choices you can make—where a gender-free product will work for both boys and girls... and products that break gender stereotypes.

Mummy Puzzle (Frank Schaffer) *p. 134*

Community Worker Costumes (Small World) *p. 113*

Red Tricycle (Radio Flyer) *p. 99*

Guitar (Woodstock Percussion) *p. 148*

Paint the Wild Kits (Balitono) *p. 138*

Koosh Loop Darts (OddzOn) *p. 149*

Soccer Barbie (Mattel) *p. 116*

StudioDesign Art Desk
(Little Tikes) *p. 104*

Polaroid Cameras (Polaroid) *p. 157*

BEST BATTERY-OPERATED TOYS 2000

Every year we test dozens of toys that run on batteries. Some lose their interest before the batteries run out. That's why battery toys often get a bad rap. In looking at our Platinum and Gold winners over the years, however, we realized that a surprising number of vehicles and building toys as well as music and learning game machines run on batteries. Many of the best are variations of classics—with the added bells and whistles that batteries can provide. For kids with special needs, the lights, sounds, and motion of such toys are a plus that provides sensory feedback and greater independence.

Infants, Toddlers, & Preschoolers

Kick Start Gym (Playskool) *p. 8*

Magic Talking Kermit the Frog (Fisher-Price) *p. 75*

Music Blocks (Neurosmith) *p. 59*

Little People Fun Sounds Garage (Fisher-Price) *p. 57*

Pretend & Play Teaching Telephone
  (Learning Resources) *p. 71*

Walk 'n' Wag Baby Pluto (Mattel) *p. 74*

RadioGo Race Car (Little Tikes) *p. 79*

Sonny the Seal (Milton Bradley) *p. 86*

Barney Song Magic Bongos (Playskool) *p. 106*

Early School Years

Phonics Writing Desk (Leapfrog) *p. 135*

Laser Tennis (Tiger) *p. 126*

Air Cushion Hockey (Hedstrom) *p. 148*

Tyco RC Hot Rocker (Mattel) *p. 119*

X-V Racers Scorcher Chamber Stunt Set (Mattel) *p. 118*

Polaroid Cameras (Polaroid) *p. 157*

Rokenbok Expandable RC Building System
  (Rokenbok) *p. 118*

TOP-RATED MAKE-A-GIFT-TO-GIVE LIST *2000*

Teaching kids to give, not just get, can be fun with any one
of these craft kits. These are just a few of our newest
favorite kits that make finished product kids can give with
pride to family, friends, or teachers.

TOP RATED SCIENCE PRODUCTS *2000*

One of the best ways to excite kids about science is to make it a hands-on experience. Here are our favorite picks of this year's top science toys. Many require some adult involvement—providing a chance to make discoveries together. Be sure to check our science books, videos, and software recommendations.

TOP RATED TOYS: $20 OR UNDER 2000

These are just a few of the many items for $20 or under that will make a big hit for birthday parties or a "just because" gift.

Infants and Toddlers

Earlyears Soft Busy Blocks (International Playthings) *p. 15*

Scoop, Pour 'n' Squirt Water Fish (Sassy) *p. 23*

Little People School Bus (Fisher-Price) *p. 52*

Animal Stackables (Little Tikes) *p. 46*

Tolo Activity Cube (Small World) *p. 14*

Preschoolers and Early School Years

Madeline Hand Puppet (Eden) *p. 77*

Construction Helmet (Small World) *p. 69*

Sea Plane Hauler (Nylint) *p. 79*

Les Minis Calins (Corolle) *p. 72*

Sonny the Seal (Milton Bradley) *p. 86*

Animal Match Puzzles (Lauri) *p. 89*

Construction Truck & Hat (Little Tikes) *p. 79*

Tug Boat Craft Kit (Creativity for Kids) *p. 104*

BIG TICKET ITEMS 2000

While we don't think you need to break the bank to find great gifts, we are often asked what big items are worth the extra investment. Sometimes having the whole family chip in to buy one special big item is better than bringing home lots of smaller items.

Deluxe Gymini 3D Activity Gym (Tiny Loves) *p. 8*

Music Blocks (Neurosmith) *p. 59*

Kitchen (various makers) *p. 55, 71*

Wooden Unit Blocks, Train Set, & Accessories (see Preschool Chapter) *p. 80–84*

Desks (Learning Curve/Little Tikes) *p. 104*

Puppet Theater (Alex) *p. 78*

Trap Set or Guitar (Woodstock Percussion) *p. 148*

Air Cushion Hockey (Hedstrom) *p. 148*

Muffy VanderBear Trunk (North American Bear Co.) *p. 117*

American Girl Collection (The Pleasant Company) *p. 116*

Chaos (Chaos) *p. 123*

Lego Mindstorms (Lego) *p. 260*

Rokenbok Expandable RC Building System (Rokenbok) *p. 118*

I • Toys

1 • Infants
Birth to One Year

What to Expect Developmentally

The Horizontal Infant
Learning Through the Senses. Right from the start, babies begin learning by looking, listening, touching, smelling, and tasting. It's through their senses that they make sense of the world. In this first remarkable year, babies progress from gazing to grasping, from touching to tossing, from watching to doing. By selecting a rich variety of playthings, parents can match their baby's sensory learning style.

Reaching Out. Initially, you will be the one to activate the mobile, shake the rattle, squeeze the squeaker. But before long, baby will be reaching out and taking hold of things and engaging you in a game of peek-a-boo.

Toys and Development. As babies develop, so do their needs for playthings that fit their growing abilities. Like clothes, good toys need to fit. Some of the toys for newborns will have short-term use and then get packed away or passed along to a new cousin or friend. Others will be used in new ways as your child grows. During this first year, babies need toys to gaze at, listen to, grasp, chomp on, shake, pass from one hand to another, bang together, toss, chase, and hug.

Time was when infants' rooms and products were all pastel. Not any more—research has shown that during the early weeks of life babies respond to the sharp contrast of black-and-white patterns. But does that mean your whole nursery needs to be black and white? Not at all. In no time, your baby is going to be responding to bright colors, interesting sounds, and motion.

Your Role in Play. To your newborn, no toy in the world is more interesting than you! Babies are more interested in people than things. Your smiling face, your gentle touch, the sound of your voice, even your familiar scent make you the most perfect plaything. Don't worry about spoiling your newborn with attention. Responding to your baby's needs now will make him less needy later. Playing with your baby is not just fun—it's one of the most important ways babies learn about themselves and the world of people and things!

BASIC GEAR CHECKLIST
FOR THE HORIZONTAL INFANT

✓Mobile
✓Musical toys
✓Crib mirror
✓Soft fabric toys with differing sounds and textures
✓Fabric dolls or animals with easy-to-grab limbs
✓Activity mat

Toys to Avoid

These toys pose choking and/or suffocation hazards:

✓Antique rattles
✓Foam toys
✓Toys with elastic
✓Toys with buttons, bells, and ribbons
✓Old wooden toys that may contain lead paint
✓Furry plush dolls that shed
✓Any toys with small parts

Crib Toys
Mobiles, Musical Toys, and Mirrors

Mobiles

A mobile attached to crib rail or changing table provides baby with fascinating sights and sounds. During the first three months, infants can focus only on objects that are relatively close. Toys should be between 8" and 14" from their eyes. Before you buy any mobile, look at it from the baby's perspective. What can you see? Many attractive mobiles are purely for decoration and do not have images that face the baby in the crib. Reject mobiles that are so pale and bland that there is nothing for the baby to see except the motion. Here are our favorites:

■ Baby Bed Bugs Mobile *2000*
PLATINUM AWARD

(North American Bear $54) Bugs are big in toyland and cribland. These cheerful bugs move to "Feelin' Groovy." Also recommended, **Flatso Farm Mobile,** friendly farm animals dangling from a red barn. Plays "Farmer in the Dell." (800) 682-3427.

■ Sensational Circus Musical Mobile

(Manhattan Toy $40) Baby can watch these bright eye-grabbers as they spin. Newest from an appealing series of mobiles with different themes. Also recommended, **Merry Meadows** (PLATINUM AWARD '98) or the **Enchanted Garden Mobile.** Designed from the horizontal baby's perspective with faces smiling down at baby. All play Brahms' "Lullabye." (800) 747-2454.

> **ACTIVITY TIP: Sing, Sing a Song!** Okay, it doesn't matter if you sing off key or you don't know all the words. To your baby, you deserve a Grammy! Singing can soothe a fussy baby.

■ Sesame Street Musical Mobile

(Fisher-Price $24.99) This is the only mass market mobile we found with the characters looking down at your baby. Plays "Sunny Day." (888) 892-6123.

■ Wimmer-Ferguson Infant Stim-Mobile BLUE CHIP

(Manhattan Toy $20) Newborns will be fascinated with the black-and-white, high-contrast patterns of the ten vinyl 3" discs and squares that dance and dangle on this nonmusical mobile for the crib or changing table. May not look as cute as other mobiles, but babies do react to the visual stimulation of this early crib toy. (800) 747-2454.

🖝 **SAFETY TIP:** Mobiles should be removed by the time baby is five months, or whenever baby can reach out and touch them, to avoid the danger of strangulation or choking on small parts.

■ Enchanted Garden Mini-Mobile 2000

(Manhattan Toy $20) Technically, this fabric sunflower with brightly-colored bugs and safe stitched features is not a mobile. Velcro straps attach it to crib rail or bassinet. A good toy for early gazing and reaching out. Also top-rated, **Enchanted Garden Sunflower Pull Musical** ($20) with a perky bug that inches up the long green sunflower stem to the tune of "Beautiful Dreamer." PLATINUM AWARD '97. (800) 747-2454.

Musical Toys

Few toys are as soothing to newborns as a music box with its quiet sounds. Many musical toys for infants come inside of fabric dolls. We prefer some of the newer pull-down musical toys to the fabric dolls with hard metal wind-up keys that older babies may chew or get poked with by accident. When baby starts turning over, use musical wind-up key dolls with supervision, not as crib toys.

■ Action Musical Peter Rabbit ★2000★

(Eden $23) There are a lot of Peter Rabbit products for babies. This cheery 10" velour version of Peter moves his head as the music plays. We still recommend the BLUE CHIP **Peter Rabbit Musical Pillow** (Eden $20), an 8" embroidered pillow that ties onto a newborn's bassinet, crib, or stroller. A small comforting take-along for trips away from home. (800) 443-4275.

■ Flatso Farm Musical Pulldown

(North American Bear $36) Framed in a soft red barn, sheep, duck, and cow watch a wiggly piglet ride up to the tune of "Old MacDonald." PLATINUM AWARD '99. Bring home with soft velour **Flatso Rattles** ($10), with eye-catching patterned bodies and gentle sounds. This company's PLATINUM AWARD-winning **Crib Notes Watering Can** ($36), with a friendly spider hanging down from the green and pink velour watering can, plays "Eensy Weensy Spider." (800) 682-3427.

■ Playtime Butterfly Spinning Musical ★2000★

(The First Years $15.99) An innovative musical, the colorful butterfly with scrunchy wings is mounted on a fabric wheel that turns slowly as it plays. This ties onto crib rail where baby can eventually reach out and touch. Also charming, **Home Sweet Home** ($9.98), a small pull-down yellow bird flies up to its little house, playing "Yellow Bird." Ties on crib or carriage. Two great finds! (800) 533-6708.

■ Slumbertime Soother

(Fisher-Price $34.99) Everyone's been there—the baby is almost asleep but the music has stopped. If you walk into the room to turn it back on, you start the whole process over again. To the rescue—an innovative remote-controlled musical toy that can be restarted from 20 feet. Has lights that change with the music, or nature sounds. Plays

10 lullabies that can be adjusted for volume (a plus). Takes 4 C and 2 AA batteries. PLATINUM AWARD '99. Also, **Lights'n'Sound Aquarium** looked promising but was not available for testing. (800) 432-5437.

■ **Tolo Musical Activity T.V.** *2000*

(Small World $20) You can attach this musical toy to crib rails and use it later on as a take along musical. Totally low tech, this music box with a handle plays "It's a Small, Small World" as bunnies and bear pictures scroll slowly on the "tv" screen. Tots can wind the knob, spin a roller or beep a button. (800) 421-4153.

ACTIVITY TIP: Some new parents feel awkward about speaking to a baby who can't yet talk. What can you talk about? Anything. The words aren't important. Talk about what you are doing. Imitate baby's coos & gurgles. For starters you'll do most of the talking . . . but soon baby will answer with gurgles and goos. Be sure to pause so baby can take turns—before long you'll be having real "chats."

Crib Mirrors

Even before he can reach out and touch, a crib mirror provides your baby ever-changing images. It will be a while before baby knows whose face and hands he sees. In time, he'll be babbling to that face and studying the reflection of his hands. Our favorite BLUE CHIP winner is **Wimmer-Ferguson Double-Feature Crib Mirror** (Manhattan Toy $34) because it has a truly distortion-free safety mirror. Comes with mirror on one side and high-contrast graphics on the other side; the latter will be of greatest interest to younger babies. The mirror ties at all four corners, so it can't be used as a lift-and-bang toy like many other crib mirrors. (800) 747-2454. Also top-rated, **Glow-in-the-Dark Crib Mirror** (Infantino $15). Framed in soft fabric with glow-in-the-dark designs, this 10" x 14" infant-safe mirror is also distortion-free and ties on to the crib rail. (800) 365-8182.

> **☞ SAFETY TIP:** Many catalogs and picturebooks show baby cribs overflowing with quilts, pillows, and toys. These are pretty to look at, but totally unsafe!

> **ACTIVITY TIP:** Here's a little baby science lesson. Hold your hand up in the air in baby's sight line, saying: "Everything that goes up comes down, down, down!" (Slowly spiral your hand down, down, down 'til you gently tickle baby under the chin or on the tummy.) Before long baby will anticipate the tickles, and giggle before your fingers touch!

Equipment for Playtime

Babies are such social beings that they are happiest when they are in the midst of the action. While many of these products have a short lifespan, they serve an important function by providing a special place for viewing the world.

■ Funtime Soft Bouncer Seat BLUE CHIP

(Summer Infant $50) This fabric chair provides the perfect perspective for young infants who are ready for a little elevation but are not able to sit up. Comes with spinning toys on a bar that baby will first gaze at and later activate. Use with adult supervision only. Up to 25 pounds. (800) 268-6237.

> 📝 **SAFETY TIP:** Never place any type of baby carrier on a table, bed, or counter. Even though the baby has never done it before, there's no way of predicting when he will make a move that can tip the carrier.

Playmats

Avoid playmats with lots of doodads that may pose a choking hazard. We found that many of the most expensive mats had more ribbons, buttons, and fuzzy trims. Avoid mats with activities all over with no really comfortable place for baby to lie down.

■ Deluxe Gymini 3-D Activity Gym BLUE CHIP

(Tiny Loves $39.95–$50) This play mat remains our favorite with two arches and dangly toys baby can gaze and eventually bat at. It gets high marks for keeping baby entertained. We prefer this design to the classic plastic activity gyms. Available in high-contrast black, white, and red version. Not for babies who are beginning to pull themselves up. Deluxe version is slightly larger. (800) 843-6292.

■ Enchanted Garden Playmat 2000

(Manhattan Toy $60) This new colorful mat is also a good choice with a "bumper" ring to define baby's play space. There's a flower mirror, a sunflower that turns with a ratchet sound, a textured caterpillar to feel, a peek-a-boo ladybug, and a teether that tucks away. These sensory items make for an interesting environment even before baby has much mobility. (800) 747-2454.

■ Kick Start Gym 2000 PLATINUM AWARD

(Playskool $34.99) We usually don't like plastic activity gyms because they are typically tippable. This innovative gym is more stable than most but, as with all play equipment, should be used with supervision. Here, baby can activate music, sounds, and motion with a swipe of a hand at the dangling toys above or by kicking the foot pad. Accidental hits will do for starters. If the sound startles baby, turn it off. Spinners above will still be activated. Takes 3 AA batteries. (800) 752-9755.

> 👉 **SAFETY TIP:** Many parents find the back-and-forth action of a swing a soothing diversion for a restless infant. However, we find it difficult to recommend any infant swings because they can entrap limbs and necks or even collapse. If you choose to use one, we urge you not to leave the room. Use it with constant supervision.

First Lap and Floor Toys: Rattles, Sound Toys, and More

Infant toys can help adults engage and interact with newborns. A bright rattle that baby tracks visually, a quiet music box that soothes, or an interesting doll to gaze or swipe at are ideal for getting-acquainted games. These toys can be used at the changing table or for lap games during playful moments after a feeding, before a bath, or whenever.

■ Lamaze First Mirror

(Learning Curve $19.99) A fabric-covered wedge with a mirror for baby to peer into, covered in eye-grabbing bold black & white patterns with red piping. The mirror in a soft fabric frame can be removed and used separately. PLATINUM AWARD '98. (800) 704-8697.

■ Tolo Gramophone Music Box 2000 PLATINUM AWARD

(Small World $20) Wind the knob and a teddy bear cranks the roller wheel as the music plays. An old-fashioned gramophone horn ratchets when turned; there are beads to finger and a small mirror for peeking into. (800) 421-4153.

■ Lamaze Peek-a-boo Puppet

(Learning Curve $15) Here's a reversible puppet that changes from a black-and-white spotted bunny to a green turtle with a checkered back and a squeaker in its head. Fun for early tracking, talking, and peek-a-boo games. We prefer this to the fuzzy lamb version. PLATINUM AWARD '98. (800) 704-8697.

ACTIVITY TIP: Peek-a-Boo has many variations. For beginners start by covering your eyes with your hands and saying, "Where's (baby's name)? Now uncover your eyes and say, "Peek-a-boo!" A note of caution: some babies find this game scary. If so, try again in a few weeks. This classic game helps baby understand that you go away and you come back!

■ **Wimmer-Ferguson**
   My First Photo Album *2000*

(Manhattan Toy $12) Share this fabric book with your early "reader." Book contains bold graphics in black and white and color and has two vinyl pages for adding your own photos. Nice for lap-time sharing, turning, focusing, talking, and touching. (800) 747-2454.

■ **Visual Cards**

(Sassy $6.99) New babies will enjoy gazing at these two cards with high contrast images and licks of primary colors on all four sides. Flip them for a change of visual interest from time to time as they stand on the changing table or in the crib, or enjoy as a book for lap time. One side has a mirror, another a smiling face, a spiral pattern, and a puppy's face. Birth & up. (800) 323-6336.

Rattles

Many rattles are too noisy, hard, and heavy for newborns. While most will be used by adults to get baby's attention, the best choices for newborns are rattles with a soft sound that won't startle and a soft finish that won't hurt. During the first months, an infant's arm and hand movements are not yet refined. Here are some of the best rattles for early playtimes:

■ Baby Bed Bugs *2000*

(North American Bear $13) You'll never find sweeter bees or butterflies! Covered in eye-catching, high-contrast knit jersey, these bugs have stitched features, floppy wings, a velvety heads. Soft to the touch, some rattle, some chime—all are machine-washable. (800) 682-3427.

ACTIVITY TIP: Following a moving object is no small feat for the new baby. Use a boldly patterned soft toy with quiet rattle or squeaky sound to get baby's attention. Move it slowly from side to side in baby's line of vision. In time baby will reach out to touch, but for now looking and listening is the name of the game. Remember, newborns can't focus on objects more than 8–14 inches from their eyes.

■ Colorfun Grabbies *2000*

(Gund $5) Soft and easy for baby to grasp and shake, these velour chick and frog rattles have stitched features. Also fun, **Red** ($10) A jolly-looking red puppy with jingle sound and easy-to-grab legs with bright licks of color. Also recommended, BLUE CHIP winner, **Tinkle, Crinkle, Rattle, & Squeak** ($10), a velour caterpillar-shaped toy with multiple sounds and bright primary colors for eye-grabbing attention. (732) 248-1500.

NOTABLE PREVIOUS WINNERS: **Elephant Sensory Teether** (Manhattan Toy $9) Teething babies will appreciate the soft, chewy teether on an adorable little red velour elephant with purple ears and rattle inside. But for now it's soft and safe for batting at and tracking. Infants & up. **Wimmer-Ferguson Pattern Pals** BLUE CHIP (Manhattan Toy $14.95 set of 3) These soft black and white toys with licks of primary color are visually inviting. (800) 747-2454.

ACTIVITY TIP: Patty-Cake.
Flat on his back or sitting up,
this is a favorite. Take baby's
hand in yours and clap as you say:
Pat a cake, Pat a cake, Baker man. Bake
me a cake as fast as you can! Roll it up
(roll baby's arms) and roll it up,
And mark it with a B (trace a B on
baby's tummy). And put it in the
oven (Put baby's arms over head) for baby and me!

The Vertical Infant

Once babies can sit up, they have a new view of
and fascination with the world of things. Now
they don't just grasp at toys, they can use their
hands and mouths to explore and feel objects. At
around nine months, babies gain fuller control of
their separate fingers and begin to use their
index fingers to point and poke at openings. Now they can activate toys with
spinners. It's also at this stage they can
handle two objects at the same time.

Watch how your baby explores any
toy, examining every angle. She looks at it, fingers it, tastes it.
Using two hands, she bangs two blocks together, or spends
many moments passing a toy from one hand to another. This is
serious work, a way of discovering how things work and what
she can do to make things happen.

During this exciting time your baby will begin to crawl and
even pull herself up on her two little feet. Some may even take
their first steps. In a matter of just a few months your baby grows
from needing others to lead a game of patty-cake, to putting out
her hands and leading others to play patty-cake with her.

Many of the toys from the horizontal stage will still be
used. By now, however, the mobile should be removed from
the crib, and new, interesting playthings should be added gradually. As new toys are introduced, put some of the older things

away. Recycle toys that have lost their novelty by putting them out of sight for a while; then reintroduce them or give them away. A clutter of playthings can become more of a distraction than an attraction.

 BASIC GEAR CHECKLIST FOR THE VERTICAL INFANT

✓ **Rattles and teething toys**
✓ **Manipulatives with differing shapes, sounds, textures**
✓ **Washable dolls and animals**
✓ **Musical toys**
✓ **Soft fabric-covered ball**
✓ **Rolling toys or vehicles**
✓ **Plastic containers for filling and dumping games**
✓ **Cloth blocks**
✓ **Bath toys**
✓ **Cloth or sturdy cardboard books**

 Toys to Avoid
These toys pose choking and/or suffocation hazards:

✓ **Antique rattles**
✓ **Foam toys**
✓ **Toys with elastic**
✓ **Toys with buttons, bells, and ribbons**
✓ **Old wooden toys that may contain lead paint**
✓ **Furry plush dolls that shed**
✓ **Any toys with small parts**

These toys are developmentally inappropriate:
✓ **Shape sorters and ring-and-post toys call for skills that are beyond infants.**

Rattles and Teethers

Now is the time for manipulatives that encourage two-handed exploration while providing interesting textures, sounds, and safe, chewable surfaces for teething. You can't teach eye-hand coordination, but you can motivate exploration by providing toys that develop baby's ability to use their hands and fingers in new and more complex ways.

■ Ambi Ted Triple Teether *2000*

(Learning Curve $5.99 each) The body of this teddy bear teether has three different colors and textures for baby to feel and taste. Also highly recommended, **Twin Rattles** ($5.99) BLUE CHIP that look like two interlocking gears. (800) 704-8697.

■ Earlyears Earl E. Bird

(International Playthings $12) Soft and interesting textures and patterns make this easy-to-grab "bird" a good choice for newborns and beyond. There's something for all the senses on this colorful toy with crinkle and squeak sounds as well as chewable rings for teething. PLATINUM AWARD '99. Birth & up. Also recommended for teething, **Chewing Rings** ($9.95). (800) 445-8347.

■ Tolo Activity Cube *2000*

(Small World $10) We were really impressed with this new but classic-looking line of baby toys, crafted of sturdy primary-colored plastics. An **Activity Cube** for little fingers to activate has a mirror, squeaker, roller and spinning ball. The **Gripper Ball** has four easy-to-grab rounded handles and a see-through hourglass in the middle with beads that roll from side to side. Also highly recommended: **Triangle Rings**, **Abacus Rings**, **Roller Rattle Ball** ($5 each) with a jolly sound, and **Reflector Rattle** ($16) with colorful marbles that look almost liquid as they spin around a mirrored triangular well. (800) 421-4153.

■ Cuddly Teether Pals *2000*

(The First Years $5.99 each) Choose the red **Puppy Pal** with black and white trim, crinkle ears, jingle rattle, and chewy teether bone, or the orange **Monkey Pal** rattle with banana teether attached. These appeal to all the senses with interesting sounds and textures to touch and taste. (800) 533-6708.

ACTIVITY TIP: Who's That? Your baby in arms will be amazed to catch sight of herself and you in a mirror. Watch her surprise as she sees you twice—the real you and your reflection. Talk about what she sees and let her touch your face and your reflection. In time you can play little games of "Where is my nose? Where is baby's nose?" Move baby in and out of the sight line of the mirror playing yet another variation of Peek-a-Boo!

Floor Toys

First Blocks

■ Enchanted Garden Shapes *2000*

(Manhattan Toy $13) Here's a new twist to a classic combo—a colorful ball and block. Baby will enjoy investigating the interesting textures, patterns, and sounds of these fabric toys. The block and ball have a jolly jingle, interesting textures, and bright patterned graphics. Still top-rated, **Mind Shapes** ($20) for 3 shapes with bold black and white graphics and licks of primary colors. (800) 747-2454.

■ Lamaze Clutch Cube

(Learning Curve $11.99) A chime inside this cube makes a quiet sound as baby investigates the patterns on the cube as well as the differing textures on the four grabbers. (800) 704-8697.

■ Earlyears Soft Busy Blocks *2000* PLATINUM AWARD

(International Playthings $12) These blocks have more give than most so baby can easily grasp them. One has a gentle rattle safely inside, another crinkles when touched, and the other squeaks. (800) 445-8347.

ACTIVITY TIP: Booom! Before baby starts stacking blocks he'll like knocking them down. Use fabric blocks or a stack of plastic ones. How high can they go before your little playmate makes them go BOOOOOOOOM? Baby loves the powerful feeling of making this happen, especially if you laugh it up.

Filling and Spilling Games

With their newly acquired skills of grasping and letting go comes the favorite game of filling and dumping multiple objects in and out of containers.

■ Baby's First Blocks and Snap Lock Beads BLUE CHIP

(Fisher-Price $8 & $3.99) Babies will enjoy these toys long before they can do what the boxes promise. **Baby's First Blocks** is technically a shape-sorter, but the blocks will be used to fill, spill, and throw long before baby can fit them into the shape-sorter lid. Put the lid away for now. Similarly, long before baby can put the lemon-sized *SNAP-LOCK* plastic beads together, they'll use them for chomping on, picking up, and little games of fill and dump. Great for developing fine motor skills and the ability to litter the floor. (800) 432-5437.

■ Dunk & Clunk Circus Rings

(Sassy $8.50) Multi-textured rings and rattles slip into special slots in the lid of this see-through container. Beginners will like tasting, tossing, and dropping pieces into the plastic box with polka-dotted handle, but older tots will like this unusual shape sorter that develops fine tuning of wrist and finger action. (800) 323-6336.

■ Lamaze My First Fish Bowl 2000

(Learning Curve $19.99) For some reason fish bowls are big this year! This one rises to the top of our list. Babies explore the interesting textures and sounds of a rattling star fish, a crinkly crab, a jingly fish, and a squeaky crab. All come in a fabric fish bowl with clear vinyl sides for filling and dumping. (800) 704-8697.

Q ACTIVITY TIP: Give & Take. Once baby can release objects at will from her hands, she will enjoy little give-and-take games. Just don't tease! Ask baby to give you a specific toy. Say thanks and give it back to her. It's a new twist on taking turns that baby can enjoy again and again. Remember, repetition is fun to baby.

THANK You —

■ Lego Primo

(Lego Systems $10 & up) These colorful chunky plastic blocks are ideal for grasping, filling, spilling, and eventually stacking. Choose a slightly larger container that includes a wheeled base that can be used for stacking and rolling back and forth. For more rolling fun, bring home **Lego Primo Caterpillar** ($9.99) Bumps on the chunky caterpillar are just right for attaching a yellow-and-black bee or a spotted lady bug. 6 mos. & up. PLATINUM AWARD '98. (800) 233-8756.

■ Wimmer-Ferguson Puzzle Cube

(Manhattan Toy $16) A fabric cube of black-&-white high contrast graphics reverses to bold primary patterns. A crinkle crescent, squeaker star, and rattle heart with interesting textures and sounds fit into cut-out openings on the cube. Unlike shape sorters for older tots, these soft shapes fit into any opening. 6 mos. & up. PLATINUM AWARD '99. (800) 747-2454.

> **FREEBIE: What's Inside?** Put five or six interesting small toys and baby books in a paper bag or box for baby to explore. This is one way to help baby establish short independent playtimes. Small boxes with toys inside motivate exploration and make happy surprises.

Toys for Making Things Happen

Some of the best infant toys introduce babies to their first lessons in cause and effect. Such toys respond with sounds or motion that give even the youngest players a sense of "can do" power—of making things happen!

■ Tomy Bouncing Billy 2000

(International Playthings $14) Press down on Billy's head and he makes a "coo-coo" sound and he makes other funny sounds as his barrel-shaped body bounces and boings. His little green arms turn with a clicking sound. Billy's broad-based feet keep him steady for tabletop play. 10 mos. & up. Also new and unusual, **Spin'n'Grin** ($16.75), with textured "ears" that spin, a mirror, and multiple turning sights to explore. (800) 445-8347.

■ Earlyears Floor Spinner

(International Playthings $14.95) There are plenty of sights and sounds to explore as baby turns and manipulates this intriguing floor toy. Each of the four cones has a distinctive activity: beads, beeper, mirror, and tracking ball. Ideal for two-handed play. PLATINUM AWARD '95. (800) 445-8347.

■ Nesting Action Vehicles 2000

(Fisher-Price $8.99) A versatile set of four chunky vehicles can be stacked in a tower, rolled along the floor, lined up, or nested inside each other for peek-a-boo surprises! Our tester just liked rolling them. Stacking and nesting comes later! (800) 432-5437.

Chime Balls 2000
Comparison Shopper

For precrawling babies, chime balls respond to a swipe of the hand without rolling out of baby's reach. Here are two favorites—you can't go wrong with either of these: **Tomy Balancing Elephant** (International Playthings $13) A playful, but noisier twist on a chime ball. Give the ball a swipe of the hand and the elephant's legs turn as a tune plays. It's designed to roll around a bit, but if you leave the ball attached to the stand it can be enjoyed by precrawlers. Remove the stand later and it has a new play dimension. 6 mos. & up. (800) 445-8347. **Lamaze Rolly Cow** (Learning Curve $14.99) A happy-looking cow bobs around with beads swirling around his middle. Satin ears and face make this a good choice for babies to hear, see, and touch. (800) 704-8697.

Q ACTIVITY TIP: Light Up the Sky! Talk about making things happen—lift baby up and let him switch the lights on and off as you enter a room. What magic!

■ Pop'n'Spin Top BLUE CHIP

(Playskool $13) An easy-to-activate top with big, colorful hopping-popping balls and barbershop-like post that twirls inside a see-through dome. Baby just pushes a big red button to activate. Very satisfying toy for a baby who is just discovering the fun of making things happen. (800) 752-9755. Also top-rated, **Tolo Teddy Bear Carousel** (Small World $12) with cheerful teddy bears that spin inside when the knob is pushed. (800) 421-4153.

Best Highchair Toys

Good highchair toys buy a few extra minutes before dinner is ready, or allow you to eat, too! Our favorite remains **Fascination Station** PLATINUM AWARD '99 (Sassy $7.99) Our little tester liked batting at this spinning toy that attaches to a tabletop with a stout suction cup with a wobbly platform. There is plenty to see, hear, and feel as balls and clackers with bold graphics and textures turn. What a surprise to discover that the spinner detaches to become a hand-held toy to explore! 6 mos. & up. (800) 323-6336. Also top-rated: **Earlyears Activity Spiral** (International Playthings $14.95) with three activity balls that spin, squeak, and go clickity-clack! (800) 445-8347.

ACTIVITY TIP: How Big? Here's a good game for changing table time. While baby is flat on his back say, "How big is the baby?" Take baby's hands in yours and lift his arms up over his head and say, "SOOO Big!" At first you'll do all the action, but before long, when you ask how big is baby? he'll lift his arms and happily do this smart baby trick!

First Toys for Crawlers

At around seven months, most babies begin to creep. It takes a few months more before most are up on hands and knees and truly crawling. Rolling toys such as small vehicles and balls can match baby's developing mobility. Toys placed slightly beyond baby's reach can provide the motivation to get moving. But make it fun. Avoid turning this into a teasing time. Your object is to motivate, not frustrate. Games of rolling a ball or car back and forth make for happy social play between baby and older kids as well as adults.

■ Sesame Street Pop & Go Vehicles *2000*

(Fisher-Price $4.99 each) Testers loved these chunky vehicles that have popping beads safely enclosed in a see-through top. Give them a push and off they go! Choose either the **Pop & Go Cement Mixer** with Elmo or **Pop & Go Garbage Truck** with Oscar, of course! (800) 432-5437.

■ Rev'n Ring Car Phone *2000*

(Playskool $9.99) Beep Beep! The ultimate transforming toy for tots. Flip the hood on this friendly vehicle that makes several sounds as it's pushed along (not too loud either) and you'll find a real mobile phone. Not a big deal, but cute. Two "AA" batteries included. 6 mos. & up. (800) 752-9755.

■ Easy Store Activity Zoo *2000*

(Little Tikes $49.99) This colorful activity center comes with a purple door to open and close a gazillion times! There are lots of safely attached toys to spin and move about for independent play. Looked promising but was not available for testing. We prefer this toy to Little Tikes' **Garden Activity Center** because all the pieces are permanently attached. (800) 321-0183.

■ Peek-a-Boo Activity Tunnel

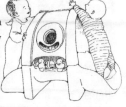

(Little Tikes $45) The gentle up-and-down ramp of this red tunnel with peekaboo window is safe for crawling babies. Our testers enjoyed going round and round again and having a covered hiding place to sit and play with the built-in chunky spinners. It's also fun to roll balls and cars down the ramps. PLATINUM AWARD '96. (800) 321-0183.

> **Q ACTIVITY TIP: I'll Catch You & You Catch Me!** Get down on the floor and take turns playing a crawling catch game. Say, "I'm going to catch you!" and crawl after baby. Or play it in reverse, telling baby to "Try and catch me!" Go slowly enough so baby can catch you. This can be pretty exciting!

■ Rainbow Sports Balls *2000* PLATINUM AWARD

(Gund $7–$12) Choose a multicolored soccer, football, basketball or baseball from this new collection of soft washable velour balls with jingle inside. Like the BLUE CHIP **Colorfun Balls,** these are perfect for crawlers to chase and for early back-and-forth roly-poly social games. (732) 248-1500. Or look for **Jingle Ball** (The First Years $2.99), a less expensive softball-sized ball, covered in washable parachute nylon with a quiet jingle inside. (800) 533-6708.

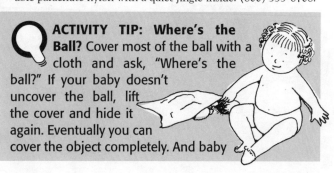

> **Q ACTIVITY TIP: Where's the Ball?** Cover most of the ball with a cloth and ask, "Where's the ball?" If your baby doesn't uncover the ball, lift the cover and hide it again. Eventually you can cover the object completely. And baby

will look for it This game helps baby learn that even if an object can't be seen, it still exists.

☞ **SAFETY TIP:** While at first glance foam balls may seem like a safe bet, they are not for infants, as small pieces may be chewed off and ingested. This is also true of Nerf-type balls that have a plastic cover that can be chewed through.

Tub Time

Bathing a baby can be one of the scariest chores to new parents. (After all, once you take off all those layers, they're so small, and that doesn't even take into account the wobbly neck situation!) For your own comfort as well as baby's, make sure you have everything ready before you begin. Some babies take to water right away, others start crying as soon as that diaper comes off. The key is to remain calm, comforting, and prepared to get wet! Little ones don't need much in the way of toys, but once they can sit securely, a few simple bath toys add to the fun.

First Tub Toys

■ Lamaze Sea Fun Bath Set 🏆 2000

(Learning Curve $16.99) There's a starfish "puppet," a squirting crab, a smiling octopus and a clam shell scoop for bath time fun. All store in mesh bucket between bathtimes. For sitting up babies. (800) 704-8697.

■ Scoop, Pour'n'Squirt Water Fish 🏆 2000

(Sassy $8) A child-friendly fish with a handle can be filled for pouring water. Comes with two small fish "balls" that squirt water. Fun! Also great for washing hair. Also recommended, **Squirting Pearls & Sea Clam.** (800) 323-6336.

SAFETY TIP: The Consumer Product Safety Commission reports 11 deaths and 17 injuries associated with baby bath "supporting rings," devices that keep baby seated in the bath tub. Never rely on such devices to keep baby safe. Going to answer the door or phone can result in serious injury, or worse, to babies and toddlers.

SAFETY TIP: Avoid foam bath toys that are often labeled in fine print, "Not for children under three." Babies can choke on bits of foam that break off if chewed.

First Huggables

Babies often receive tons of soft dolls that are too big, too fuzzy, and even unsafe for now. Although they may be decorative and fine for gazing at, fuzzy plush dolls with ribbons, buttons, plastic features that may pull out, or doodads that may be pulled off, are better saved for preschool years.

When shopping for huggables, look for:

- **Interesting textures**
- **Easy-to-grasp legs or arms**
- **Sound effects sewn safely inside**
- **Washable fabric such as velour or terry cloth**
- **Stitched-on features; no loose ribbons or bells**
- **Small enough size for infant to hold with ease**

Baby Dolls 2000 Comparison Shopper

Older babies are fascinated by dolls that look like real babies. The trick is to find dolls that are washable and safe enough for them to handle. Here are several safe choices: **Babicorolle** (Corolle $13) These French babies have all fabric velour rompers in red or blue stripes, painted faces, and a rattle to attract baby's attention. (800) 628-3655; **My Very Soft Baby** (Playskool $9.99) has a pliable vinyl face and pink terry body. African-American version available. (800) 752-9755; or **My First Dolly** (Gund $10) Choose a boy in blue striped velour, or girl in pink with stitched features on fabric faces, and available with African-American skin tone. (732) 248-1500.

■ Deecha Dolls

(Manhattan Toy $20) Inspired by young children's drawings of people, these soft velour dolls with totally stitched features are all face and easy-to-grab arms and legs. Will be a hit with the next age group, too. (800) 747-2454.

■ New Zoo Animals

(North American Bear $10 & up) Covered in bright knit jersey, these fuzz-free critters have stitched features and squiggles, stripes, and spots. They come in 10½" and 5" sizes—the smaller ones have squeakers inside. Our favorites are a lion with loopy mane, a blue and black zebra, a long-tailed monkey, and a red leopard. Also top-rated, **Tinie Dinies** ($10), ferociously friendly looking velour dinos in bright colors. Machines washable. (800) 682-3427.

■ Sleepyhead Bunny

(North American Bear $12 & $23) These are totally huggable, soft and floppy bunnies in pink or blue striped PJs. Choose either 15" or 8" rattle. The award-winning line of **Velveteenie Circus Animals** ($8–$31), in vibrant hot colors on soft velour fabric, are still a great choice for babies and beyond. PLATINUM AWARD '94. (800) 682-3427.

Best Travel Toys for Infants

Having a supply of several small toys can help divert and entertain small travelers whether you're going out for a day or away for a week. Bring along a familiar comfort toy—a musical toy or doll that's like a touch of home. Pack a variety of toys with different sounds and textures and don't show them all at once. You need to dole them out. Select several very different toys, for example:

- **Teether**
- **Hand-held mirror**
- **Highchair toy**
- **Small huggable**
- **Familiar quilt/playmat to rest on**
- **Musical toy**
- **Books and pictures to share**

■ Enchanted Garden Stroller Activity Bar 2000

(Manhattan Toy $20) Attach these soft colorful fabric flowers and bugs to provide texture, sound, visual and manipulative interest for the on-the-go baby. (800) 747-2454.

■ Wimmer-Ferguson 3 in 1 Triangle Toy

(Manhattan Toy $20) A versatile toy with 18 high-contrast graphic patterns to hang in the car for gazing at. Thanks to magnets inside, can be hung on the fridge or folded into a long wedge for floor play. There's a small mirror, and touchie feelies, as well as a squeaker that will interest older babies. Still highly recommended, the **Car Seat Gallery,** a Blue Chip choice ($12) for back-facing car seats. Hang the 4-way pattern pocket chart on the back seat of the car. PLATINUM AWARD '95. (800) 747-2454.

> **SAFETY TIP:** Links should never be made into a loop, or linked across a crib or playpen. We often see babies' strollers draped with long lengths of links. Warning labels say that a chain of links should never be more than 12" long and should be used with adult supervision.

■ Ambi Swinging Ted ✦2000✦

(Learning Curve $16.99) Ted, the friendly yellow plastic bear in red overalls swings to and fro when baby bats at it. (800) 704-8697. Also top-rated, **Paddington Bear Trapeze Crib/Stroller Toy** (Eden $7) includes a soft fabric swinging Paddington. (800) 443-4275.

■ Infant Carrier PlayCenter ✦2000✦

(Summer Infant $9.99) This activity bar attaches to any infant carrier seat and invites baby to reach out and touch. We love this one because it is uncomplicated with a smiley little figure that's easy to spin. Comes in primary colors or black, white and red. (800) 268-6237.

■ Mini Musical Mobile ✦2000✦

(Eden $20) We've been looking for a mobile that attaches to a bassinet or portable crib for years. This has a clamp fastener that really holds fast. Colorful objects spin on a red bar, but the music has a tinny electronic sound. (800) 443-4275

■ Puppet Play Mates ✦2000✦

(Tiny Love $11.95) How do you get four puppets for the price of one? This innovative glove puppet has four interchangeable heads that Velcro on. A versatile toy for interacting with baby and to use for tracking and talking games. (800) 843-6292.

Toddlers-in-Training Toys

Some of the early walking toys found in the next chapter may be ideal for infants who are seriously working on walking before their first birthday.

Best New Baby/Shower Gifts

Big Ticket ($40 & up)
: **Deluxe Gymini 3-D Activity Gym** (Tiny Love) or **Baby Bed Bug Mobile** (North American Bear) or **Sensational Circus Musical Mobile** (Manhattan Toy)

Under $40
: **Slumbertime Soother** (Fisher-Price) or **Flatso Farm Musical Pulldown** (North American Bear) or **Kick Start Gym** (Playskool)

Under $30
: **Sunflower Pull Musical** (Manhattan Toy) or **Tolo Gramophone Music Box** (Small World)

Under $25
: **Lamaze Peek-a-boo Puppet** (Learning Curve) or **Action Musical Peter Rabbit** (Eden)

Under $15
: **Earlyears Soft Busy Blocks** (International Playthings) or **Car Seat Gallery** (Manhattan Toy) or **Tolo Activity Cube** (Small World) or **Rainbow Sports Balls** (Gund)

Under $10
: **Fascination Station** (Sassy) or **Dunk & Clunk Circus Rings** (Sassy) or **Lego Primo Caterpillar** (Lego)

Under $5
: **Snap-Lock Beads** (Fisher-Price) or **Colorfun Grabbies** (Gund)

Looking Ahead:
Best First Birthday Gifts
For Every Budget

Big Ticket ($50 or more) **Push Cart** (Galt) or **Sand Box** (LittleTikes/Step 2)

Under $50 **Doors & Drawers Activity Kitchen** (Little Tikes) or **Soft Rockin' Tigger Rocker** (Little Tikes)

Under $30 **Activity Table** (Fisher-Price) or **Lego Primo** (Lego Systems)

Under $25 **Earlyears Activity Center** (International Playthings) or **Stack'n'Build Choo Choo** (Fisher-Price) or **Earlyears My Friend Earl E. Bird** (International Playthings)

Under $15 **Bigger Family Van** (Step 2) or **Baby Bed Bugs** (North American Bear Co.) or **Babicorolle** (Corolle) or **Ambi Teddy Copter** (Learning Curve)

Under $10 **Animal Stackables** (Little Tikes) or **Corn Popper** (Fisher-Price) or **Scoop'n'Strain Turtle Tower** (Sassy)

Under $5 Cardboard book (see Books section)

2 • Toddlers
One to Two Years

What to Expect Developmentally

Ones and Twos. There is a big difference between your one year old whose focus is primarily on mastering and enjoying his new found mobility and your two year old who is now running, jumping, and making giant leaps with language and imagination. Yet the second and third years are generally known as the toddler years. Many of the toys and games recommended for ones will continue to be used by twos in new and more complex ways. Since some toddlers will be steady on their feet earlier than others or talking and pretending at different times, you'll want to use this chapter in terms of your child's individual development. This chapter is not arranged chronologically. You'll find toys and games for ones and twos under each of the main headings.

Active Exploration. Anyone who spends time with toddlers knows that they are active, on-the-go learners. They don't visit long because there are so many places and things to explore. Toys that invite active investigation are best for this age group. For toddlers, toys with doors to open, knobs to push, and pieces to fit, fill, and dump provide the raw material for developing fine motor skills, language, and imagination.

Big-Muscle Play. Toddlers also need play-things that match their newfound mobility and their budding sense of independence. Wheeled toys to push, ride on, and even ride in are great favorites. So is equip-ment they can climb, rock, and slide on. In these two busy years, tod-dlers grow from wobbly walk-ers to nimble runners and climbers.

Language and Pretend Power.
As language develops, so does the ability to pretend. For beginners, games of make-believe depend more on action than story lines. Choose props that look like the things they see in the real world.

Toys and Development. As an infant your baby was involved mainly with people. Now, your toddler will spend more time investigating things. Some of the toys in this chap-ter, such as those for beginning walkers, have short-term use. However, many of the best products are what we call bridge toys, playthings that will be used now and for several years ahead. While no toddler needs all the toys listed here, one- and two-year-olds do need a good mix of toys that fit varying play modes—toys for indoors and out, for quiet, solo sit-down times, and social run-and-shout-out-loud times.

Your Role in Play. Playing (and keeping up) with an active toddler requires a sense of humor and realistic expectations. In order to satisfy their growing appetite for independence, select uncomplicated toys that won't frustrate their sense of "can do" power. For example, if your toddler does not want to sit down with you and work on a puzzle now, she may be willing in an hour, or she may be telling you that it's too difficult and should be put away and tried again in a few weeks.

Childproofing:
Setting the Stage for Learning
Childproofing involves more than putting things out of reach. It involves setting the stage for learning by providing appropriate objects that children can safely explore. To avoid a constant dialogue of "No! Don't touch!"—remove treasures and objects that may be dangerous to handle. Touching is what toddlers do—it's how they learn. Toddlers who lack freedom to explore get a negative message about learning. Your goal is to encourage their curiosity, not set roadblocks to the world around them.

Enlarging the Circle: Playmates
Your one year old will play mostly with you and the significant people in his life. But twos are ready to enlarge their social circle. Whether they go to a play group or the park or visit with neighbors, twos enjoy playing near and ultimately with other children.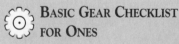
A Word on Sharing. Lacking experience, toddlers live by the philosophy that what's mine is mine and what's yours is mine, too. It's not selfishness so much as not really understanding what sharing means. Toddlers consider their toys almost as extensions of themselves—not for sharing. If playmates are coming we suggest: putting away your child's most favorite toys that he doesn't want to share; being prepared to help with negotiations since kids rarely have enough language to make their own case; having a snack prepared—tots love eating together; and keeping visits relatively short. An hour is plenty for twos—always leave them wanting more!

> ### Basic Gear Checklist for Ones
> ✓Push toys   ✓Pull toys
> ✓Ride-on toy   ✓Small vehicles
> ✓Musical toys   ✓Huggables
> ✓Toy phone   ✓Lightweight ball
> ✓Fill-and-dump toys
> ✓Manipulatives with moving parts

BASIC GEAR CHECKLIST
FOR TWOS

✓Ride-on/-in toy   ✓Pull and push toy
✓Big lightweight ball   ✓Shovel and pail
✓Climbing/sliding toy   ✓Art supplies
✓Big blocks   ✓Table and chair
✓Huggables   ✓Props for housekeeping
✓Simple puzzles/shape-sorters

🚫 Toys to Avoid

These toys pose choking and/or suffocation hazards:
✓Foam toys
✓Toys with small parts (including small plastic fake foods)
✓Dolls and stuffed animals with fuzzy and/or long hair
✓Toys labeled 3 & up (no matter how smart toddlers
   are! The label almost always indicates that there are
   small parts in or on the toy)
✓Latex balloons (Note: The Consumer Product Safety
   Commission reports that latex balloons are the lead-
   ing cause of suffocation deaths! Since 1973 more than
   110 children have died from suffocation involving
   uninflated balloons or pieces of broken ones. They
   are not advised for children under age six.)
These toys are developmentally inappropriate:
✓Electronic educational drill toys
✓Shape-sorters with more than three shapes
✓Battery-operated ride-ons
✓Most pedal toys

Active Physical Play

Between 12 and 15 months most
babies start toddling. At first, they
side-step from one piece of furniture
to another. Soon, with arms used for
balance they take their first independent
steps. In these first months of the second year they
grow from those thrilling wobbly first steps to sure-foot-

ed adventurers. Few toys lend the kind of security you give as you extend your hands to assure him you are there to catch him.

Beginning walkers will get miles of use from a low-to-the-ground, stable wheeled toy. The products on the market are not created equal. Here are some basic things to look for:

- Wobbly toddlers may use a toy to pull up on, so you'll want to find toys that are weighted and won't tip easily.

- Try before you buy. Some ride-ons are scaled for tall kids, others for small kids.

- Toddlers do not need battery-powered ride-ons! Encourage foot power, not push-button action!

- Toddlers are not ready for pedals. Few have the coordination to use pedals before 2½. Four wheels and two feet on the ground are best.

- Toys with loud and constant sound effects may be appealing in the store, but can become annoying in tight spaces.

For Younger Toddlers:

■ Grow'n'Go Walker Mower

(Fisher-Price $24.99) Our newly walking tester loved pushing this sturdy plastic mower that makes a poppity noise when pushed. Elmo, on the top of the mower, also bobs up and down as it goes. Well balanced for new walkers. (888) 892-6123.

■ Push Cart

(Galt $79.95) This recently re-styled classic wooden cart is pricier than any of its plastic counterparts but can be passed down to younger siblings! Very stable for early walkers and a perfect first wagon for carting treasures. (800) 899-4258.

Wagons, Prams, & Ride-ons for Steady-on-their-Feet Toddlers

■ Baby Walker

(LEGO Systems $25) Lego's bright plastic pushing wagon is not weighted and is designed for steady walkers—young toddlers for moving about with cargo. 1 & up. (800) 233-8756.

■ Bigger Family Construction Wagon with Blocks

(Step 2 $29.99) Bright yellow wagon with a flat cargo bed is ideal for carting about blocks and other favorite treasures. Four chunky wheels make a clicking sound when pushed or pulled with sturdy blue handle. Comes with two Bigger Family people. They say 1 & up; best suited for steady walkers. Also top-rated, **Push About Fire Truck** (Step 2 $20). PLATINUM AWARD '98. (800) 347-8372.

First Ride-Ons
■ Bigger Family Shuttle Bus Ride-On
2000 PLATINUM AWARD

(Step 2 $29.99) Our almost-two-year-old tester not only loves riding this straddle-and-drive vehicle, he loves loading the chunky play figures on and off—he even takes them to bed! The beep-beep steering wheel adds to the pretend fun. This is taller than most, so test drive before you buy! (800) 347-8372.

■ Pooh Sound Express Train *2000*

(Little Tikes $29.99) Pooh fans will enjoy riding this foot-powered ride-on that comes with Pooh as the conductor. Push the button and he says several different phrases including: "Thank you for riding the Hundred Acre Railroad." They say 1 & up, we'd say best for steady walkers. (800) 321-0183.

■ Soft Rockin' Tigger Rocker *2000*

(Little Tikes $39.99) Fabric covered and low to the ground, this huggable, easy-to-straddle rocker will fit young toddlers. Machine washable cover. Looked promising, but was not ready for testing. For toddlers who are steady on their feet. (800) 321-0183.

■ Push & Ride Racer & Semi Truck

(Little Tikes $20) The latest ride-on entries from
this company and others do not measure up to
earlier versions. Neither the new Push & Ride
Racer nor the Push & Ride Semi Truck have
true steering ability and both are harder for
new walkers to get on easily—especially if
they have short legs. That said, these are
now the best choices, but have your child test-
drive either for size. 1–3. (800) 321-0183.

■ Cozy Coupe II *2000*

(Little Tikes $44.99) The ultimate classic ride-in toy that a generation
of kids have grown up with has been updated with
a remote key clicker with four different electronic sounds. Also comes with decals for
making your own vanity license plate. These
add-ons don't detract from the coupe's value
as a terrific pretend prop. We have suggested that the company sell the key separately
because you know it's going to get lost,
just like the real kind! They say, 1½, we say
more like 2 and up. (800) 321-0183.

ACTIVITY TIP: Ask your toddler what she's
bringing as she rides by. Fuel their imagination by "opening" pretend packages they
deliver. Modeling pretend games with words and
gestures helps tots take the leap into fantasy play.

Push and Pull Toys

Push comes before pull. Instead of holding someone's
hand, young toddlers often find sheer joy in the
independence of walking while holding on to a push
toy. You probably started walking with a Fisher-
Price's BLUE CHIP **Corn Popper** ($8) or **Melody
Push Chime** ($8). They are still great choices!
(800) 432-5437. Pull toys are for older tots who are
surefooted and can look over a shoulder without tripping.

■ Walk'n'Waddle Duck 🏆2000

(Fisher-Price $7.99) Mama Duck quacks quietly and her orange feet flip flop along as tots push her with her little waddling duckling right behind her. This works better on carpet than on bare floors. (800) 432-5437.

■ Kid Classics Miss Spider

(Learning Curve $24.99) Borrowed from the Miss Spider series of books, this wooden version spins her many legs as she's pulled along. Fun! 18 mos. & up. PLATINUM AWARD '98. (800) 704-8697.

> **SAFETY TIP: Avoid pull toys with springs and beads that many toddlers will mouth. Old pull toys from the attic may have dangerous levels of lead paint.**

■ Spinning Bus

(Battat $15) Eight little animal and people passengers plus a driver spin as this pull toy rolls along. There's a ramp for taking passengers off and on. Fun for games of loading, unloading, and rearranging the multiple pieces as well as refining dexterity to fit them on their posts. 8 mos. & up. (800) 247-6144. Also recommended: Kouvalias' BLUE CHIP jaunty green wooden **Little Cricket Pull Toy** ($40). 2 & up. (800) 445-8347. For a less pricey plastic pull toy, **Ambi Max** (Learning Curve $19.99), is an adorable black-and-white pooch. 1½ & up. (800) 704-8697 or Fisher-Price's classic **Little Snoopy** ($8) that wags his tail as he walks. (800) 432-5437.

Balls

Big, lightweight balls for tossing, kicking, chasing, or social back-and-forth, roly-poly games are favorite pieces of basic gear. Twos are ready to play bounce and catch. Be sure the ball is lightweight so it won't hurt. Soft fabric balls or slightly deflated beach balls are the best choice for now. Avoid foam and balloon-filled balls that are a choking hazard if nibbled.

FREEBIE: One, Two, Three, Four. Tots love to count—any excuse will do. Count as you climb the stairs together, toss a ball, as you drop blocks into a container, or take out silverware to set the table. Make numbers and counting an everyday part of life.

Strictly Outdoors:
Climbers, Wading Pools, Sandboxes, Props for the Sandbox, Gardening Tools, and Snow Fun

First Climbers & Slides

Climbers are great for big-muscle play for toddlers who are steady on their feet. We saw a number of low-to-the-ground climbers with open platforms and some that did not have secure enough sides once tots reached the top. Many looked like an accident waiting to happen. If you are shopping for a young or especially small toddler, stick to the lowest climbers. This is not a product to grow into.

■ Junior Activity Gym BLUE CHIP

(Little Tikes $70) This pint-sized version of Little Tikes' classic Activity Gym is low to the ground, and will be used as a climber, roof-free play house, and slide. It has no steps, so toddlers must pull themselves up in order to

use the slide. 1½ & up. **Hide & Slide Climber** ($79.99) This is a
taller climber with secure sides, two big steps up, and a longer wavy
slide. Designed for big 2s & up. (800) 321-0183.

■ 8-in-1 Adjustable Playground

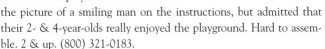

(Little Tikes $270) A combo playhouse,
tunnel, climber, and double slide that
the whole gang can play on together.
Done in hot colors, this big piece of
equipment provides for physical
and dramatic play. Parent testers hated
the picture of a smiling man on the instructions, but admitted that
their 2- & 4-year-olds really enjoyed the playground. Hard to assemble. 2 & up. (800) 321-0183.

> **Q ACTIVITY TIP: Give 'em a Hand!** Toddlers
> love an appreciative audience—don't we
> all? When they finish a puzzle, dance a jig,
> or go down a slide, clap your hands together—give
> them a hand! Keep in mind that little children see
> themselves as you see them. During this often neg-
> ative time, try to accentuate the positive.

Wading Pools

Our testers preferred inexpensive hard-vinyl wading pools
to those that had to be blown
up or filled with water to
hold a shape (most of these
had sides that were too high for younger toddlers to climb over
by themselves). Prefab wading pools are also easier to lift,
dump, and clean. You'll find an adequate no-frills pool for
under $20.

Sandboxes

While small boxes are good choices when space is a concern,
keep in mind that a bigger box will give more than one child
enough room to maneuver. We looked for smooth edges and
strong sides that will support a child's weight. The motif is
really a personal preference. You can't go wrong with any of
the following—all come with covers. Unless you can't spare

the space, this is a case where more is more. Small boxes will be outgrown quickly.

Our favorites: On the small side, **Frog Sandbox** (Step 2 $30) or **Green Turtle** (Little Tikes $30). 1 & up. Bigger choices: **Crabbie Sandbox** (Step 2 $45) or **Dinosaur Sandbox** (Little Tikes $50). Bigger still: **Tuggy Sandbox & Splasher** (Step 2 $90) There's plenty of room for several kids to play together and built-in pretend power with a captain's wheel for steering the jolly boat anywhere! 2 & up. Step 2 (800) 347-8372 / Little Tikes (800) 321-0183.

Sandbox props: A basic bucket from the store will do—just be sure to check for smooth edges. To toddlers, sand is another opportunity for spilling and dumping. Vehicles are also a great for pretend construction projects, bring along either Little Tikes' scaled-down **Loader & Dump Truck** ($12 each) or Fisher-Price's **Little People Dump Truck** and **Bulldozer (**$9.99 each) Small-scaled working vehicles that come with a figure. Both lightweight enough to take-along to the park or beach. 10 mos. & up. Little Tikes (800) 321-0183 / Fisher-Price (800) 432-5437.

FREEBIE: Pails, sieves, and a sand mill all fit their play needs. Many of the best props for the sandbox are in your kitchen: a plastic colander, empty margarine containers, strainers, squeeze bottles, etc.

Water Sprinklers

Most sprinklers on the market are too overwhelming for toddlers. We suggest low-to-the-ground ones with gentle action like the **Elmo's 1-2-3 Sprinkler** (Fisher-Price $14.99). (888) 892-6123.

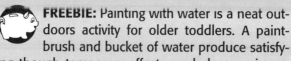

FREEBIE: Painting with water is a neat out-doors activity for older toddlers. A paint-brush and bucket of water produce satisfy-ing though temporary effects—early lessons in evaporation or magic: take your pick!

The Youngest Gardener
See Preschool Chapter

Snow Fun
■ Deluxe Toddler Sleigh BLUE CHIP

(Flexible Flyer $30) Ready for dashing through the snow, this bright-red toddler sled has high, sloping sides, molded side runners, safety seat belt, and strong yellow towrope. A great winter get-about. Toy Supermarkets.

Sit-Down Play

First Puzzles and Manipulatives

Toddlers enjoy toys that invite investigation but don't demand too much dexterity. These are toys that develop eye/hand coordination, and problem solving. Once they understand how to use them, many of the toys in this section will be enjoyed independent-ly and that is very satisfying to the "me do it myself!" set.

First Puzzles

Start with whole-piece puzzles. Take the time to introduce a new puzzle or toy. Let your child take the lead, giving time to explore the pieces and experiment with them. Those with peg handles or raised surfaces are easier for little hands to manip-ulate. Be forewarned: We continued to find many wooden puz-zles with splinters. Look before you buy!

■ Familiar Things

(Lauri $18.95) Twelve 2-piece rubber puzzles of familiar objects. 2 & up. (800) 451-0520.

■ Fruit, Farm & Pets Puzzibilities 🏅2000

(Small World $8) Toddlers will have fun fitting together these splinter-free, giant, pegged whole-piece puzzles. Lift the fish and there's a matching fish below. Each has three distinctive pieces to known, name, and match. 18 mos. & up. (800) 421-4153.

■ Barnyard Puzzle Pals 🏅2000

(Jack Rabbit Creations $16) Toddlers will have no trouble lifting the five wooden animals out of the puzzle tray since they are much thicker than most. In fact, the painted animals stand like the classic wooden figures typically used as props for blocks. 18 mos. &up. (404) 876-4225.

■ Magic Sound Animal Blocks 🏅2000

(Small World $10) When you connect these animal picture blocks, the animals moo, baa, bark, or meow. A playful way to work with putting two parts together to make a whole, and get an auditory payoff. Also recommended, **Magic Sound Vehicle Blocks.** 2½ &up. (800) 421-4153.

Manipulatives

■ Tomy Twist'n'Turn 🏅2000

(International Playthings $9.75) There are so many parts to twist, turn, and taste as toddlers develop fine motor skills. Has interesting sounds, feel, and look. Still top-rated, **Earlyears Activity Center** ($19.95). With rolling beads, clacking shapes, and rattling balls that respond to toddler's investigations. Sound, color, and action make this an appealing toy for eye/hand skills and learning about cause and effect. 1 & up. PLATINUM AWARD '96. (800) 445-8347.

■ Activity Table

(Fisher-Price $29.99) The best activity table for toddlers we've seen in years. Can be used by babies on the floor and for standing at by tots.

Table top flips from a surface for stacking with Stack'n'Build blocks to an activity center with whirling marbles (safely enclosed), mirror, peek-a-boo flippers, and chute for filling and spilling the blocks. 9 mos. & up. PLATINUM AWARD '98. (800) 432-5437.

■ Tomy Ball Party Connecting Bridge 2000
PLATINUM AWARD

(International Playthings $29) Hands down, one of the best toddler toys on the market. Two towers and multiple bridges (with ridges) become a runway for ten oversized (and safe) plastic balls that go bumpity-bumpity bump down the ramps. Can be configured (by parents) in multiple ways and combined with **Roll Around Tower** ($24.99) our PLATINUM AWARD '98. Also recommended: **Ball Party Pick Up Tube** ($9.99). 1½ & up. (800) 445-8347.

■ Beads on Wire Toys BLUE CHIP

(Anatex and Educo $15 & up) Both of these companies make wonderful tracking toys with tethered-down colored beads of different shapes and sizes that can be moved up, down, and around curved and twisted wire mazes. These abstract toys develop eye/hand skills, language, counting, and pretending. 1½ & up. Anatex (800) 999-9599 / Educo (800) 661-4142.

Comparison Shopper— Hammer Toys 2000

Kid Classics Hammer and Nail Bench (Learning Curve $24.99) looks like a traditional wooden version but with an added twist for safety—as one peg is hit, another one pops up—none come out. (800) 704-8697. Also very special, **Pound A Ball** (Battat $18), a three-level tower with a see-through window. 1½ & up. (800) 247-6144. Or **Plan Toys Punch'n'Drop** (Small World $15), a handsome wooden box with three colored balls to hammer through a chute. 2 & up. (800) 421-4153.

■ Bear City Activity Center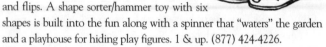

(Chicco $34.95) Talk about making things happen! Here are multiple cause-and-effect activities on target for toddlers. A push plunger spins two little vehicles with bear figures. Put one bear on the staircase and it slides down and flips. A shape sorter/hammer toy with six shapes is built into the fun along with a spinner that "waters" the garden and a playhouse for hiding play figures. 1 & up. (877) 424-4226.

NOTABLE PREVIOUS WINNERS: **Spinning Balls Top** (Battat $17) Colorful balls spin inside the see-through dome with a shiny reflective tube. 1 & up. (800) 247-6144. **Sesame Street Talking Pop-Up Pals** (Fisher-Price $20) Push the buttons to make characters pop up out of their color-coded doors. 2 & up. (800) 432-5437.

First Construction Toys

Few toys have more long-term use and learning value than construction toys. For the youngest toddlers, filling, dumping, and knocking down blocks comes before lining them up or stacking. Start with **Lego Primo** and Fisher-Price's **Stacking Blocks** (see infant chapter). Twos and up will start enjoying big cardboard blocks with adults who are willing to get down on the floor and make long roadways, towers, and bridges. Older twos will enjoy plastic blocks, such as **Duplo** and **Mega Blocks,** and even wooden blocks.

■ LEGO Primo BLUE CHIP

(LEGO Systems $4–$25) Day after day, young toddler testers returned to these colorful stacking blocks with soft edges and rounded bumps that make for an easy fit—even by little hands. Designed to stimulate the senses, some have rattle sounds, a mirror, chubby people and animal figures and wheeled bases. 6–24 mos. PLATINUM AWARD '96. (800) 233-8756.

■ Duplo BLUE CHIP

(LEGO Systems $10 & up) Chunky plastic Duplo building blocks to fill and dump, snap together, and take apart are basic gear for older toddlers and preschoolers. Small sets are good for add-ons, but be sure to start with a large enough set. 1½ & up. For a wow-wee 2nd birthday gift, look at **Duplo School Bus** ($29.99). Older toddlers can ride on top, use the roof as a base for building. Comes with 70 pieces. 2 & up. PLATINUM AWARD '98. (800) 233-8756.

■ Giant Constructive Blocks BLUE CHIP

(Constructive Playthings $15.95) These sturdy 12" x 6" x 4" cardboard blocks are printed like red bricks and great for stacking into towers, walls, and other big but lightweight creations. Strong enough to stand on, these classic blocks endure years of creative use. Set of 12. #CP-626. (800) 832-0572.

■ Mega Blocks Wagon *2000*

(Mega Blocks $30) A tot-sized red wagon loaded with 75 pieces of oversized plastic pegged blocks will be fun for making big, fast constructions. Pegs on side of wagon can be used for building up and over. 2 years & up. (800) 465-6342.

Wooden Blocks

Older twos may enjoy a beginner set of wooden blocks for loading and unloading, stacking or lining up in long roadways. For large top-rated sets, see Preschool Chapter. For a smaller set, **Radio Flyer's Block Wagon** *2000* (Radio Flyer $30) comes with 30 colorful wooden blocks in a sturdy little wooden wagon. (800) 621-7613.

Wooden Trains

See Preschool Chapter

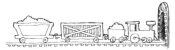

FREEBIE: Shopping Bag Fun. Filling and dumping is a favorite game that's played with a variety of objects and containers. Toddlers love moving about with their treasures. A big paper shopping bag filled with empty plastic soda bottles (without the rings or

caps) provides the bigness without much weight.
Other options: Give tots a bunch of socks or mittens
to pull out of a box.

First Stacking, Nesting, and Shape-Sorter Toys

Classic stacking toys require the ability to see and arrange
objects in size order—a skill that most toddlers do not have.
Although such toys are often labeled 6 months & up, there's
nothing wrong with your child—the problem is with the
label! In fact. many pieces are sure to be lost before tots can
put them together. Happily, there are more forgiving choices
that introduce stacking without the need for size order. These
toys are fun for toddlers to taste, toss and explore— just don't
expect them to be expert stackers. As you play with
your toddler, use color or size words to describe the
pieces. Such concepts are learned with greater ease
when they are part of everyday experiences.

For beginners, start with ring-and-post
toys with interesting textures or patterns
like the plastic **Circus Rings** (Sassy
$9.99) or the **Lamaze Stacking
Rings** (Learning Curve $19.99)
with fabric rings that stack in any order.
Sassy (800) 323-6336 / Learning Curve
(800) 704-8697.

Slightly more advanced players will enjoy **Animal
Stackables** (Little Tikes $9.99) **2000 PLATINUM
AWARD.** There's a logic to
putting heads and legs in order,
although tots will see the humor
of making mixed-up crit-
ters. Comes with two soft,
pliable heads and bases
with feet, and eight colorful stackers to make
them tall, tall, tall! 1 & up.
(800) 321-0183.

Nesting and Stacking Toys

Toddlers like the multiple pieces for pulling apart, banging, and stacking long before they can nest them. Eventually stacking and nesting toys develop hand/eye coordination, size order concepts, and even counting skills. They provide hands-on experience with concepts like bigger, smaller, taller, inside, under, top, bottom—to name but a few. You can make the language connection as you play together.

Here are some good choices: For beginners, try **Stacking Cups** (Sassy $5.50) Four boldly patterned cups with interesting textures on the rims. 1 & up. (800) 323-6336. **Tot Tower** (eeboo $19) Handsome cardboard nesting blocks with familiar objects to know and name. Their newest version, **Baby Things,** has multi-ethnic toddlers' faces and a range of feeling in their expressions. 1 & up. (212) 222-0823.

Shape-Sorters

■ Plan Toys Shape-N-Sort *2000*

(Small World $15) Three shapes fit easily in the wooden box with lift-off lid. This is simpler to use than the Lockablock below. 18 mos. &up. Also special, **First Shape Fitter** ($15), a nine-place board as pictured with tall, medium, and short shaped blocks to sort by color, shape, or size. 2 & up. (800) 421-4153.

■ Ambi Lockablock *2000*

(Learning Curve $19.99) Unlike many key and lock toys, this one has an easy action that responds with a turn of the wrist. Tots fill the block through the shape sorter top. There are just three shapes and the rim of the sorter is color-coded to match the shapes. 18 mos. & up. (800) 704-8697.

Pretend Play

As language develops, older toddlers begin their early games of pretend. So much of the real equipment tots see adults using is off-limits to them. Child-sized versions can (sometimes) offer a satisfying alternative and fuel the imagination of little ones who love to mimic what they see you doing.

Dolls and Huggables

Both boys and girls enjoy playing with dolls and soft animals. For one year olds, velour and short-haired plush are best. Huggable classics such as **Snuffles,** the polar bear (Gund) and **Spot** (Eden) may become long-loved companions. Older toddlers like oversized but lightweight huggables. Bald baby dolls to take in the tub and classics like **Cabbage Patch Kids** (Mattel) with yarn hair and soft bodies come in boy, girl, and multi-ethnic versions. Toddlers also like smaller dolls that fit in their fists. Since toddlers still chew on their toys, select uncomplicated huggables without small decorations or long hair.

■ Babicorolle *2000*

(Corolle $13 & up) When you're looking for a toddler's first baby doll you probably won't find a better choice than these soft huggable babies that feel big but light. Totally washable, **Pierrot** ($20), a clown with knitted face and parachute nylon body, is a bright, happy armful. 1 & up. Older toddlers will enjoy Corolle's bath and anatomically correct dolls. They are pricey but beautifully made. 2 & up. (800) 628-3655.

■ Earlyears My Friend Earl E. Bird *2000*

(International Playthings $20) Our PLATINUM AWARD-winner doll **Earl E. Bird** has grown into a big toddler-sized pal with crinkling beak, foot rattles, floppy legs with interesting textures, backpack mirror, Velcro wings that hug a little Squeak E. Mouse doll that fits in a pocket. 1 & up. (800) 445-8347.

■ Groovy Girls & Boys 2000 PLATINUM AWARD

(Manhattan Toy $10 & up) This year boys have been added to this funky collection velour dolls with stitched features, yarn hair and groovy flower power '60s clothes. These are still a perfect fistful for toddlers. there are also larger 20" versions that are just right for older toddlers who love lugging around a large huggable. An instant classic—move over, Raggedy Andy! 2 & up. (800) 747-2454.

■ Space Puppies 2000

(Rumpus $10.99–$16.99) Choose **Quasar, Galaxy,** or **Comet**—long legged spacey looking pups 12"–20" that are easy to grab and lug about. Interesting to the touch, they are made of colorful parachute nylon with oversized heads, legs and tails of velour. 2 & up. (888) RUMPUS1.

■ Teletubbies 2000

(Playskool & Microsoft) We agree with the critics who say that Teletubbies do little to develop toddlers' language, and that their non-verbal sounds mirror rather than expand children's verbal skills. That said, kid testers enjoyed hugging the dolls that say a few phrases. Tots also liked the new **Actimate** version with color and light shows that are activated by squeezing the dolls' hands. We wish they didn't light up with alphabet letters that they don't say. Playskool (800) 752-9755 / Microsoft (800) 426-9400.

SHOPPING TIP: Toddlers often form an attachment to one particular "lovie." This special toy or blanket often takes on a life of its own, especially when it's (horror of horrors) misplaced. Our best tip is to buy a back-up duplicate and keep both well washed and indistinguishable from each other.

> **Q ACTIVITY TIP: Yum, Yum, Teddy! Pretend Game.** Modeling games of pretend can spark toddlers to make up their own games. Stick to familiar actions, for example, pretend to feed, play patty-cake with, or cover Teddy with a little "blanket."

NOTABLE PREVIOUS WINNERS: Flatolamb and Friends (North American Bear Co. $10 & up) Soft velour farmyard critters are available as huggables (15") or luggables (25")—both will satisfy a tot's love for big, big, big. (800) 682-3427. **Wrinkles** (Manhattan Toy $60) Little floor sitters will like

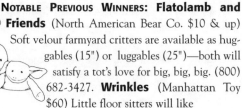

flopping over a giant 24" golden-colored, short-haired, wrinkly-faced dog. Also huggable, a smaller 14" **Wrinkles Jr.** ($20) 2 & up. (800) 747-2454. **Ragtimo Dog & Cat** (North American Bear $24 each) Made of a non-plush felt-like fabric, they wear sunny floral clothes with Velcro closures. 1 & up. (800) 682-3427.

Doll Accessories

Most toddlers will try to get into doll furniture you buy. Most plastic doll furniture is very tippable. Better to wait until the preschool years for typical baby beds, highchairs, and strollers. Older twos may enjoy a shopping cart they can push about and use for their dolls.

■ Wooden Doll Cradle BLUE CHIP

(Community Playthings $90) This solid maple cradle is designed for schools and built to last. It's 29" and big enough for kids to climb in and play baby or put a family of dolls to sleep. Sure to become a family heirloom. 2 & up. #C140. (800) 777-4244.

■ Shopping Cart

(Little Tikes $25) This bright yellow cart with baby seat is more gender free than most doll carriers. Lends itself to more open-ended pretend games. (800) 321-0183.

Vehicles

Although young walkers no longer need to crawl from place to place, playing around with wheeled toys on the floor, in the sandbox, or at the beach will continue to be a favorite way to go. Vehicles with clicky wheels, friction "motors" and passengers to load and unload provide sensory feedback. They are also great props for developing fine motor skills and pretend play. But keep in mind, this is not the time for small Matchbox or Hot Wheels cars, which have small parts and can be a choking hazard. Select simpler vehicles that are easy to manipulate and can withstand being dropped, thrown, and even tasted.

■ Ambi Teddy Copter *2000* PLATINUM AWARD

(Learning Curve $14.99) Push the jaunty little copter along and its red wheels ratchet as the round-edged propeller spins and the teddy pilot pops up and down. A pleasing floor toy that combines motion and pretend to perfection. A great companion to Ambi's classic **First Car.** 1 & up. (800) 704-8697.

■ Little People Adventure Airlines *2000*
PLATINUM AWARD

(Fisher-Price $14.99) Designed for toddlers, this jumbo plane has a handle to lift it off the ground, propellers that spin, wheels that click, and two little people to load and unload. Simple enough for beginning pretenders. Also clever, the **Little People Push'n'Pull Fire Truck** with lift-up ladder that doubles as a pushing handle. 18 mos. & up. (800) 432-5437.

■ Tolo Baby Driver Steering Wheel *2000*

(Small World $10) Attach this suction-cup toy to high chair or any table and tots will give it miles of action. An adjustable yellow steering wheel with red beeping horn makes a ratcheting sound as it's raised or lowered.

There's a gear shift that moves, too, and a suction cup that really holds on! 1 & up. (800) 421-4153. For more bells and whistles, older toddlers will enjoy the sounds and lights of V-Tech's classic **Little Smart Tiny Tot Driver** ($22) an electronic dashboard and steering wheel. 18 months & up. (800) 521-2010.

Comparison Shopper— School Buses 🌟2000🌟

Both Fisher-Price's **Little People School Bus** ($14.99) and Little Tikes' **School Toddle Tots School Bus** ($12.99) come with rear ramps, wheelchairs, and play people. Passengers are loaded in, toddler fashion, through the open roof. The new Fisher-Price model has googly eyes and passengers that bounce up and down. You can't go wrong with either. 1½–5. Fisher-Price (800) 432-5437 / Little Tikes (800) 321-0183.

NOTABLE PREVIOUS WINNERS: Bigger Family Van (Step 2 $13) Four big play figures—a mom, dad, brother, and sister—are fun to load and unload in the big family van that's scaled for toddlers' roll-about games. 1 & up. PLATINUM AWARD '98. (800) 347-8372; **Elmo and His Pet Puppy** (Fisher-Price $29.99) Squeeze Elmo's hands makes the little radio-controlled puppy walk and spin. Very neat! PLATINUM AWARD '98. 2½. (888) 892-6123. **Stack'n'Build Choo Choo** (Fisher-Price $14.99) The 10-piece set has a red engine, two cars, and plenty of other rounded blocks and characters that link the train together. Says 6–36 months. We'd say tots 12–24 months are the right target age. (800) 432-5437.

Housekeeping Props

Older toddlers, both boys and girls, adore imitating the real work they see grown-ups doing around the house. Sweeping the floor, vacuuming, cooking, caring for the baby—these are thrilling roles to play. Many of the props for this sort of pretend will be used for several years. They are what we call "bridge toys" that span the years.

■ 2 in 1 Vacuum Set

(Little Tikes $19.99) Some tots hate the loud roar of the real clean-
er, but get their courage while pretending with a tot-sized replica. We
were surprised to find the classic Fisher-Price vacuum cleaner gone
after so many years. This cleaner has colorful balls that "pop" when
the upright is pushed. Comes with a mini-vac for small pick-ups. 1½
& up. (800) 321-0183.

SHOPPING TIP: One of a toddler's favorite
toys is a child-sized broom. You'll find sets
with mops, feather dusters, and tons of
extras. But it's a basic broom that seems to make
the biggest hit. Just check handles for splinters or
badly sewn bristles. 2 & up.

SAFETY TIP: Buckets! Beware of buckets
used in the house for cleaning. Ever-curious toddlers have been known to fall into them and
drown. Old buckets from building bricks also pose
a problem. Most new play buckets have a new safety bar halfway down to prevent tots from putting
their head all the way in.

Phones

Before you buy a play phone with sound, put the receiver to your ear. Many are alarmingly loud. The quietest
of the bunch are: **Ambi City Phone** (Learning Curve
$9.99) with spinning faces, a mirror, good clicking
sounds, and lots of buttons to push. (800) 704-8697;
Pocket Phone (Chicco $10). (877) 424-4226; and
Tolo Mobile Phone (Small World $12) which
comes with a suction-based stand.(800) 421-4153.

For more bells and whistles: **Ring'n'Rattle Phone** (Fisher-
Price $12.99) Surprise! This phone not only rings, it rattles and
shakes when tots hit the big red button. Fun for early role playing.
Takes 2 "AA" batteries. This will either delight your tot or send
him in the other direction. Try before you buy! See cell phones for
fewer surprises. (800) 432-5437. **Cellular Phone** (Tomy $6) with
a pop-up antenna and flashing lights. 1 & up. (800) 445-8347.

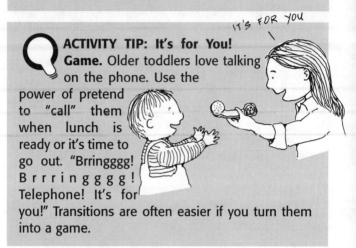

☞**SAFETY TIP:** An old real phone may seem like lots of fun, but the cord and small parts pose a choking hazard to toddlers.

Q **ACTIVITY TIP: It's for You! Game.** Older toddlers love talking on the phone. Use the power of pretend to "call" them when lunch is ready or it's time to go out. "Brringggg! B r r r i n g g g g ! Telephone! It's for you!" Transitions are often easier if you turn them into a game.

IT'S FOR YOU

Toy Dishes and Pots

Finding a sturdy, gender-free set of dishes isn't easy! Many sets we tested cracked, were too small for little hands, and were very, very pink! Stay away from sets with small parts, sharp cutlery, and of course, save the pottery and china for later.

Dishes and Tea Sets:

Little Helper's Dining Room & Pots and Pans (Step 2 $10) White, red, and yellow 22-piece set comes with dishes, pots, and utensils. (800) 347-8372.

Tea Set (Battat $10) done in primary colors with a teapot that really pours (surprisingly, not true of most!) and 4 simple cups and saucers with a sugar bowl and creamer. (800) 247-6144.

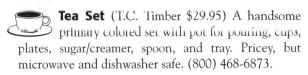 **Tea Set** (T.C. Timber $29.95) A handsome primary colored set with pot for pouring, cups, plates, sugar/creamer, spoon, and tray. Pricey, but microwave and dishwasher safe. (800) 468-6873.

Cooking sets:

My Cooking Playset (Battat $25) with 41 pieces in primary colors will appeal to junior chefs. Remove cutlery for kids who still mouth toys. (800) 247-6144.

Pretend & Play Set (Learning Resources $14.99) 10-piece cooking set in primary colors including a frying pan, a pot, big grip utensils, and our favorite—another tea kettle that actually holds water. 3 & up. (800) 222-3909.

Partyware Plus Value Set (Little Tikes $14.99) An amazing 25-piece set with pots, bowls, rolling pin, cookie cutters, plates, and utensils in bright fiesta colors. Still top-rated: **Kitchen Ware.** (800) 321-0183.

SAFETY TIP: Toddlers do not need fake food! Since they mouth most toys, you'll want to avoid small phony food that's especially tempting to "eat" and may be a choking hazard.

Toy Kitchens & Laundries

Choosing which kitchen center to bring home is really a matter of style preference and space. There are small single units, to elaborate large units that will fill up a wall! None of the plastic kitchens have sinks that hold water—which is too bad. There is also a trend back to pink kitchens—we have noted our gender-free choices because we believe strongly that both boys and girls need to know their way around the kitchen.

■ Doors & Drawers Activity Kitchen

(Little Tikes $40) This is a play setting for the youngest chefs. Our toddlers loved playing with this kitchen, which had doors to open, dials to turn, and a telephone for pretend. PLATINUM AWARD '97. (800) 321-0183.

■ Townhouse Kitchen

(Step 2 $50) This combo kitchen with stove, oven, microwave, fridge and phone takes up little space. (800) 347-8372.

■ Victorian Kitchen 2000

(Little Tikes $99) Off-white with pink and blue trim, this multi-unit ktichen comes with a microwave, stove, oven, double sink, refrigerator and, of course, a phone. Other top-rated larger-scaled plastic kitchens: Step 2's **Grand Kitchen** ($135) in yellow with licks of pink is the largest kitchen yet with doors that open and has a pass through window. For more gender-free choices look at: Step 2's **Homestyle Kitchen** ($60) with a drop down table; Little Tikes' **DoubleUp Kitchen & Laundry Center** ($79.99) includes a small kitchen center, washer, dryer and ironing board; or Little Tikes' **Family Kitchen** ($90) which has a built-in highchair. Little Tikes' ultra modern **SuperGlow Electronic Kitchen** 2000 ($69.99), with lots of bells and whistles, was not ready for testing. Step 2 (800) 347-8372 / Little Tikes (800) 321-0183.

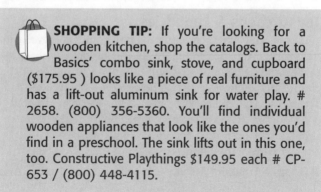

SHOPPING TIP: If you're looking for a wooden kitchen, shop the catalogs. Back to Basics' combo sink, stove, and cupboard ($175.95) looks like a piece of real furniture and has a lift-out aluminum sink for water play. # 2658. (800) 356-5360. You'll find individual wooden appliances that look like the ones you'd find in a preschool. The sink lifts out in this one, too. Constructive Playthings $149.95 each # CP-653 / (800) 448-4115.

Miniature Pretend Settings
■ Happy Crane Construction 2000

(Fisher-Price $19.99) There's so much tots can make happen on this small pretend setting in the shape of a crane (that smiles a la Thomas the Tank). Comes with a small working dump truck (that beeps) and two boulders to place down three different chutes that are easy to activate. They say 1 & up, we say 18 months & up. Also be sure to look at the classic **Little People Fun Sounds Garage** ($24.99) that has been updated with electronic sounds of the garage (horns, keys, cash register, telephone, and hammer). Purists will miss the simplicity of the original, which was easier for younger toddlers to manipulate. This has a working elevator and a ramp and buttons for a satisfying play experience. We thought two cars would have been better than one. 2 & up. (800) 432-5437.

■ Home Sweet Home

(Fisher-Price $29.99) This fully furnished take along doll house opens up for lots of pretend play. Unfortunately, it's been redesigned with lots of pink trim. In the past, we applauded the gender-free paint job. It remains a good choice for older toddlers. 2 & up. (800) 432-5437. Also, **Little People Farm** (Fisher-Price $30) a fold-and-go barn, comes with eight animals with four stalls and swinging gates. Note: While the hay and pumpkin in this set pass the choke-tube test, they are, in our opinion, still too small and should be removed. 1½ & up. (800) 432-5437.

FREEBIE: Empty, staple-free boxes are among the best toys known to toddlers. Great for sitting in, climbing out of, coloring on, lugging around, crawling through, or loading up.

Art and Music

Art Supplies

Give your toddler opportunities to explore colors and textures. Scribbling comes before drawing, just as crawling comes before walking! This is not the time for coloring books or coloring inside the lines. Twos may give names to their creations after they are done. Finished products are not as important as getting their hands into the doing.

Even one year olds get a sense of "can do" power scribbling with big, easy-to-grasp crayons on blank paper. Older tots love the fluid lines they get with fat washable markers, but keep in mind, you'll need to replace the covers or markers dry out. Twos also enjoy bright tempera paint with thick brushes, or play-dough and finger paints for lively hands-on fun!

You don't really need an easel for now. A low table that children can stand at is fine. In fact, they have less trouble with paint rolling and dripping when they work on a flat surface. If your toddler persists in eating supplies or spreading them on floors or walls, put them away for a while and try again in a month or two. (See Preschool Chapter for more on paints & easels.)

■ Kid's First Washable Crayons & Markers

(Crayola $3 & up) These washable crayons are very big to match toddler's way of grasping with a whole fist. Save the smaller crayons, which snap in tots' hands, for their school days. 1½ & up. (800) 272-9652.

Play Dough

Playing with pre-made **Play-Doh** (Hasbro $2 & up) or homemade dough is marvelous for twos who love pounding, poking, rolling, crumbling, and hands-on exploring. At this stage the finished product is unimportant. The focus is on smashing a lump flat or pulling it apart into small pieces or mixing blue and yellow to get green. Dough should be used with supervision in an established place for messy play. Beginners will try to taste: It's nontoxic but not for eating. (800) 752-9755.

> **FREEBIE:** Kids love making their own play dough by getting their hands into the bowl and mixing it up. Dough can be stored in a covered container. Mix together 1 cup of flour, 1/3 cup salt, a few drops of vegetable oil, and enough water to form a dough. Add a splash of food coloring or of bright tempera paint.

Musical Toys

Once they are steady on their feet, toddlers love to move to music. Play a variety of music for them to dance to or accompany with their "instruments." Aside from the usual music for kids, try some marches, ballet scores, or music from other cultures.

■ Little RhythmMaker Piano 2000

(Little Tikes $14.99) Toddlers can easily activate the eight big colorful keys and make music with this reworked classic. The sound is pretty good, and it has a carry handle so toddlers can lug it about. Don't worry about "reading" color-coded music now. Let your tot explore the joys of making her own music. Still top-rated, **Little RhythmMaker Rhythm Set** BLUE CHIP ($13) Safe, chunky rhythm instruments—maracas and tamborine—are perfect for the youngest music makers. 2 & up. (800) 321-0183.

■ Music Blocks 2000 PLATINUM AWARD

(Neurosmith $69.95/$19.95 for cartridges) One of the most innovative toys of the year! We were skeptical about such an expensive musical toy for kids—that was, until we played it! Imagine five colored plastic blocks,

each side with a geometric shape and representing a different sound. Match the shapes or play them in random order—there's no right or wrong way. Push on the blocks to play musical phrases! What sets this toy apart is the quality of the sound: woodwinds, trumpets, percussion. Comes with "Mozart's Night Music" cartridge. Bring home the "Rhythms of the World" cartridge right away. 2 & up. (562) 434-9856.

■ Musical Jack in the Box

(Small World $15) Turn the yellow knob to play "This Old Man" until the Jack in the box pops up with its smile and rosy red nose. May be too surprising for some tots, but most will come to love the predictable and repetitive pop! 1½ & up. (800) 421-4153.

> **ACTIVITY TIP:** Use a full-length mirror to play a "can you do-what-I-do?" game. Use big and little motions from faces to toes. Getting kids to copy what you are doing is more than fun. It helps kids begin to focus on details and translate what they see into actions. Demo a sequence of two motions—pat your head and then your tummy. Can he remember two motions? How about three?

Bath Toys

The tub is another locale for learning and play. Discovering how water spills from a cup, drips from a washcloth, and splashes when you hit it—are a child's way of finding out how things work. In or out of the tub, toddlers are becoming great pretenders. Simple toys like small buckets, boats, a rubber ducky, or a??? For the sometimes reluctant bather, a new toy or a game will do the trick.

SAFETY TIP: Foam bath toys are a choking hazard to toddlers, who may bite off pieces. Unfortunately, many of the age labels on such products are in very small print.

■ Tomy Splash Along Teddy & Swimmers
2000

(International Playthings $7) Here are two small but delightful tub toys to tempt a reluctant bather into the tub. The little blue bear on a barrel goes splish-splashing around the tub when you wind him up. Or press the tail fin on the friendly little shark **Swimmers** ($5) and it paddles across the tub. 18 mos. & up. (800) 445-8347.

■ Scoop'n'Strain Turtle Tower *2000*

(Sassy $8) One of best tub toys ever. Three turtles stack on a center post base that attaches to the side of the tub. The best part of the toy is the funnel in the center post that spins as water runs through it! 1 & up. PLATINUM AWARD '99. (800) 323-6336.

■ Ambi Rub A Dub Tub *2000*

(Learning Curve $16.99) Like the three little men in a tub, three little sailors rise up as water fills their "boat." Lift the tub for a waterfall, and the sail doubles as a whistle. Still top-rated, **Ambi Fishwheel** ($14.99). Pour water into the wheel and three fish spin. 2 & up. (800) 704-8697.

Basic Furniture

Table and Chairs

This is a basic piece of gear that will be used for years of snacks, art projects, and tea parties. Best bets are going to have steady legs and a washable surface. After that, it's a matter of budget and style to fit your home. Check the underside of tables and chairs for smooth finishes that won't snag little fingers. Twos also enjoy a rocking or arm chair scaled to their size. 2 & up.

Some basic safety and design questions you may want to check:

Can your child get on and off chairs/bench easily?

Is this a set that will work when your child gets a little bigger?

If you're looking at a wooden set, are there exposed screws or nuts (check the underside) that can cut your child?

Is the surface washable and ready for abuse? (A beautiful painted piece will be destroyed by paint, play-dough, crayons, etc.)

Comparison Shopper— Plastic Folding Tables

We compared Fisher-Price and Little Tikes foldable plastic tables. Little Tikes **Easy Store Picnic Table** ($59.99) rectangular table is easier to fold away. However, testers report that Fisher-Price's round **Grow-With-Me Patio Table** ($55) is easier for smaller children to use. The Little Tikes model requires kids to step over the plastic that connects the bench to the table. Fisher-Price has no such barrier, making it easier for toddlers to use independently. Fisher-Price (800) 432-5437 / Little Tikes (800) 321-0183.

Selecting Backyard Gym Sets

Buying a backyard gym is an investment in years of active fun that calls for care before you buy, as well as proper installation, maintenance, and supervision. Having such equipment right outside your own door provides an open-ended invitation to get out and use those muscles and that endless energy. Although the primary attraction may be the swing and slide, often these hold less long-term interest than the playhouse/climber, which is used for exercising both body and imagination.

Here are some tips on choosing equipment, installing it, and supervising its use. Shop where you can see and compare gym sets that are set up. Ask yourself:

 Is the set sturdy?

 If it's wooden, is it smooth or likely to turn splintery? Is it made with pressure-treated wood? If so, you should know that the Consumer Safety Commission now reports that the quantity of chemicals used is not considered hazardous.

 Whether it's wood, metal, or plastic, are there sharp or rough edges?

 Are the swing seats like soft straps that conform to a child's body? These are safer and easier to get on and off.

 If swings are hung on chains, are they sealed in vinyl so they won't pinch fingers?

 Are the spaces between ladder rungs wide enough so a child's head can't get caught? All openings should be at least 9". Avoid sets with climbing bars that run the length of the set above the swings.

 Is the bottom of the slide no more than 12" off the ground?

 Are nuts and bolts embedded so they can't snag fingers and clothing?

 Is the set scaled to your child's physical and developmental needs? Many sets come with climbers and slides that are not really appropriate for preschoolers. Do platforms have guardrails?

 What's the weight capacity recommended by the manufacturer?

 Who will install the set and how will it be anchored? Sets should be installed with stakes or in concrete "footings" so they won't tip, and on surfaces such as sand or wood chips 6"–12" deep to cushion falls. Grass is no longer considered safe enough for falls.

⚠ Do you really have room for it? Equipment should be at least six feet from fences, buildings, or anything that could endanger kids.

⚠ What's your budget? Most of the basic wooden sets start at $500, but that's just for the basic unit. After adding a slide, climber, and/or playhouse you're talking about $1,000 and up.

Here are the names of several major gym set companies:

⚠ **Childlife.** Top-rated. Distinctive wooden green finish is smoother and less likely to splinter than the cedar and pine gyms used in many other sets. $450 and up. (800) 462-4445.

⚠ **Rainbow Play Systems.** Steel parts are vinyl dipped, wood is chemical-free, built of redwood & cedar. Cadillac of gym sets, starts at $1100 & up. (800) 724-6269.

⚠ **Hedstrom.** Metal sets from $149 and up. Available from Sears and many toy supermarkets.

⚠ **Little Tikes.** Their plastic **SkyCenter Playhouse Climber and Swing Extension** ($650) has an attachable metal swing set extension that also needs to be anchored with concrete for stability. 3 & up. (800) 321-0183.

Best Travel Toys For Toddlers

We ask almost the impossible from toddlers when we travel by car. Sitting still for long stretches is physically stressful for this age group. Having a plan before you get in the car may help make the transition a little bit easier. The most obvious tip would be to try to plan your car travel to nap time. Of course, that's not always possible. While some kids find the movement of the car soothing and fall asleep easily, others seem to feel the need to co-drive the car—staying alert the entire way!

It's at this age that kids do that straightening-of-the-back-trick when being put into their car seats. It will help if you:

- Give your child a heads-up about getting ready to go into the car.

- Leave a special toy in the car that they can look forward to playing with only in the car.

- Bring along favorite tapes to listen to in the car.

- Bring snacks and drinks—especially good if you get caught in traffic!

- Be sure to bring along a favorite huggable and/or blanket.

- Bring big washable crayons and pad of paper in a travel sack small enough to fit into a diaper bag or glove compartment.

- An inflatable ball for out of the car breaks and when-you-get there fun.

- Small cardboard books they can handle themselves when in their car seats.

- For extended stays: a small set of big plastic blocks or the "favorite toy of the week," one you know she'll be happy to play with while you're unpacking!

FREEBIE: Wrap small items for toddlers to unwrap along the way-little books, a box of cereal, a manipulative toy. Don't show your bag of tricks all at once. Dole them out as you go! Toddlers love surprises and unwrapping is part of the fun.

Best Second Birthday Gifts
For Every Budget

Over $100   **Climber** (Little Tikes) or **Toy Kitchen** (Step 2/Little Tikes)

Under $75   **Music Blocks** (Neurosmith) or **Sandbox** (Little Tikes/Step 2) or **Junior Activity Gym** (Little Tikes)

Under $50   **Cozy Coupe II** (Little Tikes) or **Snuffles** (Gund)

Under $30   **Duplo School Bus** (Lego) or **Bigger Family Shuttle Bus Ride-On** (Step 2) or **Tomy Ball Party Connecting Bridge** (International Playthings)

Under $25   **Shopping Cart** (Little Tikes) or **Little People Fun Sound Garage** (Fisher-Price)

Under $20   **Tomy Ball Tower** (International Playthings) or **Ambi Fishwheel** (Learning Curve) or **Groovy Girls and Boys** (Manhattan Toy)

Under $15   **Tolo Mobile Phone** (Small World) or **Little People School Bus** or **Airplane** (Fisher-Price) or **Pretend & Play Set** (Learning Resources) or **Familiar Things** (Lauri)

Under $10   **Scoop'n'Strain Turtle Tower** (Sassy) or **Crayola Big Bucket** (Crayola) or **Fruit, Farm & Pets Puzzibilities** (Small World)

Under $5   **Play-Doh** (Hasbro)

A Word about Balloons. Despite the fact that latex balloons are considered unsafe for children under six, people continue to give them to kids in stores, parks and at parties. The problem is that kids can suffocate on pieces of latex if they bite and/or inhale a balloon they break or try to blow up. Yes, they are an old tradition—but a dangerous one. Why take the risk? Stick to Mylar!

3 • Preschool
Three to Four Years

What to Expect Developmentally

Learning Through Pretend. Preschoolers are amazing learning machines! Watch and listen to them at play and you can hear the wheels of their busy minds working full tilt. From sunup to sundown, preschoolers love playing pretend games. Playing all sorts of roles gives kids a chance to become big and powerful people. Providing props for such play gives kids the learning tools to develop language, imagination, and a better understanding of themselves and others.

Social Play. Your once-happy-to-be-only-with-you toddler has blossomed into a much more social being. She enjoys playing with other kids. Sharing is still an issue, but there's a budding understanding of give and take.

Solo Play. Unlike the toddler who moved from one thing to another, preschoolers become able to really focus their attention on building a bridge of blocks, working on a puzzle, or painting pictures.

Toys and Development. Although preschoolers love to play at counting and singing or even trying to write the alphabet, informal play is still the best path to learning. Building a tower with blocks, they discover some very basic math concepts. Digging in the sand or floating leaves in puddles, they make early science discoveries.

Big Muscles. Threes and fours also need time and space to run and climb and use their big muscles to develop coordination and a sense of themselves as able doers.

Your Role in Play. A child who has shelves full of stuffed animals or every piece of the hottest licensed character may seem to have tons of toys, but the truth is that, no matter how many trucks or dolls a kid has, such collections offer just one kind of play. Take an inventory of your child's toy clutter to see what's really being played with and what needs to be packed away or donated.

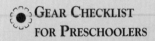

GEAR CHECKLIST FOR PRESCHOOLERS

✓ Set of blocks and props (small vehicles, animals, people)

✓ Trike	✓ Dolls and/or soft animals
✓ Dress-up clothes	✓ Housekeeping toys
✓ Transportation toys	✓ Matching games
✓ Picture books	✓ Sand and water toys

✓ Art materials—crayons, paints, clay

✓ Simple puzzles (eight pieces and up)

✓ Tape player and music and story tapes

🚫 **Toys to Avoid**

These toys pose a safety hazard:

✓ Electric toys or those that heat up with light bulbs that can burn

✓ Toys with projectile parts that can injure eyes

✓ Toys without volume control that can damage ears

✓ Two-wheelers with training wheels

✓ Latex balloons

These toys are developmentally inappropriate:

✓ Complex building sets that adults must build while children watch

✓ Teaching machines that reduce learning to a series of right or wrong answers

✓ Coloring books that limit creativity

Pretend Play

This is the age when pretend play blossoms. Some kids pretend with blocks, trains, and miniatures they move around as they act out little dramas. Others prefer dressing up and playing roles with their whole being. Either way, such games are more than fun. They help children learn to stretch their imaginations, try on powerful new roles, cope with feelings and fears, and develop language and social skills.

Dress-Up Play and Let's-Pretend Props

There are a lot of dress-up kits around. Truth be told, most kids enjoy dressing up in real clothes as much as the store-bought variety. Old pocket-books, briefcases, jewelry, hats, and such are treasures to kids. For very specific role-playing, a hat, a scarf, or a homemade badge is often all that's needed to transform young players. Below are a few specialty items you may want to buy.

■ Construction Worker & Helmet or Fire Chief *2000*

(Small World $15 each) Testers liked this orange vest with wooden Stop & Go traffic sign for serious road work and the yellow slicker Fire Chief's coat with whistle. Hats are sold separately. New for *2000*, a yellow hardhat **Helmet** ($7) with a light! Outfits in this collection are cut for kids who are not big for their age. (800) 421-4153.

■ Create a Clown or Princess *2000*

(Creative Education of Canada $25) Either of these costumes is bound to please young pretenders. The Clown set comes with a supply of bells, stars, and pom-poms that kids can Velcro and design their pointed jester's hat, vest, and jingly wand. The Princess's kit comes with pointed hat, tutu, and jewels. Still top-rated, **Create-a-Fireman** & **Dress-a-Police** ($23–$25). With all sorts of silvery Velcro badges, golden stars & buttons, and belts, either of these well-made costumes will see plenty of action. Also, **Create-a-Crown** ($12), an adjustable crown with Velcro gems for young royals. PLATINUM AWARD '98. 4 & up. (800) 982-2642.

■ School Bus & Ice Cream Truck　2000 PLATINUM AWARD

(Play-hut $29.99) Here's a new twist on play tents. Choose **School Bus, Ice Cream Truck, Space Shuttle,** or **Fire Engine** (app. 28"L x 55"W x 36"H). Kids love enclosed spaces where they feel big and imagination takes off. A bit more literal than a tent made of a blanket, but either makes a great rainy day prop for pretending. We wish the ice cream truck were a little less pink and lavendar. Also top-rated, **Crawl N Peek,** a 60" long tunnel done half in nylon and half in see-thru mesh for crawling, hiding, and pretending. 3 & up. (800) PLAYHUT.

Doctor's Gear

 Comparison Shopper—
Doctor's & Vet's Kits

Doctors no longer make house calls and even the traditional little black bag from Fisher-Price is gone. Their new **Sesame Street Medical Kit** (Fisher-Price $18) in a blue bag doesn't work quite as well as the original black bag, but the basic gear is almost the same as the original. (800) 432-5437. For even more props, Battat's **Medical Kit** ($25) is amazing—with all the usual tools plus scrubs, a mask, and a beeper (with a loud sound)! Comes in a big white attaché case (slide catches are slightly tricky). 3 & up. (800) 247-6144. For a work-

ing **Stethoscope** (Constructive Playthings $7.95).
#MTC 261. (800) 255-6124.

Housekeeping Tools

Both girls and boys use props for cleaning,
cooking, and childcare. Few toys will get
more use by both boys and girls than a mini-
broom or mop. This is an inexpensive favorite
that you'll find in most toy supermarkets. Just
check for smooth finish. Kitchen toys will be
used for playing house and running restaurants.
As children's experiences broaden, so does the
scope of their games of make-believe. For
more kitchens and toy dishes, see
Toddler section.

■ Call-Back Phone *2000*

(Fisher-Price $7.99) It looks and sounds real!
Like the most current cell phones, it has a
flip-down front, flashing lights, and authentic sounding tones. It shuts off after three rings
and is not too loud—a real plus! Takes 2 AAA
batteries. 3 & up. (800) 432 5437.

■ Pretend & Play Teaching Telephone *2000*
PLATINUM AWARD

(Learning Resources $39.95) You can program in any
phone number and leave a message. When your child
calls that number they hear your message. A great way to teach important phone numbers and the
concept of 911. Even the concept of taking messages is built
into the pretend. Takes 4 AA batteries. 4 & up. (800) 222-3909. For
other phones, see Toddler Chapter.

■ Shop & Cook Kitchen

(Fisher-Price $64.99) This combo toy with store and cash register on
one side and a kitchen on the other is loaded with play value. Done
in gender-free primary colors, this can be passed from sister to broth-

er. Comes with accessories and "working" sink—you can actually put water in it and then lift and dump. Note: We were unable to get the screws in all the way, but the toy holds together. PLATINUM AWARD '99. One of the best small add-ons from this line is the **2-in-1 Musical Cake** ($14.99), a novelty cake that flips from wedding to birthday with a special candle or bride and groom that trigger the cake to play "Happy Birthday" or "Here Comes the Bride." Takes 2 AA batteries. (800) 432-5437.

Dolls and Huggables

Preschoolers love soft animals and dolls as huggable companions for bedtime and playtime. At this age, playing with dolls gives both boys and girls a chance to try out new roles and language.

■ Multicultural Dolls

Just a few years ago, there were few options that reflected our diversity. **Cabbage Patch Kids** (Mattel) were almost alone in this category. They are still a good affordable choice, but happily there are now more options in all price ranges. The Pleasant Company's **Bitty Baby Dolls** ($38 each) are 15" soft-bodied dolls available with Caucasian, African-American, Asian-American, or Hispanic features and skin tones. PLATINUM AWARD '96. (800) 845-0005. Manhattan Toy's **Groovy Girls** (see Toddlers) now come with easy on/off clothes. Corolle has added Asian- and African-American dolls to its affordable 8" doll collection of **Les Minis Calins** ($15). **Baby carrier** ($12) or **spring chair** ($16) or **one doll in a wicker carrying case** ($50) is trés jolie! PLATINUM AWARD '97. 3 & up. (800) 628-3655.

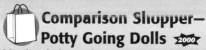

Comparison Shopper— Potty Going Dolls

Hard to believe there are so many choices in this depart- ment! This year there were lots of dolls that talk and giggle while they tinkle—we found all that chatting a distraction. We prefer the pricey (but tubbable), anatomically correct **Fan-Fan** boy or girl drink-and-wet dolls ($80) from Corolle. A smaller, newer, and less expensive boy doll with potty seat ($44) looked promis- ing but was not ready for test- ing. (800) 628-3655.

Favorite Characters

■ Arthur & D.W.

(Eden $22 each) While the origi- nal Arthur's book series is tar- geted to school age kids, many preschoolers have become fans of the television show. Books and merchandise have been designed for the 5 & under crowd. (800) 443-4275.

■ Steve & Blue

(Eden $16 each) There are talking, singing, and bark- ing versions of these two popular characters. We found some of the talking versions too loud. Our preference is for the non-talking types who say whatever kids imagine. It's nice to have a boy doll for this age group! 2½ & up. (800) 443-4275.

■ Rugrats Collection

(Mattel $20 & up) If you have a Rugrats fan at home, these novelty dolls will be a hit. New for 2000 , **Baby Dil** and **Bathtime Rugrats** (good for reluctant bathers). 4–8. (800) 524-TOYS.

■ **Dressable Madeline Doll** BLUE CHIP

(Eden $30) Oo-la-la! That's what any Madeline fan will say who receives a 15" soft doll that seems to step right out of the storybook (complete with appendix scar). Soft and huggable, she has an amazing wardrobe available, like her green coat with gray woolly collar, hat, and skates outfit ($15). Bring home the books & videos, too. 4 & up. (800) 443-4275.

Bears of the Year *2000*

No need to wonder if bears that say and do nothing are out of fashion. They're still as desirable as ever. Among our favorites of the year are **Snoodles** (Gund $15 & up), a silky plush with contrasting muzzle and floppy legs, and **Squeezer** (Gund $15 & up), a toffee-colored bear in string plush with eyes that give it an astonished look. (732) 248-1500. Still top-rated, **Sassafras** PLATINUM AWARD '99. (Manhattan Toy $10 & up), with jointed limbs, a bandanna scarf, silky-soft body, and a sweet face (800) 747-2454.

Dogs of the Year *2000* PLATINUM AWARD

We actually found more delightful dogs this year than bears. Besides **Blue,** our favorites range from zany to cuddly. Here are our top picks: A PLATINUM AWARD goes to **Walk'n'Wag Baby Pluto** (Mattel $30) a novelty toy that's the cat's meow! His leash is a remarkably responsive remote control that makes Pluto shake his head, walk, wag, and bark. 3 & up. (800) 524-TOYS. You'll find **Space Puppies** (Rumpus $20), those zany pooches with over-sized snouts, in the toddler chapter. Also lovable and huggable, **Bonehead** (Gund $20) a soft two-toned pooch with floppy ears. If your preschooler prefers monkeying around, you'll find **Flapjack** (Gund $25) a memorable choice, or **Curious George** ($25) is a classic. Gund (732) 248-1500.

Interactive Dolls

The big news this year is that Elmo and Ernie play their own guitars. Our testers found these dolls to be "one-note" toys, with very little for kids to do but watch. That said, they have novelty appeal and will play well on tv and be heavily promoted. We also found a doll that giggles when she goes to the potty and apologizes for wetting her pants.

Our favorites remain:

■ ActiMates Barney

(Microsoft $99) Barney remains the most magical interactive doll because it was expertly designed to match the skills of preschoolers. Barney not only sings, plays games, and engages players in active give-and-take—he also interacts with the VCR and the computer. Takes 6 AA batteries. 2½ & up. Platinum '98. (800) 426-9400. We found the skills programmed into **ActiMates Arthur** and **D.W.** off the mark for preschoolers.

■ Hug & Learn Little Leap

(Leap Frog $39.99) This big green frog can count and say its ABCs—and it also says "please" and "thank you"! Kids can push Leap's shirt and he says letters, or they can play in search mode that teaches letter names and sounds. A third game looks for letters and numbers that come before and after. We found this doll better than many quiz machines that work on the same skills. Takes 4 AA batteries. They say 2–5, we say 4 & up. (800) 701-5327.

■ Magic Talking Kermit 2000 PLATINUM AWARD

(Tyco $30) Kids and adults alike fell in love with this fly-catching, singing amphibian. Push his tummy and he sings; press his mouth and he says how good it tastes! Hard to believe, Kermit is 30 years old this year. Still top-rated, **Talking Big Bird,** who plays peek-a-boo and patty-cake. (800) 488-8697.

Comparison Shopper— Doll Strollers and Furniture

Budget and taste will go into making the choices here. Just like the real equipment, there are doll carriers for the silver-spoon set and more practical models for your average doll.

Doll Strollers 🎗2000🎗

We like Pleasant Company's gender-free white and red umbrella stroller ($18) designed for their 15" **Bitty Baby Dolls.** (800) 845-0005. Little Tikes' plastic pink and white doll stroller ($25) can hold a doll up to 18". 2 & up. Also top-rated, Little Tikes' **Shopping Cart** ($23) fills the bill for a gender-free, more open-ended prop with a doll seat. (800) 321-0183.

■ Wooden Doll Cradle BLUE CHIP

(Community Playthings $90) A solid maple cradle designed for schools and built to last. The large 29" model is big enough so kids can climb in and play baby or put a family of dolls to sleep. Sure to become a family heirloom. 2 & up. #C140. (800) 777-4244.

Puppets and Puppet Stages 🎗2000🎗

Through the mouths of puppets, kids can say things that they might not otherwise speak about; so puppets are a way of venting feelings and developing imagination and language skills. Young puppeteers replay stories, create original ones, and develop skills that link to reading and writing. Animal puppets from Gund and Applause are widely available. Since kids know familiar characters from **Sesame Street** (Applause) and **Disney** (Gund), it's easy for young puppeteers to step into familiar roles. Gund (732) 248-1500 / Applause (800) 777-6990. See Early School Years for more puppets and stages.

■ Family Puppet Sets

(Constructive Playthings $24.95 per set) For realistic role-playing, try this four-piece family with Mom, Dad, brother, and sister. Caucasian, Hispanic, African-American, and Asian American sets available. All-fabric heads and bodies. Company will customize families! #FPH721L. (800) 832-0572.

Puppets of the Year ⚡2000

We dare you to pick one favorite! Manhattan Toy outdid itself with **Electralips** ($15), funky, vibrant, velour, polka-dotted bugs with gossamer wings ready for fantasy flights of imagination. Or consider the humanoid **Beakniks** ($15), or swamp-dwelling **Knitwits** ($12.50) Lizigator, Turtellini, & Sluggo done in soft chenille with big easy-to-move mouths. Testers also loved **Morphing Marty** ($15) an ever-changeable puppet with 22 features that attach with Velcro. Straight from storybook-land comes **Madeline** (Eden $14), a full-body puppet dressed in her yellow hat and blue dress. Madeline is ready to retell stories or make up new ones. Our testers gave the PLATINUM AWARDS to the Beakniks and Knitwits—but all of these are winners. Manhattan Toy (800) 647-2454 / Eden (800) 443-4275.

■ Puppet Theatre ⚡2000

(Alex $80) A large but stable floor model that's 48" high, with painted trim on one side and chalk surfaces for messages, is ideal for theatrical productions. Small tabletop model is also available ($25). 3 & up, up, up. (800) 666-2539.

FREEBIE: Do it yourself—a large appliance box can be turned into an excellent puppet stage, and so can a cloth-covered card table that kids can hide behind. Another great option is a spring curtain rod and length of fabric that can be used in any doorway.

Pretend Settings:
Doll Houses and Parking Garage

Some of the mini-settings listed in the Toddlers section will be used in more elaborate ways now. If you put them away, try bringing them out again and see how differently your child plays with them. Here are descriptions of recommended settings that are more complex.

Doll Houses *2000*

Dollhouses should be kept simple for little hands. That's what we liked about the Little Tikes Place, which is no longer available. Fisher-Price's new **Loving Family Dollhouse** ($49.99) has all the amenities of home but is very, very pink (did we mention how pink?). (800) 432-5437. Simpler, with a more open plan, **Plan Toys Wooden Doll House** (Small World $99 & $139). Choose either of their modern-looking A-frames with open roofs for easy access. The pricier one has sliding doors and wallpaper. Furnishings for bedroom, bath, living room, and kitchen are beautifully crafted in wood ($20 per room). (800) 421-4153.

■ FELTKids Playhouse Playmat & Playscenes *2000*

(Learning Curve $14.99) Where space is tight, a two-dimensional felt Playhouse unfolds into four colorful rooms that kids can decorate with FELTKids characters and furnishings ($9.95 per room). These felt cutouts are ideal for language development, pretending, and storytelling. Top-rated playscenes & playboards: **Madeline's Birthday, Space Adventure,** and **Blue's Clues.** 3 & up. (800) 704-8697.

■ Farm House

(Battat $45) Larger and more elaborate than most, this big red barn with carrying handle opens to reveal a double-sided two-story barn with windows, gates, working doors, and plenty of barnyard critters. 3 & up. (800) 247-6144.

Comparison Shopper—Garages 2000

We were disappointed that Fisher-Price discontinued the Big Action Garage and replaced it with their smaller **Little People Sound Fun Garage** that's loaded with electronic sounds (see Toddler chapter). We were also disappointed that ALEX's ($80) spiffy-looking wooden garage was not ready for testing.

Trucks and Other Vehicles

Preschoolers are fascinated with all forms of transportation. The real things are out of reach and on the move, but toy trucks, cars, boats, jets, and trains are ideal for make-believe departures, both indoors and out. Choose vehicles with working parts to use with blocks, in the sandbox, or at the beach. BLUE CHIP choices such as **Mighty Tonka Trucks** are perfect gifts for now. So are **Matchbox** or **Hot Wheels** cars, which are now appropriate and often the first "collectible."

■ Construction Truck with Hard Hat

(Little Tikes $20) If you're looking for a showy gift at a reasonable price, you won't do better than this set. These vehicles are articulated for easy action and made to withstand sand and water. Choose a working dump truck or loader. 3 & up. (800) 321-0183.

■ Sea Plane Hauler 2000

(Nylint $11) A sleek white semi that carries a seaplane that floats. 4 & up. For this company's BLUE CHIP trucks see Early School. (800) 397-8697.

Comparison Shopper—Remote Control Cars 2000

Both of these radio control cars have two speeds and free wheeling mode. **RadioGo Race Car** (Little Tikes $29.99) has a futuristic look with bright red knobby textured wheels. Controller is easy to operate, with two large buttons clearly marked with arrows for forward, reverse, and turn actions. Takes 1 9 volt and 4 AA batteries. **2-in-1 R/C Truck** (Fisher-Price $34.99) raises from racer to monster truck look, and controller has a wheel that turns the vehicle as well as a button for forward and reverse. Testers liked both but report that Little Tikes Racer corners better. 3 & up. Little Tikes (800) 321-0183 / Fisher-Price (800) 432-5437. Tomy's new **IRC Jumbo Jet** looked promising but was not available for testing. (800) 445-8347.

First Trains and Track Toys

What They Learn

A non-electric train is a classic toy that will keep growing in complexity as you add working bridges, roundhouses, and other extras. (Note: Preschoolers are not ready for electric trains, except to watch!)

Trains are really open-ended puzzles with no right or wrong answers. Making the track work often becomes more important to many kids than actually playing with the trains.

Many stores display their trains on tabletops with track glued down, but much of the open-ended play value is lost when you do that at home. Making ever-changing settings is half the fun. Skip the table and invest in more tracks and bridges.

Train-Buying Tips

Most starter sets come with just a circle of track that will lose its appeal quickly. Start out with enough tracks to make it interesting.

Most wooden track sets are compatible with Brio trains, the best-known line. ▦ For econo-my and multiple choices, add accessories from various makers.

Good starter sets

■ Intermediate Suspension Bridge Set BLUE CHIP

(Brio $76) Brio's top-of-the-line wooden train set has 18 pieces of track (135"), one suspension bridge that looks like the Golden Gate, ascending tracks, and a three-piece train. New for 2000, a smaller **Classic Figure 8 Set** ($39.95) comes with 24 pieces.

■ Wooden Train

(T. C. Timber $72.95) Set comes with 37 pieces—enough track to form a figure eight, a tunnel-bridge, trees, and four-piece train. (800) 468-6873.

■ Thomas the Tank Engine Around the Barrel Loader Set

(Learning Curve $100) Thomas fans will be thrilled with the 50-piece set that includes 3 trains, tunnel, barrel loader, a shed, signs, trees, and play figures. Note: Some Thomas trains are too tall for other makers' bridges. Also great & less pricey, a figure 8 set with one tunnel/bridge ($40). (800) 704-8697.

Best New Wooden Train Props

New accessories can inspire fresh layouts and keep interest chugging along.

■ Cranky the Crane 2000

(Learning Curve $29.99) Young engineers can raise and lower cargo with this magnetic crane. Looked promising, but was not ready for testing. Also new this year, a **Water Tower** ($19.99) in which the water level changes with a turn of the switch (like magic baby doll bottles). For young readers there's a **Stop & Go Station** ($15) that controls traffic. (800) 704-8697.

■ Light and Sound Level Crossing 2000

(Brio $35) This little crossing has lights that flash and a bell that pings for 10 seconds as the trains go by. Looked promising, but was not ready for testing. Also new for 2000, **Autostop & Start Battery Engine & Track**

($36) a 2-piece set with a little green engine and a track with a switch that stops and starts the engine. Still top-rated, **Sky Bridge** ($55). Lots of high bridges for wooden trains with tricky descending tracks are too hard for beginners to build. This two-piece bridge goes together with ease and has a center tunnel underpass wide enough for a double track. 3 & up.

■ Suspension Bridge

(Learning Curve $49.99) Even the most jaded train buff will say WOW! This elegant suspension bridge has flexible tracks, green suspension "wires," and brick arches. Putting this together is not hard, but challenging. Also neat, **Thomas the Tank Engine Curved Viaduct** ($44.99). Four arched and curved pieces with "stone-work" decals connect to form an amaz-

ing raised viaduct for wooden trains to cross. Does not come with ascending tracks, although you'll need them. A beauty! (800) 704-8697.

> ☞ **SAFETY TIP** Many toy train sets come with very small accessories (trees, people, and animals) and the trains also have small parts. They are not appropriate for toddlers or even preschoolers who still mouth their toys.

Construction Toys

If there's one toy no child should be without, blocks are it! Few toys are more basic. Stacking a tower, balancing a bridge, setting up a zoo—all call for imagination, dexterity, decision making, and problem solving. Built into the play are early math and language concepts that give concrete meaning to abstract words like "higher," "lower," "same," and "different." Best of all, blocks are wonderfully versatile—they build a space city today, a farm tomorrow.

Kids will enjoy both wood and plastic types of blocks, which encourage different kinds of valuable play experiences. Choosing blocks depends largely on your budget and space. Although many of these sets are pricey, they are a solid investment that will be used for years to come.

Wooden Blocks

Unit blocks come in many shapes and lengths and should be carefully proportioned to each other. Many catalogs offer unit blocks in sets of different sizes. Parents are sometimes disappointed when kids don't use the small starter sets they buy. Keep in mind that kids really can't do much with a set of 20 blocks and no props. This is one of those items where the more they have, the more they can do.

■ Master Builder Block System *2000*

(T. C. Timber $25 & up) These wooden blocks are 40 percent smaller than regular unit blocks but maintain their size relationships. Most interesting in this system are architectural sets: **Maya** *2000*, **Romantic, Medieval, Russian,** and **Japanese.** PLATINUM AWARD '96. Old 4s & up. (800) 468-6873.

Comparison Shopper— Unit Blocks

No two catalogs have the same number of blocks or shapes in any set, so there's a small difference in all the sets listed. The cost of shipping will vary depending upon where you live, and the weight and price of the item. Our best suggestion is that you call around and compare. Here's a sampling of what a good basic set will run:

Back to Basics set of 82 blocks in 16 shapes. (#133). $124 (800) 356-5360.

T. C. Timber set with 87 pieces in 23 shapes. (#50-6674). $275 (800) 468-6873. (Higher price reflects greater number of shapes with architectural accessories.)

Constructive Playthings set of 85 pieces in 15 shapes. (#CP-U305L). $169. (800) 832-0572.

Grand River: Super Set of 101 dark hardwood blocks with 88 pieces in 16 shapes plus a 7-piece Roman arch and 6 classical columns. (#A60). $88 (800) 567-5600.

Small World set of 50 unit blocks in 9 shapes comes in sturdy storage cardboard box with rope handles. (*829739) ($50). (800) 421-4153.

Props for Blocks

Providing a variety of props, such as small-scaled vehicles, animals, and people, enhances building and imaginative play. Here are some props designed to inspire young builders. Our favorites:

■ Rainbow Blocks

(Guidecraft $48.95) Kids will love looking through these 14 smooth hardwood blocks with "window" panels of colored Plexiglas. Scaled to unit blocks, there are rectangles, triangles, arches, and squares. Pricey but special for adding accent shapes to constructions. Also, **Mini Traffic Signs** ($12). Six wooden signs come in a neat carrying case. 4 & up. (800) 544-6526.

■ Safari Playset 2000

(Simplex/Battat $45) We loved the old-fashioned set of 20 painted wooden animals, trees, people, and vehicle. The animals will be used for zoo, safari, circus, and other dramatic play. 3 & up. (800) 247-6144.

■ Windows and Door Blocks

(Constructive Playthings $16.95) Scaled to fit standard unit blocks: a five-piece set of 4 windows and one door. (#PCR-62L). (800) 832-0572.

ACTIVITY TIP: Playful Cleanup. Preschoolers often need help cleaning up. You can get some learning in by saying, "I'll find the trucks, you pick up all the cars," or "Let's find all the smallest blocks first." Set up open shelves for blocks and baskets for props to avoid having a constant jumbled mess!

Cardboard Blocks

See Toddler Chapter.

Plastic Blocks

Plastic building sets call for a different kind of dexterity. Here's what you should look for:

Beginners are better off with larger pieces that make bigger and quicker constructions.

Encourage beginning builders to experiment rather than copy or watch you build.

■ Duplo   **2000** PLATINUM AWARD

(LEGO Systems $10 & up) Chunky plastic Duplo building blocks to snap together and take apart are basic gear. We recommend starting with a large bucket with lots of pieces. Here is an example of more being more. Duplo's new **Brick Mixer** ($24.95), which comes with Duplos in a see-through drum for filling, spilling, and transporting, wins our PLATINUM AWARD for **2000**. This is the first year Lego has ventured into licensed characters. For some children, familiar characters, animals, and vehicles may spark their interest in building. New for **2000**, **Winnie the Pooh** ($25) comes with his friends and setting from the 100 Acre Wood. The large 49-piece **Deluxe Harbor Highway** ($29.99) is for more advanced builders, with 2 vehicles and 10 roadway pieces. Putting the curved roadway together calls for some adult help. (800) 233-8756.

■ Multi-Activity Table

(Nilo $200) This Cadillac of play tables (33" x 48" x 20") is a piece of wooden furniture that's more versatile than most with a raised edge to hold everything from train tracks to building blocks. (800) 872-6456.

> **SHOPPING TIP:** Older preschoolers will enjoy mixing their old chunky Duplos with the smaller-scaled Lego bricks. The latter demand more dexterity, so don't rush kids into frustration. See Early School Years Chapter for more advanced sets.

■ Mega Blocks BLUE CHIP

(Mega Blocks $10 & up) These oversized plastic pegged blocks are easy for preschoolers to take apart, fit together, and assemble into B-I-G constructions with a minimum of pieces. Select a set with wheels and angled pieces for more flexibility. (800) 465-6342.

Early Games

Preschoolers are not ready for complex games with lots of rules or those that require strategy, math, or reading skills. Best bets for family fun are games of chance such as lotto, picture dominoes, and classics such as Candyland, where players depend upon the luck of the draw rather than skill. Taking turns is often hard, and so is the concept of winning or losing. We've selected games that can be played cooperatively and those that are quick and short so there can be lots of winners. Some of the best games here can also be played as solitaire matching games.

Active Games

■ Bullfrog Bullseye 2000

(Playskool $12.99) Three silly-looking frogs are sitting on a very plastic log. The object is to hit the frogs off their log with three bean bags. We were surprised by how much our mixed-aged testers enjoyed this game. Younger kids will of course need to stand closer to make a hit. 3 & up. (800) 752-9755.

■ Sonny the Seal 2000 PLATINUM AWARD

(Milton Bradley $19.99) Toss your rings and Sonny, a blue motorized seal, tips his head and bobs about. He barks and claps his flippers when you get a ring around his neck. Fun for solo or two kids. Requires 2 C batteries. 3–6.

NOTABLE PREVIOUS WINNERS: Hot Potato (Parker Brothers $14.99) An electronic musical spud. 4 & up. **Create-a-Word Supermat** ($34.99) Kids push letters printed on the giant talking mat and it says letters or sounds. 4 & up. (800) 701-5327.

Color, Counting, and Dominoes
■ Barnyard Boogie Woogie 2000

(International Playthings $20) Most of the action happens "off the board" as players must move and sound like the animal they land on before they can collect a playing piece. First to collect five animals wins. Playful fun for preschoolers with an adult to keep it together. 4 & up. Also top-rated, **Maisy Game** ($20), a handsome color game featuring Maisy. Players roll the color die to move down the path to Maisy's farm, school, playground, or home. (800) 445-8347.

■ Elephant Ride 2000

(Ravensburger $20) Players match monkey cards and lean them against the big elephant playing board. First to reach top of elephant wins the round. Handsome graphics and fun game for 4 & up. Still top-rated and easier, **Busytown Board Game** ($20). (800) 886-1236.

■ Farm Friends 2000

(Ravensburger $20) Older preschoolers collect farm animals and construct corrals as they move along playing board. A game of chance for pre-readers. 4 & up. (800) 886-1236.

NOTABLE PREVIOUS WINNERS: Farm Animals To Go! (Learning Resources $11.95) Play several fast sorting and memory games with these 48 pleasing rubber animals (kids love them). 3–5. (800) 222-3909. **Curious George Match-a-Balloon** (Ravensburger $20), a color matching game. (800) 886-1236.

Matching and Memory 2000

Pre-readers match pictures before they match words. These
games provide playful ways to develop vocabulary, memory,
and visual skills. While there are lots of choices, many sets
either have too many images or are not sufficiently distinct for
young players. We found the following to be graphically clear-
er for kids to follow. Here are our top picks:

■ Maisy Memory Game 2000

(Briarpatch $19.95) Features popular story-
book character Maisy, with easy-to-identify
objects. Still top rated, PLATINUM AWARD
winner **Goodnight Moon Game** ($19.95),
a simple matching game for 2½ & up or
more challenging, **I SPY Preschool Game**
($14.95) a terrific getting-ready-to-read
game. 4 & up. (800) 232-7427.

■ Theodore Tugboat Rootin' Tootin' Card Game 2000

(International Playthings $15)
Players turn their cards one at a
time at the same moment. The
first player to see a match and
hit the special "tooting" bell
takes all the cards that have
been turned so far. Player with
the most cards at the end of the game wins. Requires looking at details
and rapid reflexes! For a more traditional Lotto game, see **Picture Pairs**
with clear photo images from DK. 4 & up. (800) 445-8347.

Puzzles

A word about puzzles. Preschoolers gradually move from
whole-piece puzzles to simple puzzles that challenge them to
see how two or more parts make a whole. For kids with no previous experience, start with 5–7 pieces in a frame. Children's
skills vary, so take your cue from the child. Some fours can
handle 20–30 pieces, while others are still working on 10–15
pieces. Large pieces are easier for little hands. A word of warning: With some notable exceptions listed below, many of the
wooden puzzles that came our way continued to be badly finished and were rife with splinters.

■ **Airplane** 🎖**2000**

(Lauri $7.50) Lauri's puzzles come with rubber pieces and a pattern printed in the container/tray for beginners to follow. For building confidence, these are the perfect place to start. BLUE CHIP favorites: **Dump Truck, Airplane, Choo-Choo** or **Backhoe.** New for 🎖**2000**, **Animal Match Puzzles**, a dozen two-piece animal puzzles with each pair of animals in different positions —a step beyond simple matching. 3–7. (800) 451-0520.

■ **Big Dump Truck Puzzle** 🎖**2000**

(Frank Schaffer $14.95) Truck lovers will enjoy building this 26-piece floor puzzle of a dump truck that can be tipped after it's built. 4 & up. A 50-piece **Racetrack** comes with four tiny pull-and-go cars that are zippy, but run straight rather than round the track. 4 & up with help. Also, **Firefighter** ($13.95) and BLUE CHIP winner, **Number Train.** 3 & up. (800) 421-5565.

■ **Form & Shape Boards** 🎖**2000**

(Plan Toys/Small World $15 & up)The **Form Board,** with 9 solid pieces to lift and match, is easier than the 19-piece **Shape Matching Board** with each shape divided in two. Still more advanced, **Geometric Sorting Board** challenges beginning counters to fit shapes on 1–4 pegs. 3–5. (800) 421-4153.

■ **Go, Dog, Go!** 🎖**2000**

(Mudpuppy Press $14.95 & up) This company continues to make marvelous puzzles from picture book art. There are 12-piece frames ($7.95), and 24–36 piece floor puzzles in handsome, sturdy storage boxes. Among our favorites this year are **Go, Dog, Go!, Today I Feel Silly, Bunny My Honey.** 3 & up. (212) 354-8840.

■ **Inside Outside Puzzles** 🎖**2000**

(Straight Edge $5) Pick of any one of these handsome 12-piece cardboard puzzles shaped like a tugboat, space shuttle, bulldozer, or farm.

Lift the pieces out to reveal the inner workings and information to read. 4 & up. (800) 732-3628.

■ Three Pigs & Other Puzzibilities *2000*

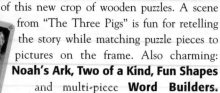

(Small World $11 each) We liked the innovative raised pieces of this new crop of wooden puzzles. A scene from "The Three Pigs" is fun for retelling the story while matching puzzle pieces to pictures on the frame. Also charming: **Noah's Ark, Two of a Kind, Fun Shapes** and multi-piece **Word Builders.** Testers liked **City Life** and **Our Home** with geometric shapes that call for looking at fine details. A clever **Alphapatterns** has patterns on each letter that are enlarged details of the animal shown below. 3–5. (800) 421-4153.

■ Little Bear Puzzles *2000*

(Great American Puzzle Factory $9.95) Fans of Sendak's Little Bear will like putting together the 24-piece floor puzzles of **Little Bear's Friend** or **Birthday Party.** They say 3; we'd say more like 4 & up. Also new for *2000*, **Giant 1-2-3 Train** ($10), a 6-foot-long 20-piece puzzle for number sequencing. Toot toot! 3s with help. (800) 922-1194.

Lacing Games *2000*

Kids dive right into lacing activities without knowing it's a great way to develop fine motor skills they'll need for writing. While stringing beads, they can also sort by color and make patterns, learning to see likes and differences. Three favorites: **Jumbo Stringing Beads** BLUE CHIP (T. C. Timber $20) 31 large wooden beads in different colors and shapes. (800) 468-6873. **Cotton Reels** (Galt $9) Big colorful plastic spools to sort and string. (800) 899-4258. New for *2000*, **Lacing & Tracing Dinosaurs** (Lauri $6.95), seven colorful dinos of sturdy chipboard punched with holes that kids "sew" with colorful laces. 4 & up. (800) 451-0520.

Science Toys and Activities

Floating a leaf in a puddle, collecting pebbles in the park, making mud pies in the sandbox, watching worms wiggle— these are a few of the active ways children learn about the natural world. Here are our favorites for early science exploration:

Magnets and Observation Tools
■ **Giant Super Magnet & Magnifier** *2000*

(Constructive Playthings $3.95) A giant horseshoe magnet. Easy to hold and powerful enough to pick up several metal objects. Item # MTC-405. Also special, a **Hardwood Giant Magnifier** on legs ($39.95) that fits over objects preschoolers can examine. Item #WB-4. (800) 832-0572.

Q ACTIVITY TIP: Give your preschooler a sheet of peel-off stickers to put on anything they find that the magnet sticks to. Or give kids a bag full of household items to sort into two baskets. Have them put all the things that are attracted to the magnet in one basket and all the others in another.

Garden Work

Preschoolers love the magic of seeing things grow. Apartment dwellers can garden on a windowsill. For the backyard set, more elaborate child-sized tools are available. **Plastic Garden Tools** (Little Tikes $13) are safer for preschoolers than scaled-down metal versions from other companies. An accidental swing in the wrong direction will not mean a trip to the ER. They also don't have splintery handles as some metal tools do, and won't rust when they are inevitably left outside.

Garden Sets
■ **Little Landscaper Lawn & Garden Cart**

(Little Tikes $17) For young gardeners, this BLUE CHIP gardening cart has pockets that hold watering can, trowel, and cultivator. Unlike a tippy wheelbarrow, it has two front wheels for stable pushing action. Also recommended, plastic **Garden Tools** ($13 set of three). 2–6. (800) 321-0183. For somewhat bigger kids, **Tot Deluxe Garden Set** (Battat $34). This blue wagon kids can push or pull comes with large sturdy plastic shovel, rake, hoe, sprinkling can, and hand tools for serious gardening. 3 & up. (800) 247-6144.

Lawn Mowers

Choose either the classic Little Tikes **Little Land-scaper Mulching Mower** ($20), Fisher-Price's **Bubble Mower,** or Ertl's **John Deere Kids Action Push Mower** ($26.99) Pull-back handle makes a whirling sound as it "cuts" (too noisy for inside) and the see-through dome lets you see the grass inside. Little Tikes (800) 321-0183 / Ertl (800) 553-4886 / Fisher-Price (800) 432-5437.

SAFETY TIP: Kids should be nowhere near real mowers in action. Flying pebbles travel at 200 mph and can cause deadly accidents. Ditto on riding with adults on power mowers!

■ Push/Pull Wagon

(Radio Flyer $60) Bigger than the classic red wagon, this plastic update has higher sides, a well, and a stout handle for pushing or pulling kids or cargo. This and the BLUE CHIP classic version are ideal for carting plants, tools, imaginary playmates—you name it. (800) 621-7613.

Sand, Water, & Bubble Toys

Sand and water are basic materials for exploring liquids and solids, floating and sinking, sifting and pouring. An inexpensive pail and shovel are basic gear and less upsetting to lose than the high-priced spread. A sand mill is also basic for sandbox or beach. Older preschoolers will be delighted with a set of turrets and tower molds for building beautiful sand castles—kids will add moat, imagination, and who knows what else! Some other sand tools are also worth considering.

■ Brio Waterway

(Brio $41 & up) Learn how locks lift ships with this wet and entertaining hands-on waterway. We've seen waterways before, but this system goes together with greater ease and no leaks. An adult will need to assemble and supervise, but this is a great poolside, backyard water toy for 4–8s. (888) 274-6869.

ACTIVITY TIP: Does it float? Gather things like a paper cup, paper dish, plastic blocks, a comb, a bar of soap, a plastic spoon that are safe but interesting. Challenge your child to discover which things float and which sink. Make float and sink piles for keeping track.

SHOPPING TIP: You can find molds in almost any toy store. Just be sure to check the edges for roughness. Most catalogs offer new combinations every season, some with handy net bags for storage.

■ New Giant Castle ⭐2000

(Battat $30) Dreaming of castles rising by the sea? This 14-piece set is designed for a group with multi-sized towers, turrets, stairs, and tools for building amazing castles. All the pieces fit into a gigantic pail that's shaped like a royal gatehouse. All ages. Still top-rated, **Deluxe Sand & Water Set** (Battat $21) 14 pieces including a sand-mill and hose sprinkler on the big bucket.(800) 247-6144.

ACTIVITY TIP: Give kids empty squeeze bottles, sieves, funnels, different-shaped cups, and tumblers for pouring, sprinkling, and spilling experiments.

■ Splash Sports *2000*

(Fisher-Price $2.99 & up) For fun ways to cool off and get wet without a pool, try this collection of sports balls and paddles. Fill them with water then bat, toss, and hit! Kids loved getting soaked with squeezable **Splash Balls** ($3) and a tether-ball-like toy called **SplashSports Sprinkler** ($24) that attaches to the garden hose. 3 & up. (800) 432-5437.

Bubbles

Blowing bubbles has come a long way from the small plastic containers of pink liquid with a small, sticky wand. For mixed-age groups: The 12-piece **Bubble Party** (Battat $17) includes wands, trumpets, giant rings, and a waffle wand (enough pieces for nine kids!). (800) 247-6144. The **No-Spill Big Bubble Bucket** (Little Kids $13.99) has three extra-large wands that can't get lost in the bottle! Testers also gave top ratings to **Little Kids Mini Bubble Tumblers** ($4.99), and **Bubble Phibians** ($4.99) which let kids blow a stream of bubbles. Both make fun party favors. (800) 545-5437.

■ Tonka Bubble Fire Truck *2000*

(OddzOn $19.99) Push the red fire truck and tons of little bubbles emerge. The faster you push, the more bubbles you get! Makes bubbles more easily than the classic Fisher-Price **Bubble Lawn Mower** that requires more speed to produce the bubbles. 2 & up. Our testers found OddzOn's new **Jumba Bubba** too loud and difficult to work. OddzOn (800) 755-6674 / Fisher Price (800) 432-5437.

FREEBIE: For super-large bubbles, mix 1 cup of Dawn liquid detergent with 3 table-spoons of Karo syrup in 2½ quarts of cold water. Stir gently. Leftovers (if you have any) need to be refrigerated. Ideal for large groups.

Portable Pools and Sandboxes

See Toddlers Chapter.

Active Physical Play

Active play builds preschoolers' big muscles, coordination, and confidence in themselves as able doers. It also establishes healthy active patterns for fitness, relieves stress, and provides a legitimate reason to run and shout. Agreeing on the rules of the game and taking turns promote important social and cooperative skills. For tips on buying swing sets, see Toddlers section.

Basketball Sets: Hoops Recalls

Right after we went to press with last year's book, the Consumer Product Safety Commission issued a recall on most child-sized basketball sets. The detachable netting on the hoops posed a strangulation hazard. You can call the CPCS hotline, (800) 638-2772, for more details, but the recall involved Fisher-Price, Ohio Arts, Little Tikes, and Today's Kids. Companies are offering to replace the hoop portion of the sets.

While the hoops have been fixed, we found a new safety concern with almost all new sets. In the past, manufacturers suggested filling the base with water or sand, but the base was pretty stable without filling. Unfortunately, the newer designs tip easily unless they are loaded with the recommended sand because the posts are placed closer to the front of the whee-lable base. We understand now why you need the wheels!

■ Jam & Go Basketball Set 2000

(Little Tikes $44.95) Adjustable to five different heights from 4 to 6 feet, here's the newest basketball set that will grow with your child. The base has two wheels which make it easier to move about once you've filled the base. Comes with one junior-size basketball. Also recommended, the **Easy Store Basketball Set** (Little Tikes $44.95) which is larger—adjustable to five heights from five to seven feet. Folds for storage and has wheels for portability. Both must be filled with sand to avoid tipping. 3 & up. (800) 321-0183.

■ Bing Ball Hopper BLUE CHIP

(Hedstrom $11.99) Hop-on balls are classics for active play and building coordination. This new version has colorful balls inside that bounce and make noise as child bounces on the big ball. Great for building big muscle action and coordination. 4 & up. (800) 765-9665.

■ Gertie Balls

(Small World $5 & up) These gummy inflatable balls are soft enough for kids who may be scared of big heavy balls coming towards them. We particularly like the **Nobbie Gertie.** 3 & up. (800) 421-4153.

■ 3-in-1 Baseball Trainer 2000

(Little Tikes $29.99) As kids grow, this baseball teaching tool goes from a simple tee ball to a pop-up pitching machine. At first an adult steps on the pedal to launch the ball for a young player to try to hit. Later the player can remove the tee and step on the pedal to launch the ball independently. Comes with five balls and flat-sided bat for beginners. They say 3 & up, we say 4 & up. (800) 321-0183.

Comparison Shopper—Golf Sets

Young Tigers-in-training have a variety of choices for teeing off. **Golf Set** ⟨2000⟩ (Fisher-Price $19.99): If playing golf is big in your family, your preschooler will no doubt want to try it, too. Here's the perfect set to start—comes with two clubs, a rolling case that also holds and dispenses the golf balls. 3 & up. (800) 432-5437.

Still recommended: **Tournament Golf Set** (Little Tikes $30) has a no-nonsense look with three challenging putting greens. Comes with wedge, putter, and six balls for indoors or out. Says 2 & up; we'd say 4 & up. (800) 321-0183. For clubs on wheels, our testers loved **Today's Kids Golf Cart** ($40) complete with clubs, balls and putting cup. (800) 258-8697.

■ Rocking Rider Horse BLUE CHIP

(Today's Kids $75 & up) A splendidly stable rocking horse with broad base and innovative rubber hinges that replace the usual metal springs. **Midnight Mustang**, a black stallion, comes with motion-activated horse sounds that can be turned off. 3 & up. (800) 258-8697.

■ Roller2 Inline ⟨2000⟩

(Fisher-Price $23.99) Older preschoolers are likely to want skates like their big sibs. These cleverly designed skates start as four-wheeled rollers that convert to in-lines. There's a forward-only option for beginners. Worn over shoes, these grow from shoe sizes 8–12 to 1–2. Our 4- and 7-year-old testers gave these a thumbs up. Skaters should always wear helmets and knee, wrist, and elbow pads. 4 & up. (800) 432-5437.

Water Sprinklers

For a crowd we still recommend **Waterpark Twist'n'Spout Sprinkler** (Little Tikes $20), a tall sprinkler with four different spray patterns including straight up in the air. Testers preferred this to the new **Waterpark Soak 'n' Spray Sprinkler** which did not work well. 3 & up. (800) 321-0183. Testers did love **Funnoodles' Giggle Wiggle Sprinkler** (Kidpower $10). Water flows through the soft foam tubing, making the tubes wiggle, and testers certainly did giggle—loving the unpredictability of the water spray. 3 & up. (800) 545-7529.

Wheel Toys—
Trikes and Other Vehicles

Preschoolers will still use many of the vehicles featured in the Toddlers section. Vehicles such as the **Kiddie Coop, Fire Engine for Two,** or **Pickup Truck** with no pedals remain solid favorites. Older preschoolers are also ready for tricycles and kiddie cars with pedals. The battery-operated vehicles that go 5 mph look tempting, but they won't do anything for big-muscle action. Here's what to look for in a three-wheel drive with pedal action:

- Bigger is not better. Don't look for a trike to grow into.

- Take your child to the store to test-drive and find the right size trike. Kids should be able to get on and off without assistance.

- Preschoolers need the security of a three-wheeler, which is more stable than a two-wheeler.

- A primary-colored bike can be reused by younger sibs regardless of their gender.

- See Safety Guidelines section for new safety standards for helmets.

Top-Rated Wheel Toys

Every year we test some of the newest wheeled toys—both trikes and four-wheelers. Our "ride-off" testers ranged in sizes and ages from 3 to 7. One common problem that affects the ride-ability of far too many vehicles remains the absence of treads. Kids are frustrated with plastic wheels that tend to spin without going anywhere.

■ Red Tricycle 2000

(Radio Flyer $54 & up) You probably had one of these! A classic little red metal trike with rubber tires and a little basket for treasures. Available in 10" or 12". (800) 621-7613.

■ Tough Trike

(Fisher-Price $29.99) This blue and yellow sporty trike with underseat storage is well sized, sturdy, but lightweight. A good value! (800) 432-5437.

■ Kettrike Happy

(Kettler $129.90) Gender-proof primary-colored trike with detachable push bar for adult. High-back seat for added security. Adult testers like the innovative control feature in the front wheel—an optional push/pull safety hub that adjusts for fixed drive or automatic coaster freewheeling. (757) 477-2400

Four-Wheel Drives

■ '57 Chevy 2000

(Today's Kids $50) Just like Grandpa's red '57 Chevy convertible, this foot-to-the floor kid-powered car has white walls, tailfins, and lots of "chrome" accents. There's a clicking key, beeping horn, and pivoting front wheels. Was not ready for testing. 2–5. (800) 258-8697.

■ Fire Engine for Two

(Step 2 $50) Our testers loved the flashing lights and sounds of this bright red fire engine that has a rear seat for an extra firefighter. Runs on foot power sans pedals and is scaled for smaller kids from 2–4. For a larger child, consider the **Farm Tractor** ($40) PLATINUM AWARD '99. (800) 347-8372.

■ Pickup Truck

(Little Tikes $59.99) Kids will get great pretend mileage from this yellow pick-up truck. Flatbed has a drop-down tailgate equipped with hardhat and tool kit for emergency repairs. Runs on foot power for developing muscles and has a working steering wheel with horn. Big 2 & 5. (800) 321-0183.

> **SHOPPING TIP:** Little Tikes suggests using a little liquid detergent or cooking oil on the connecting pieces of their toys if you are having difficulty putting them together.

Stand-Alone Climbers

■ Little Tikes Playground

(Little Tikes $450) This top-of-the-line climber is part playhouse, part climber. It does not provide the kind of big-muscle climbing, dangling, and jumping that classic monkey bars do, but kids had no complaints. They loved the multiple play areas with mini-tunnel, slides, and platforms for imaginative play. Expensive but a solid investment. 3 & up. PLATINUM AWARD '95. For a small climber, we recommend the BLUE CHIP **Activity Gym** (Little Tikes $160). A durable climber with four colorful panels that lock together to form an all-purpose play environment. Has dominated the market for years because of its sturdiness. 3 & up. (800) 321-0183.

Playhouses

A playhouse is the ultimate toy for pretend that will be used for years of solo and social play. Kids as young as two love the magic of entering their own domain—being the owner of a space that's scaled to size. Toddlers love opening and closing the door, looking out the windows, or playing with the toy kitchen (in some models). You'll find houses to fit a variety of tastes and budgets. Little Tikes' **Playhouse,** just 46"H ($130), will be outgrown before their 52"H pastel **Country Cottage** ($180). For still grander and thematic housing, consider the 59"H **Log Cabin** ($250) or a huge **Victorian Mansion** ($400) that's 5'H and opens on one side. Step 2's **Sunshine Playhouse** ($110) is just 48"H and has working door, shutters, and a pass-though window. Or for the long haul, consider their **Welcome Home Playhouse** ($400) that's 66"H, has a skylight, and is designed for kids as old as 10. If you prefer a wooden structure and price is no object, you'll do best at a roadside fence dealer who also sells prefab sheds. Little Tikes (800) 321-0183 / Step 2 (800) 347-8372.

■ **My Playhouse/Theatre** 2000
PLATINUM AWARD

(Alex $200) Here is imagination center! A giant combo playhouse, puppet stage, and store. Sure to be the focal point of any playroom, this sturdy wood and laminated play center is done in Maisy-like primary stripes and dots. It has a shelf for puppet stage and side window "ticket" office, front and back curtains and a working door. 3 & up. (800) 666-2539.

FREEBIE: For temporary indoor housing, don't overlook the charm of a big cardboard box with cut-out windows and door or a tablecloth draped over a table for little campers to use as a tent. A great way to overcome rainy-day cabin fever.

Art Supplies

Markers, crayons, chalk, clay, and paint provide different experiences, all of which invite kids to express ideas and feelings, explore color and shapes, and develop muscles and control needed for writing and imagination. A supply of basics should include:

- ✳ Big crayons
- ✳ Glue stick
- ✳ Finger-paint
- ✳ Tempera paint
- ✳ Washable markers
- ✳ Safety scissors
- ✳ Colored construction paper
- ✳ Plain paper
- ✳ Molding material such as Play-Doh or plasticine

SHOPPING TIP: Our testers were disappointed with fancy-shaped crayons that give less colorful results than regular wax crayons. Preschoolers' little hands also have better control with fatter crayons than with the standard size.

Paints and Brushes

Tempera paint is ideal for young children because of its thick, opaque quality. Watercolors are more appropriate for school-aged children. Young children will have more success with thick brushes than skinny ones, which are harder to control. To reduce the number of spills, invest in paint containers sold with lids and openings just wide enough for a thick paintbrush. Buying paint in pint-sized squeeze bottles is more economical than buying small jars of paint that will dry out. Look for both nontoxic and washable labels on any art supplies you buy.

■ Construction Paper Crayons 2000

(Crayola $2.99) Remember how hard it was to get colors to show up on construction paper? Now a special set of 16 colors solves that problem. (800) 372-9652.

■ Preschool Puppets Kits

(Creativity for Kids $16 each) While most craft kits are designed for older kids and are end-product-minded, these kits provide enough open-ended materials to give preschoolers an opportunity to explore clay or making puppets. Develops kids' dexterity, creative thinking skills, and imagination. 3s & up. (800) 311-8684.

ACTIVITY TIP: Painting with straws is a great outdoor game. Take a large piece of construction paper and pour puddles of tempera paint on the paper. Preschoolers love blowing the paint with a straw to create their own designs. Or take an easel outside for painting the great outdoors!

■ Magna Doodle *2000*

(Fisher-Price $10 & up) An updated version of a classic with new magnetic drawing shapes that stay in place better. Kids and parents love this no-mess magnetic drawing board for home or on the go. Kids draw directly on the board with stylus or shapes. 3 & up. A talking **Pooh Magna Doodle** was not available for testing, but the **Barbie Magna Doodle** appealed to older preschoolers who don't have the dexterity to dress the real Barbie, but liked the fun of doing so with the magnetic clothes patterns. 4s & up. (800) 432-5437.

ACTIVITY TIP: Magic Painting is great fun. Have child draw on paper with a piece of wax or a white crayon. Then water down a bit of tempera and have child paint over invisible drawing. Abracadabra! The drawing appears!

■ Tug Boat Craft Kit 2000

(Creativity for Kids $14) Easy to assemble, the pieces of the jaunty wooden tugboat need little sanding—except for the fun of sanding. With some easy pasting and painting, preschoolers create a real floatable tugboat and barge for floor or tub play. Don't just look at the picture on the front of the box. This is one kit that shows you photos of how real 3–6 year olds will paint their boats. A dandy gift kids could make for a cousin or sibling. 3 & up. (800) 311-8684.

Easels

A flat table may still be easier for preschoolers since the colors won't run. However, preschoolers are better able to adjust the amount of paint they load on brushes, and many enjoy painting at an easel. Avoid watering down paint, so it's easier to control. Having an easel set up makes art materials accessible whenever the mood moves young artists.

Plastic Easels 2000

Depending on your space and needs, the following are top-rated choices: **Double Easel** (Little Tikes $50) This bright red easel has a chalkboard on one side and a large clip that holds a pad of 17" x 20" paper. Also top-rated, the **9-in-1 Easy Adjust Easel** (Little Tikes $25). Takes little space and adjusts to nine different heights for tots to preteens. New for 2000, the **StudioDesign Art Desk** (Little Tikes $69) has a slanted easel desktop, built-in lamp, two storage compartments for paints, crayons, and markers, a chair and a stylish "iMac" look. (800) 321-0183. If space permits, look at **Creative Art Center** (Step 2 $40). This art center has two easels and a work table in between. 2 & up. (800) 347-8372.

Wooden Easels 2000

If you prefer wood, here are our top-rated choices: New for 2000, **Kid Classics Activity Desk** (Learning Curve $100). Handsomely crafted like and old-fashioned school desk in gen-

der-free colors, with top that lifts and becomes an easel. Assembles well but takes a minimum of one hour. (800) 704-8697. **Tabletop Easel** (Alex $40) If floor space is tight, consider a sturdy dual-sided table top hardwood easel with four-place paint-cup holder, 16" x 18" eraseboard and painting surface, and a chalkboard on reverse side. Folds flat for convenient storage. PLATINUM AWARD '98. (800) 666-2539. For a traditional floor model, testers gave high rating to those with chalkboards on one-side and write-and-wipe marker boards on the other (Back to Basics $89.95 & up). We suggest using big clips to hold paper rather than rollers, which kids often pull to create a real paper trail! Item #998. (800) 356-5360.

Modeling Materials 2000

These totally pliable, unstructured materials invite kids to use their hands and imagination to shape something from nothing. Fun for pounding, stretching, kneading and rolling—three-dimensional experience that preschoolers love. Older preschoolers may name what they make after the event. Few set out to design something. The focus here is on the process and not on making something realistic. Some of our favorite materials:

■ Model Magic 2000

(Crayola $5.39) This newly improved material comes packaged in several colors along with cookie cutters, roller and paint. Soft and pliable, it can be painted and dries like magic without crumbling as kids work with it. 3–8. (800) 372-9652.

■ Play-Doh

(Hasbro $2 & up) Classic Play-Doh is still a favorite. We prefer the dough without the doodads since most of the kits are less open-ended and tough to do. This self-hardening dough dries out if left uncovered. 3 & up. (800) 752-9755.

■ Plasticine

(Alex / Crayola, $4 & up) This oil-based material is what your old "clay" set probably contained. Unlike Play-Doh or clay, plasticine never hardens, though you may need to soften it up by kneading it before your child can work with it. It can be reused.

■ Self-Hardening Clay

(Adica Pongo / Alex $4 & up) This is more responsive to the touch than either Play-Doh or plasticine. This material dries in the air and can be painted. (800) 247-6144 / (800) 666-2539.

FREEBIE: Cookie cutters, rolling pins, baby bottle rings, and other items around your kitchen make great tools for molding.

Four top-rated clay kits: Crayola Magic Modeling Critter Kit ☆2000 PLATINUM AWARD (Crayola $15.99) This super set of Model Magic comes with six bags of newly improved self-hardening modeling material, plus tools and even a box for keeping your critters! Great present! (800) CRAYOLA. **Preschool Clay** (Creativity for Kids $16) Comes with non-hardening modeling clay in a rainbow of colors with googly eyes and other doodads. (800) 311-8684. **Clay Model Maker Kit** or **Clay Bears** (Alex $17) A mix of self-hardening and air-dried clay, roller, cutters, and paint or a Bear kit, less open-ended but better for some kids who feel more comfortable trying new material with more direction. (800) 666 2539. All 4 & up.

Music and Movement

■ Lollipop Drum

(Woodstock Percussion $22) Preschoolers can easily hold onto the handle of this lollipop-shaped drum. Makes a pleasing sound, according to both kid and parent testers. (800) 422-4463.

■ RainBoMaker

(Small World $19) A see-through plastic "rainstick" with colorful beads that makes a soothing sound. Or shake it for a maraca-like sound. 3 & up. (800) 421-4153.

■ Barney Song Magic Bongos ☆2000

(Playskool $29.99) Last year we raved about the **Song Magic Banjo** which used a light motion detector to activate the stringless banjo that plays 8 instruments

and 8 songs, including "I Love You..." Comes with 3 AA batteries. PLATINUM AWARD '99. This year's **Bongos** are also
quite magical! Kids hit the bongos to activate 11 songs.
Another button changes to one of five instruments. There's
a learning curve here for kids to discover that
the speed with which you hit the drums directly affects the pace of the music you hear. 2–5.
(800) 752-9755.

Q ACTIVITY TIP: Use drum to beat out someone's first name. For example, Sa-man-tha
would get three beats. Take turns guessing
whose name is being clanged.

Preschool Furniture Basics

Table and Chairs

These convenient pieces of basic gear will be used for artwork,
puzzles, tea parties, and even lunch. You'll find many choices
in both plastic and wood. This is a decorating choice as well
as a functional one. For safety and buying checklist, see page
61 in the Toddlers chapter.

Best Travel Toys

Preschoolers can entertain
themselves for short periods of
time with toys and art supplies. A
well-loved soft doll or mini-set-
ting with multiple pieces makes
for a cozy pretend play. At
this stage, a piece of home, whether it's
a toy or a blanket, is still important. One
of the best ways to make time fly is to bring along a tape player with favorite songs or stories to enjoy. For restaurant stops,
pack a plastic baggy filled with simple games, cards, or crayons
and paper to fill time before the breadbasket arrives. Bring
along a handful of paperbacks to share and for independent
"reading." Here are some of our favorites:

Top-rated take-alongs

■ Baby Nurse Doll Car Seat/Carrier

(Berchet/International Playthings $19.95) Perfect for dolls on the go, this cotton car seat has a safety harness just like the real thing, and converts to a backpack. Fits an 8"–16" doll or stuffed animal. 3 & up. (800) 445-8347.

■ Discovery Channel 3D Viewer Binoculars *2000*

(Fisher-Price $4.99 & up) Remember your old View-Master? Well, now there's are wildlife images that spring to life and with a turn of the button kids can convert their viewer into working binoculars. Also amazing, the new **View-Master Virtual Viewer** with a real 3-D look! 4 & up. (800) 704-8697.

■ FELTKids Interactive Playbooks *2000*

(Learning Curve $19.99 each) These books, with lots of felt pieces for pretending and arranging, are ideal for travel. Top-rated books: **Goldilocks, Decorate & Play House,** & **Let's Put On a Show.** Great for language, storytelling, and good parent/child connections. (800) 704-8697.

■ Magic Cloth Paper Dolls & Play Board *2000*

(Schylling $12) Cutout magnetic dolls and familiar characters (such as Curious George, Arthur, Rugrats) with outfits, and a play board. New for *2000* : A newly designed 13" x 12" board with pockets on the back for storing playing pieces. Great for pretend play and storytelling. 3 & up. (800) 541-2929.

■ Arthur's Four in a Row *2000*

(Great American Puzzle Factory $5) A quick card game for two. Players try to be first to put down four cards of Arthur or DW in a row. Big, easy-to-handle cards with pleasing graphics. 4 & up. (800) 922-1194.

■ Mr. Potato Head Electronic Game 2000

(Playskool $14.99) Although this little hand-held game has a grammatical goof, it still is an entertaining way to learn body parts. Players dress Mr. Potato Head with a push of his buttons. We just wish he didn't say, "You're doing good!" Also newly packed, **Silly Suitcase** ($14.99), the classic Mr. Potato Head with 25 parts that are a tight fit. 4 & up. (800) 752-9755.

■ Three Bears House

(Pockets of Learning $35) Every child's favorite tale comes to life with this little zip-and-carry fabric house. Fitted out with fabric bears, Goldilocks, and, of course, chairs and beds that are too hard, too soft, and just right. Perfect for retelling the original and making up your own adventures. 2½ & up. (800) 635-2994.

■ Travel Magna Doodle

(Fisher-Price $10) This no-mess magnetic drawing tool with tied-on "pen" is perfect for drawing, tic-tac-toe, and even writing letters and numbers. (800) 432-5437.

Best Third and Fourth Birthday Gifts for Every Budget

Big Ticket ($100 Plus)	**Set of wooden blocks** or **Playhouse** (Little Tikes/Step 2/Alex)
$100 & under	**Wooden Train set** or **Shop & Cook Kitchen** (Fisher-Price) or **Actimates Barney** (Microsoft)
Under $75	**Red Tricycle** (Radio Flyer) or **Easel** (various makers), or **StudioDesign Art Desk** (Little Tikes)
Under $50	**School Bus** (Play-Hut) or **Walk'n'Wag Baby Pluto** (Mattel) or **Fire Engine For Two** (Step 2) or **Easel** (Alex)
Under $25	**Lollipop Drum** (Woodstock Percussion) or **Arthur/D.W. Dolls** (Eden)

Under $20 **Duplos** (Lego) or **Sonny the Seal** (Milton Bradley) or **Electralips** Puppets (Manhattan Toy)

Under $15 **Tugboat Craft Kit** (Creativity for Kids) or **2-in-1 Musical Cake** (Fisher-Price) or **Sea Plane Hauler** (Nylint)

Under $10 **Puzzle** (Lauri) or **Gertie Ball** (Small World) or **Model Magic** (Crayola) or **Arthur's Four in a Row Card Game** (Great American Puzzle Factory)

4 • Early School Years
Five to Ten Years

What to Expect Developmentally

Learning Through Play. During the early school years, as children begin their formal education, play continues to be an important path to learning. Now more complex games, puzzles, and toys offer kids satisfying ways to practice and reinforce the new skills they are acquiring in the classroom.

Dexterity and Problem-Solving Ability. School-aged kids have the dexterity to handle more elaborate building toys and art materials. They are curious about how things work and take pride in making things that can be used for play or displayed with pride.

Active Group Play. These early school years are a very social time when kids long for acceptance among their peers. Bikes and sporting equipment take on new importance as the social ticket to being one of the kids. Children try their hand at more formal team sports where being an able player is a way of belonging.

Independent Discovery. Although these are years when happiness is being with a friend, children also enjoy and benefit from solo time. Many of the products selected here are good tools for such self-sufficient and satisfying skills.

BASIC GEAR CHECKLIST FOR EARLY SCHOOL AGE

✓ Sports equipment   ✓ Dolls/soft animals
✓ Craft kits   ✓ Board games
✓ Musical instruments   ✓ Tape player and tapes
✓ Water paints, markers, stampers
✓ Two-wheeler with training wheels
✓ Lego and other construction sets
✓ Electronic game/learning machines

🚫 Toys to Avoid

These toys pose safety hazards:

✓ Chemistry sets that can cause serious accidents
✓ Plug-in toys that heat up with light bulbs and can give kids serious burns
✓ Audio equipment with volume controls that cannot be locked
✓ Projectile toys such as darts, rockets, B-B guns, or other toys with flying parts that can do serious damage
✓ Super-powered water guns that can cause abrasions
✓ Toys with small parts if there are young children in the house

The following is developmentally inappropriate:

✓ An abundance of toys that reinforce gender stereotypes; for example, hair play for girls and gun play for boys

Pretend Play

School-age kids have not outgrown the joys of pretending. They like elaborate and realistic props for stepping into the roles of storekeeper, athlete, or race car driver. For some, mini-settings such as puppet theaters, doll houses, and castles are a preferable route to make-believe. This is also the age when collecting miniature vehicles and action figures can become a passion. Such figures generally reflect the latest car toon or movie feature. Nobody needs all the pieces, although many kids want them all. At this stage, owning a few pieces of the hottest "in" character represents a way of belonging.

Puppets and Puppet Stages

Puppets provide an excellent way for kids to develop language and storytelling skills that are the underpinning for reading and writing. Kids who can "tell"a story have less trouble writing a story. Many of the puppets and stages in the Preschool section will get lots of mileage now. Older kids may also become interested in making shadow, stick, or hand puppets of their own.

■ Finger Puppet Theater   **2000**

(Manhattan Toy $30–$50) Last year's PLATINUM AWARD winning theater now comes trimmed with stars and packed with four **Spellbinder** finger puppets. Both the original and the update are wonderful fabric stages with working curtains and fold-out platforms on which finger puppets can perform. Fold up for easy portability with storage space for puppets. Other top-rated finger puppets ($5 each) for **2000**, **Royal Rumpus, Traipsing Tutus,** and **Groovy Girls.** 4 & up. (800) 747-2454.

■ Community Street or Medieval Castle Theater

(Creative Education of Canada $25 each) These cardboard tabletop theaters are surprisingly sturdy, have curtains, and come with three felt hand puppets that match the themes. 4 & up. (800) 982-2642.

Favorite Hand Puppets

■ Emergency Rescue Squad Puppets
   BLUE CHIP

(Learning Resources $19.95 set of 4) Multicultural workers—doctor, paramedic, police officer, and firefighter with vinyl heads and cloth bodies. 4 & up. (800) 222-3909.

■ Lacing Puppets 2000

(Lauri $9 & up) Choose from a variety of pre-cut felt puppet sets with different themes that kids lace together and then use. Choose pre-cut **Bunnies, Bugs,** or **People** puppets. Kits come with yarn and big plastic needle for sewing (which develops fine motor skills kids need for writing). New for 2000, **Cinderella** with six cast members and two finger puppets (the mice, of course!) ($11.95). (800) 451-0520.

■ Tiger 2000

(Folkmanis $60) Realistic full-bodied tiger is just the newest and biggest in this wonderful line of puppets. We also found the black **Labrador Puppy** ($24) irresistibly cuddly and the **Large Rabbit in a Hat** ($15) fun. 5 & up. (800) 443-4463.

■ Spellcasters

(Manhattan Toy $10 each) A wizard, dragon, and unicorn with licks of gold and silver on velour cast their spells. Five-finger control makes for very animated story telling. 6 & up. (800) 747-2454.

Dollhouses, Castles, and Other Pretend Environments and Props

Kids are ready now for finer details in house and furnishings. Specialty dollhouse shops and crafts stores sell prefabs and custom houses to fit all budgets. The play settings recommended here require construction skills and adult involvement. For simpler wooden and plastic dollhouses, see Preschool Chapter.

■ Playmobil System X 2000

(Playmobil $99 & up) Here's a pretend setting that will provide hours of dramatic play. Made of sturdy plastic, this building with police headquarters, hospital and heliport, required an adult to put it

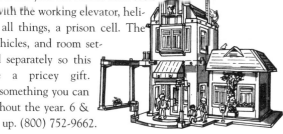

together, but our six-year-old testers soon took over playing with the working elevator, heliport, and, of all things, a prison cell. The helicopter, vehicles, and room settings are sold separately so this can become a pricey gift. However, it's something you can add to throughout the year. 6 & up. (800) 752-9662.

■ Victorian Doll House BLUE CHIP

(Playmobil $199 & up) Don't try to set this up before you give it! Putting it together is part of the fun. A challenging but well-designed model to construct together. When the deed is done, it will be used for dramatic play. (800) 752-9662.

Castles 🏰 2000

(LEGO Systems/Playmobil $50 & up) This year, castles really do seem to cut down gender lines. Playmobil's new **Fairytale Castle** is extremely lavendar (if you know what we mean) while Playmobil's **Monster Castle** and Lego's latest line of castles are both more ghoulish with trap doors, dragon, and other spooks. 7 & up. Playmobil (800) 752-9662 / Lego (800) 233 8756.

Props for Pretend

See Preschool chapter for this year's best costumes.

■ Let's Pretend Restaurant BLUE CHIP

(Creativity for Kids $17) If food service is a big theme, a kit with chef's hat, order pad, menus, signs, checked tablecloth, money, and fake food will be a hit. We still love **Paraphernalia for Pretending Kit** ($17) a classic kit with gear for restaurant as well as theater, stores, and offices. 4 & up. (800) 311-8684.

■ Kitty Vet Kit

(Battat $28) For vets in the making, this kit has detailed props for setting up an office and curing ailing pets—not to mention a plush kitten. 5 & up. (800) 247-6144.

Pretend & Play Calculator Cash Register

(Learning Resources $39.95) A solar-powered register with working calculator and digital display, comes loaded with play money and a credit card. Expensive but better made than any other. A marvelous tool with pretend and math skills built into the action. Marked 4 & up, but a solid choice for school-aged kids who are learning to use a calculator. (800) 222-3909.

Dolls

Now's the time when girls often get heavily invested in dolls with tons of paraphernalia. Although five- and six-year-old boys often find ways to play with a cousin's or sister's doll or dollhouse, they are more likely to choose action figures for this kind of play. Both boys and girls continue to enjoy soft stuffed animals, the zanier the better.

For many years, the only kinds of dolls around were blonde with blue eyes but, happily, more manufacturers today are creating dolls that reflect our cultural diversity. Here are some of the best:

■ American Girl and American Girl of Today

(Pleasant Co. $82) This mail-order-only company has made its name with exquisite dolls from different periods in American history. There are books for each doll—a wonderful way to introduce history to kids. The American Girl of Today collection allows you to choose one of 20 contemporary-looking dolls with Caucasian, African-American, Hispanic, and Asian-American skin tones and features. Each comes with a journal for writing. New for *2000*, new sporting outfits, PLATINUM AWARD *2000*. 6 & up. (800) 845-0005.

■ Barbie UPDATE *2000*

(Mattel $12 & up) We like the idea of Barbie emulating real female sports figures. Last year it was WNBA Barbie. This year she's with the World Cup Champions. **Soccer Barbie** *2000* **PLATINUM AWARD**

($20) really can kick! Also on a positive note, there's **Pilot Barbie** ($12) with her own **Airplane** ($63.99) with electronic sounds and working microphone to welcome passengers aboard. Her plane was not ready for testing, nor was **Super Gymnast Barbie** ($33.99) who promised to work the parallel bars—via remote controls (we could do it that way, too). As for Ken, he's gone back to shaving. (800) 524-8697.

■ Les Mini Corolline 🎀*2000*

(Corolle $20 each) You won't know which to pick from this group of 8" blonde or brunette dolls. Each comes with two outfits. We love the the ballerina, the horseback rider, and, new for *2000*, an ice skater. PLATINUM AWARD '99. Amazing furniture such as a bed, table and chair set, or armoire ($25 each) are scaled to size and beautifully finished in white. Also very special, **Corolline** ($50), an 11" beauty who comes with a small china tea set. Ooh-la-la! 4–8. (800) 628-3655.

■ Muffy VanderBear and Hoppy VanderHare 🎀*2000*

(North American Bear Co. $20 each) Collectors of Muffy will adore the combo trunk/bunk beds ($90) for playing and storing two dolls and accessories. Very pricey but very special! Still top-rated, the exquisite blue & white **Pagoda Collection,** PLATINUM AWARD '99. Accessories include a tea-set with both characters printed on the fabric and china. **Muffy Starter Set** ($29.95), with Muffy in her underwear, a signature dress, and shoes, is a good place to begin at a great price. 6 & up. (800) 682-3427.

Electric Train Sets

Many train buffs will tell you that this is the stage when their romance with trains began.

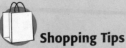 **Shopping Tips**

▪ Select HO gauge for beginners. Smaller trains and tracks can be frustrating and tricky to put together. Larger-gauge sets take up a tremendous amount of space, so you generally end up with just a boring circle of track.

▪ Start with a basic set and enough track to make an interesting roadbed.

▪ Since trains are plug-in electrical items, they are labeled for 8 & up. Younger children may enjoy them, but they should be used only with adult supervision.

Racing Car and Track Sets

Over the years, our testers have been disappointed with the performance of most racing car sets. "This looked great on TV, but we can't keep the cars on the track," or, "Is this all it does?" Most kids want more options. These sets delivered as promised: **Hot Wheels Starter Set** (Mattel $17) is a super-fast motorized cloverleaf track. For best results tape down the track. (800) 524-8697. Best of the lot:

▪ X-V Racers Scorcher Chamber Stunt Set 2000
PLATINUM AWARD

(Mattel $24) This is the newest in the line of X-V Racer track sets and is even more fun because the vehicles now light up as they travel. We still are great fans of PLATINUM AWARD winning **Triple Loop Set** and **The Cyclone,** with tighter triple loops. Both deliver! Use the power charger to rev up the specially motorized X-V racer and watch it zoom. An extra car is a must even though it's an additional $11! PLATINUM AWARD '99. Also top-rated, larger **Off Road X-V Racers.** 5 & up. (800) 524-8697

▪ Rokenbok Expandable RC Building System 2000

(Rokenbok $149 & up) Forget about those big racing car set-ups, this does more than just race in circles! This innovative system is expensive, but it is also more open-ended and expandable, and offers greater

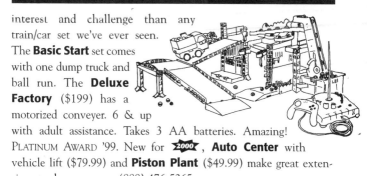

interest and challenge than any train/car set we've ever seen. The **Basic Start** set comes with one dump truck and ball run. The **Deluxe Factory** ($199) has a motorized conveyer. 6 & up with adult assistance. Takes 3 AA batteries. Amazing! PLATINUM AWARD '99. New for **2000**, **Auto Center** with vehicle lift ($79.99) and **Piston Plant** ($49.99) make great extensions to the starter set. (888) 476-5265.

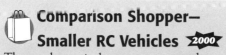

■**Super Jet Stunt Set** **2000**

(Mattel $53.99) We are eager to test this new track system designed for airplanes that will do loops and barrel rolls on innovative pipe-like plastic track. Looked great but was not ready for testing. 5 & up. (800) 524-8697.

Trucks and Cars

Comparison Shopper— Smaller RC Vehicles **2000**

The good news is that you can enter the world of RC at a much lower price. Our testers especially liked the **Tyco RC Hot Rocker** (Mattel $29.99) which has a roll cage for rollover action. Our testers also liked smaller versions of past winners: **Mini Psycho** ($29.99) and **Mini Tantrum** ($14.99)— these take regular batteries which means, on the downside, you'll go through lots of batteries. But on the upside, you don't have to wait to recharge an expensive power pack. Also novel, **Tyco RC Canned Heat** ($19.99). A car pops out of a can-shaped container and the control is in the can's lid. Nice—but difficult to get back into the can! 5 & up. (888) 557-8926.

■ **Tyco TMH Wild Sting** and **TMH Super Rebound** 🌟*2000*

(Mattel $59.99 each) Testers were thrilled with the
eight-wheeled action of the **Wild Sting** that
whips, flips, and does spirals and wheel-
ies. Uses a rechargeable battery and
one 9V battery. 6 & up. An
updated **Rebound** is bigger
than the '96 PLATINUM winner
and has a rotating power arm that
allows it to do amazing stunts. (888) 557-8920.

■ **Sound Machine Water Cannon** BLUE CHIP

(Nylint $46) The ultimate fire engine, with electronic sounds repro-
duced from a real fire truck—including air brakes, warning signals,
and sirens. Has flashing lights and a 35" boom that pivots. New for
🌟*2000*, **Search & Rescue Playset** ($25). Comes with 4x4 and
floodlight. 5 & up. (800) 397-8697.

■**Playmobil Construction Vehicle Sets** 🌟*2000*

(Playmobil $35 & up) Our 6-year-
old tester had no trouble putting
these kits together independently by following
pictorial direc-
tions. Once built,
the sturdy trucks are
ready for dramatic play. Pricey but simpler
to assemble than typical Playmobil sets with tiny details that are better for older kids. 5 & up. (800) 752-9662.

Construction Toys

What kids learn from construction toys

Builders learn to follow directions and develop
dexterity, problem-solving skills, and stick-to-
itiveness. Success is not always instant. Updated
classics such as **Lincoln Logs** and
Tinkertoys, are more appropriate for
this age even though they are labeled
for preschoolers. Glueless **Snap**

Models are also a good place to start for beginning model builders.

What you should know before you buy:

📦 **As their dexterity develops, kids can handle smaller pieces and more complex building sets.**

📦 **Provide a variety of building sets rather than just one type because building with Legos, K'nex, and Erector Sets involves different, but equally valuable, skills.**

📦 **Start with open-ended sets that can be built in multiple ways. As your child becomes a more confident builder, move on to small models.**

📦 **Age labels on most building sets are not accurate. If the box says 5 & up and your 5 year old needs a lot of assistance, the problem is with the label and not your child.**

📦 **On the plus side, working on one of these sets together can be rewarding. Be careful not to take over; break the project into do-able parts to build confidence.**

📦 **Keep in mind that less can be more. Start with do-able sets in the $15–$20 range that help your child to learn the particular building strategies.**

📦 **Girls as well as boys need to develop spatial/visual skills that are built into construction toys.**

Top-Rated Open-Ended Construction Sets

■Block-N-Roll *2000*

(Taurus $19.99 & up) A new twist on marble runs, this engrossing multi-piece set (60 or 100) has blocks (that are compatible with LEGO Duplo) with grooves, drop-throughs, ramps, and turns that link together to make an endless variety of runways. 6 & up. (877) 267-2565.

■Expandagon Hoberman Kit *2000* PLATINUM AWARD

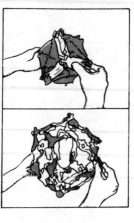

(Hoberman $40–$60) One of our favorite toys of the year. You've probably seen Hoberman's spheres in science museums, but now kids can create their own flexible spheres, cubes, and other geometric shapes with simple connections. Both the Advanced and Expert sets have six expandable squares, key to making big structures. The manual could be a little more user friendly, but once you get started this is an addictive toy (with great math and science lessons built in). If you're lucky, your kids will let you play with it, too. 8 & up. (888) 229-3653.

■LEGO System Classic Building Sets BLUE CHIP

(LEGO Systems $1.99–$44.99) The granddaddy of plastic building blocks, Legos are a must-have for this age group. New sets include a mix of bricks,

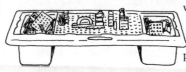

wheels, doors, and mini-figures. Also a great value, **Lego Classic Play-table** ($15) comes with 300+ pieces. 5–7. (800) 233-8756.

■Puzzle Pipes *2000*

(Kahoot $30) A truly open-ended construction toy. Kids put the pipes and joints together and then load the balls in and race them through the tubes. This is also fun to load with water and sparkles for a special look. No right or wrong ways to do this 75-piece set. 6 & up. (770) 985-5460.

PREVIOUSLY RECOMMENDED: Toobers & Zots (HandsOn Toys $5 & up) An innovative bendable foam shapes set, this '96 PLATINUM AWARD winner remains a hit with testers who liked the **Kit & Kabooble Set** ($49.95). 5 & up. (781) 932-8774. **Zolo** (Wild Planet $15 & up) An abstract and open-ended creative building set with endless constructions children can build. Works on the same principle as your old Tinkertoys, with post-and-hole pieces. Done in plastic, in Memphis-style colors and shapes. (800) 247-6570.

Theme and Pattern Construction Sets
■ LEGO Play Systems 🎖2000

(LEGO Systems $15 & up) The big news in Lego this year is Star Wars. Our testers gave these top ratings: From Episode I, the **Naboo Fighter** 🎖2000 PLATINUM **AWARD** ($19.99/174 pieces) and **Gungan Sub** ($49.99/375 pieces). From the original Star Wars, the **X-Wing Fighter** ($29.99/263 pieces) with **R2-D2,** and the **TIE Fighter** and **Y-Wing** ($49.99/407 pieces) with **Darth Vader.** For non-Star Wars sets, top ratings went to the exciting new **Lego System Mission Control** ($79.99/479 pieces) with **Space Shuttle** with lights and sound and an amazing launching pad with moving arms. This project is designed for 8–12 year olds and will necessitate adult assistance for the younger builder. For older builders, **Lego Technic** ($10 & up) are designed to teach kids how gears, pulleys, wheels, and axles work. New for 🎖2000, **Indy Storm Racer** ($39.99/440 pieces) 10 & up. To power any model, use **Power Pack** ($39.99). (800) 233-8756. See Computer Chapter for **Lego Mindstorms.**

Top-Rated Motorized Sets
■ Chaos 🎖2000

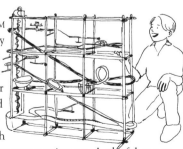

(Chaos $135) This PLATINUM AWARD winner has been totally redesigned to create even larger (7' tall!) Rube-Goldberg-like inventions. In answer to our question, "What did your child like about this toy?" the answer was, "EVERYTHING!" Both boys and girls tested this amazing construction set. A playful way to give kids a hands-on experience with basic science and engineering principles, problem solving, spatial relationships, and creative thinking. Adult help needed. Smaller sets available. 10 & up. PLATINUM AWARD '98. (314) 567-9097.

■ Erector Playsystem and Erector

(Irwin $20 & up) For beginners, stick with Erector Playsystem plastic models, such as PLATINUM AWARD-winning **Desert Raider** ($29.99) which makes three different models with pull-back friction motors. Testers liked playing with their vehicles almost as much as building them. For older builders, classic metal building sets are still challenging. Look at sets: **Evolution 2** and **3** both come with battery-operated motors and enough pieces so kids can build a variety of models. (800) 268-1733.

■ K'nex 2000

(K'nex $5 & up) K'nex really took off when they started building kits with friction-, battery-, or solar-powered motors. Beginners should start with small friction motor sets. Testers report that you need more finger strength with K'nex than with Legos. **All Terrain Trekker** 2000 PLATINUM AWARD ($39.99/280 pieces) will appeal to advanced K'nex builders. While not easy to do, it comes with larger pieces for faster results. Teaches about pulleys and comes with a dual speed battery motor. See Comparison Shopper below on robots. 8 & up. (800) 543-5639.

Comparison Shopper— The Battle of the Robots 2000

This year both Robotix (Learning Curve) and K'nex have motorized and remote-controlled robots. Robotix is introducing its newly styled line with **Galactisaurus Rex** ($99), the pet **2 K-9** ($99) and **Vox Centurion** ($199), a life-size defender that will talk with a wireless remote control, 400 parts and four motors. Unfortunately, none were ready for testing. (800) 704-8697. K'nex also introduces a **Robot World** with

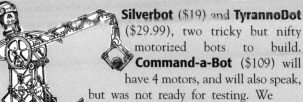

Silverbot ($19) and **TyrannoDot** ($29.99), two tricky but nifty motorized bots to build. **Command-a-Bot** ($109) will have 4 motors, and will also speak, but was not ready for testing. We look forward to having **Vox Centurion** and **Command-a-Bot** face off! (800) 543-5639. For building your own computerized robot, see **Lego Mindstorms** in the Computer Chapter. For a premade, 2-foot-tall robot that works by remote control, look at **Emiglio** (GP Toys $100), with a built-in microphone. (847) 955-0483.

Games

Classic and New Games

Now's the time when kids begin really to enjoy playing games with rules, with both friends and family. Of course, winning is still more fun than losing, and playing by the rules isn't always easy. That's the bad news. The good news is that many of the best board games are both entertaining and educational. Many games can improve math, spelling, memory, and reading skills in a more enjoyable way than the old flash card/extra workbook routine. Game playing also builds important cooperative social skills. For 5s & 6s, now's the time for classic BLUE CHIP games such as:

Parcheesi	**Dominoes**	**Chutes and Ladders**
Checkers	**Lotto**	**Trouble**
Uno	**Pick-up-Sticks**	**What's My Name?**
Connect 4	**Lite-Brite**	

For 7s, 8s, and up, try classics such as:

Othello	**Yahtzee**	**Monopoly Jr.**
Sorry	**Pictionary Jr.**	**Clue**
Chess	**Scrabble**	**Twister**
Upwords	**Bingo**	**Music Maestro II**
Boggle	**Life**	**Scattergories Junior**
Battleship	**Chinese Checkers**	**Quarto!**

■ Alpha Animals Junior 2000

(Great American Puzzle $14.95) Players move along the board by naming an animal that starts with the letter they land on. First to reach the end of alphabet wins. In a more advanced version, players name animals found on land, air, or water. A playful combination of initial sounds, language and classifying skills. 5–8. (800) 922-1194.

■ Dig'n Dinos Monopoly Jr. 2000

(USAopoly $20) Join Uncle Pennybags and collect dinosaur fossils as you and other paleontologists make your way around the board. Players collect fossil cards and charge when other players land on their fossils. (888) 876-7659. Like **Monopoly Jr.,** both the subject and math are geared to 5–8s. For older kids, the new **Star Wars Edition** (Hasbro $45) or **Millennium Edition** 2000 PLATINUM AWARD (Hasbro $39) are likely to be hits.

■ Ice Blocks 2000 PLATINUM AWARD

(Gamewright $13.99) In this two-person strategy game, players take turns stacking their blue or clear "ice" cubes in an interlocking pyramid trying to connect their own colors horizontally or diagonally while blocking their opponent. Game time is about 20 minutes. Testers liked the look and feel of the game. 8 & up. (800) 638-7568.

■ Laser Tennis 2000 PLATINUM AWARD

(Tiger $39.99) Our testers were amazed that the tennis ball is really an LED light that moves across the playing board when hit with a special reflector racket. "This rocks!" exclaimed one tester. This won't replace Ping Pong, but it takes a lot less space and you can play against the computer. A great rainy day game. (847) 913-8100.

■ Rainbow Fish 🎖2000

(Ravensburger $18) There's a lot of close looking needed to match the fish on the handsome glittery cards with the fish on the board. So this is more than a simple matching game. We suggest adapting the rules so that all players benefit from the "free" fish roll of the die. 5 & up. (800) 886-1236.

■ Rolit 🎖2000

(Pressman $14.99) This is a strategy game like Othello for four. Instead of black and white tiles, Rolit playing pieces are four-sided marbles with four colors. Players try to capture their opponents playing pieces by trapping them between two pieces of their own color. 8 & up. (800) 800-0298. Still top-rated, **Kuba** (Patch Products $30), a more challenging marble game where players push and capture marbles off the board. Both are fun and easy to learn, and develop flexible thinking. (800) 524-4763. 8 & up.

■ Space Walk 🎖2000

(Ravensburger $18) If you have a child who likes mancala, this game requires the same kind of strategy. Each player moves his nine space ships around the universe, but watch out—there are black holes in the board to fall into. The size of ships determines how the pieces move about the board. The player with the most space ships at the end wins! (800) 886-1236.

■ Stick Around 🎖2000

(Great American Trading $15) Quick 5-minute rounds make this two-player game fast & fun with plenty of chances to win! Players must place their red or yellow "sticks" so that they abut their own color. Object is to be the first to use all your sticks. Some strategy, simple rules make this good for 6 & up. (800) 225-7449.

■Where the Wild Things Are 2000

(Briarpatch $19.95) Fans of the Sendak
classic will try to be the first to connect
Wild Things puzzle playing pieces to
build a muddy path, vine, or stream. Play
involves looking at details and some
strategy skills. An easier domino-type
game for younger players can be enjoyed
by younger sibs, but the regular game is
best for 5s & up. (800) 232-7427.

NOTABLE PREVIOUS WINNERS: Three great games for developing visual discrimination (and having fun!): **Dog Dice** (Gamewright $10), a
clever twist on Bingo in which players must look for two matching
attributes (800) 638-7568; **I Spy Memory Game** (Briarpatch
$19.95), where players must match pairs of objects shown from dif-
ferent perpectives. 5 & up. (800) 232-7427; **Round the Bend**
(International Playthings $20), where players build a pipeline from
one side of the board to another, translating one-dimensional images
on cards to 3D forms. 5 & up. PLATINUM AWARD '99. (800) 445-8347.

Top-Rated Card Games

The game of the year is
Pokemon (Wizards of the
Coast), which is much more
about collecting than playing.
Aside from a deck of cards for
a fierce game of Rummy, War,
or Old Maid, don't overlook
classics like **Uno** or **Mille Borne.**

Here are other card games to play that are fun and quick,
and even have some learning power built in:

• **I Scream** 2000 PLATINUM AWARD (M.J.
Moran $9.95) Cool-looking ice cream graph-
ics grabbed our attention in this game, which
is basically a simple variation of Hearts in
which players pass cards until one player
manages to the get four matching ice
creams. Yum! Can be played by three, but
best for four or many more! In **Dog Pound**
players match dogs and "look-alike"

humans. Both games are fast-paced, with simple rules and lots of laughs. (800) 656-6726.

- **Suds** (Gamewright $10) A fast-paced sequencing game, a bit like War. Players must get rid of all their clothing cards in order from caps to shoes. No turn-taking here—it's a free-for-all! 6 & up. PLATINUM AWARD '98. Also top-rated, **Aliens** (a harder variation on War). (800) 638-7568.

- **The Wild Rumpus Card Game** ★2000★ (Briarpatch $5.95) Three fast-paced rummy-style games, played with a deck featuring characters from the Sendak classic. (800) 232-7427.

Math Games and Equipment

■ Mad Math

(Patrick Comm. $17.99) Knowing your multiplication tables is not required, but Mad Math provides a playful way to reinforce them. You play on a multiplication table so the answers are on the board. Kids not only learn to read the grid, they begin to see patterns. It's not like some dreaded "game" that's good for you—it's actually "edutaining." 9 & up. (888) 834-2380.

■ Peppino the Clown ★2000★

(Ravensburger $18) A seemingly simple color game turns out to be a sequencing game with attention to small details and the need for speed. Players flip a card and the object is to be the first player to match the pattern and color sequence shown. 5 & up. (800) 886-1236.

■ Pie in the Sky ★2000★

(Learning Resources $12.95) If fractions have anyone in your family tense, here's a fun board game where the object is to get three pies in a row. Players spin the fraction wheel and need to find the matching pie on the board. For more advanced fraction play, see **Beginning Fraction Zone Bingo.** (800) 222-3969.

■ Rhombo Continuo ★2000★

(U.S. Games $12) A quick colorful game that sharpens visual discrimination and counting skills. Players take turns connecting rhombus-shaped cards to make long continuous runs of the same colors.

Can be played by 1–5 players. 5 & up. (800) 544-2637.

■ Sum Swamp

(Learning Resources $12.95) Players toss three dice, one with plus or minus signs as they move their critter through the swamp where they sometimes have to deal with odds and evens. Right on the mark for late first, early second grade. Also top rated, **Timing it Right** (good for reinforcing clock concepts). 7 & up. (800) 222-3909.

NOTABLE PREVIOUS WINNERS: For playing around with greater and less than: **Pivot** (Wizards of the Coast $6.99) (800) 324-6496 and **Rat-a-Tat Cat** (Gamewright $10) (800) 638-7568.

Money Concept Games

■ Bunny Money

(International Playthings $20) If they know the storybook, they'll love this young math game. Like Max and Ruby, players have a shopping list and have to buy what's on their list before they run out of money. For younger kids than Monopoly Junior. 5 & up. (800) 445-8347.

■ Money Bags *2000*

(Learning Resources $12.95) A much more advanced money game where players move along the gameboard by earning money for different activities (which they must take from the bank). Provides lots of opportunity for making change and exchanging values! 7 & up. (800) 222-3909.

Math Manipulatives

Concrete materials give kids a greater understanding of counting and calculating. Don't rush to take these materials away from kids. They help make the transition to abstract thinking easier. BLUE CHIP choices are: **Math in a Bag** (Water Street $25) Giant-sized cuisenaire rods. (800) 866-8228. **Unifix Cubes** (Didax $19.95) Beginning math students use these cubes for understanding early math concepts. (800) 433-4329. **Primary Time Teacher Learning Clock Junior**

(Learning Resources $14.95) As kids move the minute hand, the synchronized and color-coded digital display also tells the time in 5-minute increments. (800) 222-3909.

Math Electronic Quiz Machines

Most math quiz machines are like electronic flash cards—good for drilling basics in addition, subtraction, multiplication, and division. Kids often prefer them to flashcards, since they can quiz themselves and work at their own speed. Be forewarned: On most electronic quiz toys, two-digit answers have to be answered with tens first. This is contrary to the way kids are taught to do math, especially when regrouping is involved, so machines may be confusing. Many quiz machines also go too far and fast. Try them before you bring one home. Remember, machines can't clarify repeated mistakes but they can provide practice and speed, and reinforce what kids know.

Our top choices: **Number Wise** (Tiger $14.99) Handheld game that works as both a calculator (good for checking homework) and a quiz game machine. (847) 913-8100. **Math Safari** (Educational Insights $99.95) Machine uses quiz books with pictorial images so child has more to work with than abstract symbols & calculations. (800) 933-3277. **Twist & Shout Addition** or **Multiplication** (Leap Frog $19.95 each) A flashlight shaped, hand-held toy with 3 modes of play: One tells the answers; Two is a quiz with multiple choice answers; Three asks for missing factors. We wish it had a volume control. 6 & up. (800) 701-5327.

Puzzles and Brainteasers

Putting jigsaw puzzles and brainteasers together calls for visual perception, eye/hand coordination, patience, and problem-solving skills. During their early school years, kids should build from 25-piece puzzles to ones with 50- and 100-plus pieces.

Beginners' Puzzles—Under 50 pieces
■ A–Z Panels BLUE CHIP

(Lauri $8.95) Not only does fitting the rubbery letters in and out of the puzzle frame help kids learn to know and name the letters, but handling the 3-D letters also gives kids a feel for their shapes. Updated this year with useful pictures under each letter. Also, **Kids Perception Puzzle**

($7.50), figures in slightly different poses that help kids look at small differences, just as they must when reading words that look almost alike, such as "cap" and "cup." 4–7. (800) 451-0520.

■ Backyard Bugs

(Frank Schaffer $14.95) Forty-eight big pieces and an identification key for learning the names of the bigger-than-life-sized bugs are found in this 5'-long beautiful garden scene. Also, **Endangered Animals** (48 pieces become a 5'-long mural). 5 & up. (800) 421-5565.

■ I Spy 1, 2, 3... Floor Puzzle

(Briarpatch $14.95) Our testers loved working on this oversized 35-piece floor puzzle taken from the pages of I Spy School Days. After kids put together the puzzle, they have to locate the objects in the riddle. A good parent-and-child activity. Also top-rated, **63–100-piece I Spy puzzles** in this series. (800) 232-7427.

■ My Size Puzzles *2000*

(Mattel $6.95) Hot Wheels fans will be thrilled when they put together these 3' wide Hot Wheels racers with 46 big pieces. These shaped puzzles are challenging because they have no flat edges. For Barbie fans, there is also **My Size Barbie.** They say 4 & up, we say more like 5 & up with help. (800) 524-8697.

■ Parquetry Blocks and Cards Blue Chip

(Learning Resources $26.95) Thirty-two geometric-shaped tiles are arranged on top of 20 colorful patterns. Advanced players can use tiles without the pattern. Develops skills in matching and sequencing patterns—skills that are needed in putting letters together to make words. 5–8. (800) 222-3909.

Intermediate—50+ Pieces and Shaped Puzzles

■ Metamorphosis of a Butterfly *2000*

(Frank Schaffer $14.95 each) A beautiful monarch graphic shows the larva, chrysalis, and wide-winged butterfly. This 50-piece floor puzzle is marked 4 & up but it is really difficult! We'd say more like 6 & up. Also challenging, the leggy 24-

piece **Giraffes** puzzle. And the 50-piece **Rainforest Frogs** ($14.95) says 4 & up, but we'd say more like 5. (800) 421-5565.

■ Endangered Species

(Anything's Puzzable $17.95) One of an amazing collection of circular puzzles with whole creatures that fit together. Interesting facts appear on back of each puzzle piece. Testers also loved the 69-piece **World Beneath the Sea** and the 75-piece **World of Dinosaurs.** With adult help, 5 & up. PLATINUM AWARD '98. (800) 984-8486.

NOTABLE PREVIOUS WINNERS: Arthur Goes to School (Great American Puzzle Factory $6) 60-piece puzzle that includes an alphabet trail. (800) 922-1194. **Puzz-3-D** (Hasbro $5.99 & up) We liked these miniature three-dimensional puzzles with fewer pieces than the originals, but super-challenging. Try the **Empire State Building** or the **Eiffel Tower.**

Comparison Shopper— USA and World Maps Puzzles 2000

USA puzzle maps in frames are the place to start. You can't go wrong with either the wooden version from Small World ($22) with graphics of products, landmarks, capitals, and a vinyl sheet for arranging pieces out of the frame, or Battat's new puzzle with states, capitals, and a topographical map below. 6 & up. Small World (800) 421-4153/ Battat (800) 247-6144. For a cardboard puzzle, **Carmen Sandiego US** or **World Map Puzzle** (Great American Puzzle Factory $11.95 / 60 pieces) also have magic-rub clues for solving crime cases. 6 & up. (800) 922-1194. Testers liked the huge **World Map** (Frank Schaffer $13.95) 100-piece 20" x 30" puzzle. Names of the continents and oceans are printed on map and includes 21 geography cards to match icons on the map. Says 5 & up, we'd say 7 & up. (800) 421-5565.

More Advanced Puzzles—100 Pieces + and Brainteasers

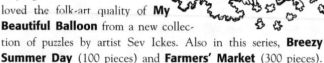

■ Bugs! & My Beautiful Balloon 𝟮𝟬𝟬𝟬

(Great American Puzzle Factory $5/$9.95) A spectacular 100-piece cardboard puzzle that features dazzling pictures of beetles, dragonflies, and ladybugs. Our testers also loved the folk-art quality of **My Beautiful Balloon** from a new collection of puzzles by artist Sev Ickes. Also in this series, **Breezy Summer Day** (100 pieces) and **Farmers' Market** (300 pieces). (800) 922-1194.

■ Mummy Floor Puzzle 𝟮𝟬𝟬𝟬

(Frank Schaffer $14.95) Harder than most, this two-sided 100-piece puzzle is 3' long with painted or golden designs for kids who are smitten with Egyptology. 8 & up. Still top rated: **Statue of Liberty** PLATINUM AWARD '99. (800) 421-5565.

■ Puzzles in Motion 𝟮𝟬𝟬𝟬

Puzzle in Motion   DISCOVERY

Totally in Charge
with eith... ...card

210 PIECES

(BePuzzled $9.99 each) Inspired by the Discovery Channel, these 210-piece nature puzzles have great graphics, and each comes packaged with a holographic card of the featured theme (e.g., elephants, asteroids, sharks, and lions) that fits in the center of the puzzle. A must-have for advanced puzzlers. (800) 347-4818.

■ Railroad Rush Hour 𝟮𝟬𝟬𝟬

(Binary Arts $15) The object of this brain teaser is to get your red locomotive out of the freight yard by sliding the other trains and baggage out of the way on the board. Opening patterns move from beginner to advanced level. Develops visual perception, strategy, and patience! This is a variation of **Rush Hour,** PLATINUM AWARD '98. 8 & up. (800) 468-1864.

It's Magic!

Some kids like to impress friends and family with magic tricks. Learning to do them takes time, practice, and real reading skills. Reluctant readers may become avid readers of books that involve doing things such as magic or science experiments that are like magic. Our top picks for beginners are T.C. Timber's small kits, **Magic Disks** and **Abracadabra** ($9.95 each). 6 & up. (800) 468-6873. For a more elaborate set, **Hocus Pocus** (Small World $46) with dozens of tricks, props, and a video. 8 & up. (800) 421-4153.

Electronic Equipment & Learning Tools

Kids tend to love the novelty of electronic teaching machines, which don't actually teach new skills but do reinforce and provide the kind of practice some kids need.

■ Phonics Writing Desk 2000

(Leap Frog $39) Phonics go in and out of style. The fact is, most kids learn to read with a mix of approaches. If you're going to buy only one electronic phonics toy, this is it! From learning letter names and sounds, to spelling and even writing, this toy is one of the most amazing phonics toys we've ever tested! It provides visual, auditory, and tactile feedback in a playful way. Kids get to practice writing letters with a stylus on a magic-slate-like surface that's below an electronic window that beeps as it demonstrates how to shape each letter. There's even a button to switch from upper- to lowercase letters. 4s might like it, but this is really a great tool for 5–7s. Takes 3 "AA" batteries. For bilingual games, see **Phonics International English/Spanish** ($45). (800) 701-5327.

■ GeoSafari and GeoSafari Jr.

(Educational Insights $99.95) We prefer the original **GeoSafari Jr.,** to the version featuring Richard Scarry's Busytown. While Scarry appeals to preschoolers, this product skills level (reading) is really for beginning readers. (They say 3 & up, we say more like 6 & up). **GeoSafari,** designed for 8 & up, includes pictorial quiz cards that focus on reading, math, weather, and history. The bells and whistles make head-to-head games more like playing Jeopardy. 8 & up. PLATINUM AWARD '94. (800) 933-3277.

Comparison Shopper— Talking Globes

■ GeoSafari Talking Globe Jr.
(Educational Insights $99.95) This "junior" version is much better suited to beginning geography skills than the original. This simpler globe is easy to read and use for finding answers to interactive questions. Pictorial/color cues help kids in guided explorations for 6–10s. PLATINUM AWARD '99. The original **GeoSafari Talking Globe** is still fine for 10s & up. (800) 933-3277. The **Odyssey Globe** (Explore Tech $299) is a much pricier interactive tool. Touch the sensor pen to this globe and it names the locale. In quiz mode, players must find a locale. Globe gives clues, and in search mode, you find atlas info such as climate, population, and money, and even hear national anthems. 5–55+. (800) 701-5327. A new touch-sensitive globe from Leap Frog looked promising but was not ready for testing.

■ Talking Whiz Kid Super Animated
(Vtech $49.99) We tested a slew of these "laptop" type quiz machines and this turned out to be the best fit for early school years. Many are just too hard for early school years and often the math answers need to be typed in with tens before ones—not the way kids do it on paper. This machine is on the mark and includes math (single- and two-column addition, subtraction, multiplication, and division), spelling, grammar, time, and music. It's easy to key in the activity of choice. 6–10. (800) 521-2010.

Activity Kits and Art Supplies

For school-aged kids, art class is seldom long enough. Besides, such classes are usually teacher-directed with little chance for kids to explore their own ideas.

Giving kids the tools and space for art projects at home is more than pure entertainment. Art helps develop their ability to communicate ideas and feelings visually, to refine eye/hand skills and to learn how to stick with a task.

BASIC GEAR CHECKLIST FOR EARLY SCHOOL YEARS ARTISTS

✓Crayons, chalk, colored pencils, and pastels
✓Watercolor and acrylic paints
✓Watercolor markers of varying thicknesses & colors
✓Loom (weaving, beads, pot holders)

✓Origami paper folding	✓Sand art supplies
✓Sewing	✓Colored wax
✓Lanyard kits	✓Needlepoint
✓Rug hooking	✓Cutting/pasting
✓Woodworking	✓Fabric paints
✓Flower press	✓Air-hardening clay
✓Stamps	

Activity and Craft Kits

Both boys and girls love making things they can play with, wear, or give as gifts. Some of our favorites introduce them to art forms and crafts from other cultures and times in history. Many require adult assistance.

Drawing, Painting, Coloring

■**Hand Painted Ceramic Treat Jar** *2000*
PLATINUM AWARD

(Creativity for Kids $18) After it's painted, this ceramic treat jar makes a perfect container for treats. It's smaller than a traditional cookie jar, but big enough to make a "statement." After the acrylic paints dry 24 hours, pop it into the oven for a final finish. Adult supervision. Still top-rated,

Ceramic Piggy Bank ($12); our penny pinchers loved this one. 7 & up. Platinum Award '99. (800) 311-8684.

■ Illustory Kit

(Chimeric $19.95) Imagine the thrill of having an original story and your own illustrations bound in a real book. This kit comes with 12 sheets of paper with space for art on each and text (or you can opt for more text and less art). Mail your child's story in and get back a hard-covered book! What an inspiring way to motivate young writers. 5 & up. (800) 706-8697.

■ Paint the Wild Kits 2000

(Balitono $7.50 & up) Beautifully crafted wooden animal carvings that kids paint and display, or use as play figures. New for 2000 : **Keepsake Chest** ($14), a 7" three-drawer chest to paint for small treasures. Still top-rated, **Birdhouse Chime Kit** ($15) with a tiny songbird sitting on a miniature birdhouse. For more advanced builders, choose a **Butterfly & Ladybug Wind Chime Kit** ($15). Also, for holiday presents, testers loved the **Christmas Ornaments** ($15) and unusual **Nutcracker** ($14). 6 & up. (609) 936-8807.

■ Many Mini Messages 2000

(Creativity for Kids $10) Comes with five 3"x 2" wooden frames with slate-like centers that kids can paint messages on. A novel way to send birthday greetings to friends or family. Also fun, **Optidot Magnets.** Kids create designs and stick them to the self-adhesive magnetic sheets that are then rolled in a dish of plastic optidots that give the design a shimmery pop-art effect and dimension. 7 & up. (800) 311-8684.

■ Picture Frame 2000

(Creativity for Kids $15) Kids dab special pearlized paints on the raised floral motif of this porcelain frame. Why not give Grandma a photo in a unique frame? 7 & up. (800) 311-8684 ext. 3037.

■ Scratch-Art Fabulous Frame & Key Chains 2000

(Scratch-Art Co. $10 each) Remember doing this craft? You scratch the black surfaced paper

with a wooden drawing tool to reveal bright colors. Now this classic material has been turned into a variety of kits that are quick and fun. A plastic 5" x 7" acrylic frame comes with two sheets of "stained glass" material that's translucent when scratched. It includes a stencil for those who don't like drawing freehand. Also terrific to decorate, two acrylic key chains and a greeting card kit with 3-D cut-outs. (800) 377-9003.

■ Splash'n'Sparkle Umbrella   *2000*

(Alex $15) Just in time for rainy days, this child-sized umbrella comes with outlines of flowers and rainbows that children paint with special sparkly acrylic paints. One tester tried to paint the background as well as flowers and ran out of paint. There's plenty of paint for filling in the designs and even doing a second coat for more opaque results. Kids do need to wait 24–48 hours for paint to dry before using! 5 & up. (800) 666-2539.

ACTIVITY TIP: Make a Millennium Memory Tray. Pick up a wooden tray at a craft store. Have kids decorate with graphic images that reflect what's noteworthy to them, e.g., photos of family, friends, a ticket or postcard from a trip, a movie they saw, an ad for their favorite food. Arrange all these pieces together, add letters and dates from graphics clipped from magazine and seal them all down with special decoupage glue and seal with glaze. This memory tray will be nice to display or use for the dinner table.

■Stained Glass Clock Activity Kit 2000

(Alex $13) Kids decorate an acrylic clock frame with stained glass colors. Once the decorating is done, a real clock mechanism is plugged in and—voilà! a working clock that would make a great gift. Requires one AA battery. 7 & up. (800) 666-ALEX.

■ Wooden Treasure Box

(Creativity for Kids $16) Just right for holding special pins, rings, coins and treasures, this sturdy wooden box with a brass latch is ready to decorate with acrylic paints and brush for making it like no other box in the world. 7 & up. (800) 311-8684.

NOTABLE PREVIOUS WINNERS: Under Sea Bag Buddies (Creativity for Kids $16) Three sand-filled creatures—a dolphin, a whale, and an octopus—that kids paint with bright acrylic fabric paint. Once dry, these are fun to juggle, catch, or display. 6 & up. (800) 311-8684. **Tie Dye Wear Kit** (Jacquard $19.95) Comes with enough dyes and ideas for 16 tee shirts (not included). No heat needed. Adult supervision needed. (800) 442-0455.

Cut & Paste (and Glue!)

■ Icky Sticky Bugs

(Alex $10 each) Kids draw with colored glue onto a vinyl sheet. Once dry, they lift off and stick to windows. New Glow in the Dark kit shows bright colors on box but comes with pastels—a disappointment to our testers. 6 & up. (800) 666-2539.

■ Floppy Flower Hat 2000

(Learning Curve $14.99) Kids paint precut flowers, leaves, and butterflies and glue them onto this floppy felt hat. No two hats will be the same! A very appealing project testers loved to make and wear. Each step, however, takes a very long time to dry. 4 & up. We were disappointed that the new Best Friends Banner only had one African-American figure. Still top rated, **FeltKids Design Kits** ($16.99), precut figures and clothes for kids who love to glue, glue, glue! Choose from mermaids, fairies, or glittering gowns. (800) 704-8697.

■ Musical Jewelry Box Activity Kit 2000
PLATINUM AWARD

(Alex $15) A small ballerina pops up when you open this lavendar music box that plays "When You Wish Upon a Star." Our six-year-old tester couldn't wait to decorate her "treasure" box with jewels, ballet slipper stickers, and glitter glue. A perfect gift kids can make and use. 6 & up. (800) 666-2539.

NOTABLE PREVIOUS WINNERS: Create Your Own Scrapbook (Creativity for Kids $20) Kids are great collectors, and having a scrapbook is one way to get their collectibles organized. Kit includes a notebook, markers, stickers, paper, glue, color foam pieces, plastic sleeves, and ideas. 6 & up. (800) 311-8684. **Ballet Bag** (Alex $17) A pre-made pink and lavendar drawstring bag for slippers and leotard that ballerinas can personalize with pearls, ribbons, and glitter. 7 & up. (800) 666-2539.

Candle & Soap Making
■ Candle Decorating 2000

(Creativity for Kids $15) The latest in candle kits comes with one stout pillar candle and three good-sized dripless tapers which kids decorate with colored wax pieces that stick to premade candles. Includes cookie cutters to shape the sheet wax. No heat other than the heat of one's hands is needed. Still top-rated, **Beeswax Candles** ($16) with sheets of beeswax for rolling simple candles around a wick. 5 & up. A lovely gift kids can make and give to Grandma or another adult. 7 & up. (800) 311-8684.

■ Soap-Scape 🏅2000

(Curiosity Kits $10) This is a parent-intensive project since melting soap in the microwave is potentially dangerous! Yet testers really liked the process. You heat scented glycerine to liquid, and pour it over small rubber animal shapes, embedding them as the soap hardens. Kit includes gift wrappings. 6 & up. (800) 584-5487.

Cooking

■Garden Bugs Cookie Cutters 🏅2000

(eeboo $6) A set of five bug cookie cutters and recipes for young bakers—or a set of **Munchie Monsters** and **Out of Orbit** (space shapes) cutters. A tasty way to work on math, measuring, reading, and decorating skills with edible payoffs. 4–40+. (212) 222-0823.

■Yummy Chocolate Bugs 🏅2000

(Curiosity Kits $15) You'll need to melt the colorful chocolate disks in the microwave. Then you and your child "paint" the molds with layers of colorful chocolate until you've created bugs good enough to eat! This project takes over an hour, but there's lots of learning as kids make artistic decisions and work in a step-by-step, systematic way. The trick is not to eat the disks before you melt them! (800) 584-5487.

Modeling & Molding

■ Wax Works BLUE CHIP

(Chenille Kraft $4.95 & up) These waxy sticks (available in a rainbow of colors) can be coiled, twisted, and shaped into letters, butterflies, or free-form sculptures. Also, top-rated, **Creativity Street** ($14.95), a kit that includes Wax Works, pipe cleaners, eyes, feathers, and beads for creative fun. (800) 621-1261. 5 & up.

■ Pottery Wheel 🏆2000

(Curiosity Kits $40) Throwing pots puts a new spin on playing with clay. This pottery wheel has a powerful motor, foot control, wooden tools, clay, paint and instructions to guide the novice. Looked promising but was not ready for testing. 6 & up. (800) 584-5487.

■ Stone Sculpture Clock 🏆2000
PLATINUM AWARD

(Curiosity Kits $20) Kids stain the 7½" wooden frame and insert the battery-operated timepiece. Then they stir and pour the stone sculpture mixture. Glass gems are embedded to mark the hours and kids can carve designs or messages into the hardened surface. 8 & up. (800) 584-5487.

NOTABLE PREVIOUS WINNERS: Copy Cast BLUE CHIP (Creativity for Kids $18) An unusual casting kit that actually makes a reusable mold so that a cast of a hand, foot, or toy can be made again and again. Our testers insisted on cloning their action figures. (800) 311-0604. **Make-a-Mask Kit** (Educational Insights $12.95) Make original masks to wear or display. Comes with plastic reusable face form, plaster gauze, paint, and excellent step-by-step guide. (800) 933-3277.

Beads, Jewelry & Accessory Kits

Using beads is more than a creative craft, it helps kids develop fine motor skills. Both boys and girls like the magic of **Hama** or **Perler** bead sets where kids put beads on pegboard forms that adults iron to create plaques. Older kids like weaving Native American beads on small looms. Other kits with beads to make or simply string produce end products kids like to wear. In fact, a big kit is fun for a sleepover project.

■ Bead Bonanza

(Alex $17) Hundreds of metallic, jewel tone, letter, heart, and odd-

shaped beads in a plastic box with compartments for each color. 5 &
up. (800) 666-2539.

■ Amigo Bands *2000*

(Creativity for Kids $10) Comes with handsome ethnic beads in off-
white, coral, silver and turquoise, silk and leather cord for making ten
amigo bands. One reviewer loved them; the other thought they were
handsome but there should be more in the box. Still top-rated,
Leather Bracelets ($10). For kids who may not be up to weaving
friendship bracelets, these three leather ones snap on and can be dec-
orated in a snap with markers. A quick, easy, and pleasing project.
(800) 311-8684.

■ Butterfly Beads *2000*

(Creativity for Kids $10) You get four paint-
ed ceramic butterflies, plus smaller iridescent
hearts and butterflies and hundreds of glass
beads to string on silvery elastic string for
making many necklaces and bracelets. Kids
end up with showy end products. 7 & up.
(800) 311-8684.

Sewing Kits

Learning to sew has a realness about it
that kids find especially satisfying. It's also an ideal way to
develop fine motor skills. This category has exploded with
great choices. Here are our testers' favorites:

■ Betty's Begin to Sew Sets

(Quincrafts $4.99 & up) Small affordable kits for trying out a variety
of needle crafts. The bean bag sets (Dolphin or Butterfly) come with
plastic safety needle and pre-cut holes for easy sewing. 5 & up. Testers
also liked the **Needlepoint Activity Deluxe Kit** ($7.99) with mate-
rials for using quickpoint to make picture frames, bookmark, earring
stand, and keychain. A good place to start. 7 & up. (800) 342-8458.

■ Lacing Friends *2000*

(Alex $16) Four beautifully illustrated cardboard characters
come with a set of pre-colored clothes plus another set for kids to color. Colorful laces are used to
"dress" the cat, pig, rabbit and bear. This calls for
more dexterity and the need to line clothes up with
the holes on the figures. They say 4, we'd
say more like 5 & up. (800) 666-2539.

■ **Totes for Two** 🏷️**2000**

(Alex $15) Our testers were engrossed as they stitched together the precut felt pieces to make two different totes that were then decorated with glued-on heart and flower cut-outs. They reported that they loved the end product, but parents indicated that lots of supervision was required to help with the directions. Still top-rated, **Dress Up Bears** ($20) a stuffed bear with precut clothes to sew. 7 & up. (800) 666-2539.

■ **National Geographic: My World Quilt**

(Curiosity Kits $20) Kids create their own quilt by drawing pictures onto preprinted panels with headings such as, "This is my family," "This is my town," "...my street," then ironing the panels and sewing them together. 7 & up. Adult supervision required. PLATINUM AWARD '97. Also top-rated, **National Geographic: Mola Pillow** ($12). PLATINUM AWARD '98. 8 & up. (800) 584-5487.

Comparison Shopper— Weaving Looms

Begin to Weave (Quincrafts $4.99) has a cardboard "loom," a blunt needle, yarn, and some beads for extra finishing touches. A simple way to introduce beginners to weaving. (800) 342-8458. **PegLoom** (Harrisville Designs $18.95), a small over/under loom with large needle, is also a good choice for true beginners. 5 & up. **Create Your Own Loops & Loom Projects** (Woodkrafters $14) potholder looms are fine for beginners. This new 7" x 7" frame comes with fabric loops and a metal hook that's easier to use than most kits that come with plastic. 5 & up. (800) 345-3555.

For larger looms: Brio's **Loom** ($68) comes out of the box threaded and ready to work! Testers felt the instructions were spotty for a true novice but gave the product overall high ratings for design. (888) 274-6869. The Harrisville **Easy Weaver** ($90) also comes threaded but does not fold up like Brio's. Our testers found the instructions easier to follow and also liked the refill kits ($25.95) that slip right onto the loom! 7 & up. Harrisville's new **Needlepoint Kit** ($12.95) comes with scrumptious colors and plastic frames. (800) 338-9415.

Art with a Scientific Edge

■ Chalk Board Planter & Paint A Planter *2000*

(Alex $10 each) Try either of these two crafty techniques for decorative planting pots. The **Chalk Board** kit has chalk board paint, a small pot and chalk for decorating the pot again and again. **Paint A Planter** has white acrylic paint to cover the pot and a rainbow of colors for decorating over the white. They say 8 & up, but if you put the base coat on, younger kids will enjoy doing them. Make a great gift! (800) 666-2539.

■ Paper Making Kit

(DaMert $10) Use your blender and junk mail to make recycled paper. Kit comes with clear directions, simple tools, and dried flowers for making scented paper, too. Also, **Sun Print Making Kit,** with all the ingredients for making designs with light-sensitive paper. 8 & up. (800) 231-3722.

■ Leaf Press Activity Kit

(Alex $20) We liked the fact that this kit also came with the material for making a journal for a leaf collection. 7 & up. (800) 666-2539.

■ Super Dooper Bouncing Zooom Balls

(Curiosity Kits $10) An update of a '98 PLATINUM AWARD winner, this kit has enough material for 10 balls with new shapes—a 10-sided ball, a bumpy one, and a scalloped one, plus the original round jax-sized ball. A little science here with mixing crystals & water to change them into a solid, bounceable material in just 3 minutes. 6 & up. (800) 584-5487.

NOTABLE PREVIOUS WINNERS: **Paper Marbling** (Creativity for Kids $18) Kit includes nontoxic ink, a pan, templates for boxes, paper, and materials for making a book cover and other marbled objects. Use rubber gloves and a bigger pan than the one provided in kit. 8 & up.

(800) 311-8684. **Makit** & **Bakit Sets** (Quincrafts $10) Pour color-ful crystals into a grid, bake them in the oven. Use as keychains or suncatchers. We liked the glow-in-the-dark set with less gender-spe-cific themes. Adult supervision. 8 & up. (800) 342-8458.

Musical Instruments

■ Chimalong & Mini Chimalong BLUE CHIP

(Woodstock Percussion $20 & up) Unlike most musical toys for kids, the tone of this metal-chime xylophone is lovely. Can be played by number/color or musical notation. Can be enjoyed by a preschooler, but becomes a true musical instrument for older children that also reinforces reading from left to right. Mini version is not as sweet sounding. That said, this is a pleasant travel take-along toy. Says 3 & up; we'd say 4–8. (800) 422-44638.

■ Glockenspiel Making Kit

(Woodstock Percussion $15) As usual, this maker has designed a musical toy with beautiful sound quality as well as an innovative design. Children "construct" the playing pieces of this instrument by placing them on the frame in size and number order. Chimes attach easily with Velcro. Putting the playing pieces on, kids see and feel the progressive size and discover which keys are higher and lower. Says 4 & up, but 5–8s will get more play and learning from this kit. Also top-rated: **Rainstick Kit** ($20) and **Mbira Kit** ($20). (800) 422-4463.

■ Kids' Tom Tom

(Remo/Woodstock Percussion $40) If you're lucky, they'll let you play this colorful drum while they dance—or switch roles and boogie! Comes with mallets, but testers say that tones are better when played by hand. Also terrific: a **Kids' Konga Drum, Two-Headed Bongo,** and **Ocean Drum.** (800) 422-4463.

■ Music Maker Harp BLUE CHIP

(Peeleman-McLaughlin $50) No electronic sounds here. This is a cross between a zither and an autoharp, but much easier to learn to play. Slip one of 12 follow-the-dot song sheets under the strings and pluck. Has a soft and lovely tone. Includes folk, Beatles, and classical music sheets. 6 & up. (800) 779-2205.

■ Piano Keyboard

(Casio $40–$150) Without a huge investment, an electronic keyboard gives kids a taste of what learning to play the piano is like. Keyboards from 32 to 49 keys are for young kids. For 8s & up consider four- to five-octave keyboards ($149 & up). O.K., it's not a Steinway, but for tight space and budget, it's a place to start. 6 & up. For a less complex keyboard, **Little Smart Super Sound Works** (VTech $39.99) is a 24-note keyboard with songs, instruments, animal sounds, color-coded music, and follow-the-light mechanism. 4–7. (800) 521-2010.

■ Trap Set 🎖2000

(Woodstock $150) Most child-sized drum sets are paper toys. This is a real instrument with snare, tom-tom, bass, and cymbal. Pricey but serious. Woodstock has also introduced a child-sized **Guitar** ($50) that's a beauty for beginners who are not big enough for a full-sized guitar. (800) 422-4463.

Woodstock Drums

See Audio chapter for more instruments.

Active Play

Young school kids are often more eager than able to play many games with rules. Sometimes the real equipment is too heavy for them to use. Balls that are softer don't hurt as much and promote kids' confidence. The same is true of scaled-down bats, rackets, and other equipment.

■Air Cushion Hockey 🎖2000
PLATINUM AWARD

(Hedstrom $69) Not as big as the arcade—but great fun with family or friends. Our testers gave this table—with adjustable legs and a fan (not too loud)—high ratings. 6 & up. (800) 765-9665.

■ Koosh Loop Darts **2000**

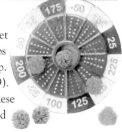

(OddzOn $16.99) This so-called "dart" set has no darts. Special Koosh balls with loops easily grip onto the prickly target. 5 & up. Still top-rated, **Koosh Catchers** ($19.99). Even poor catchers have success with these bristled disks that easily grab the looped Koosh ball. 7 & up. (800) 755-6674.

Ball Games Equipment

■ Fun Gripper Balls

(Saturnian 1 $9.95 & up) Designed for beginners, these balls are covered with nylon and non-slip grips. There's a lightweight bat and ball, a terrific football, soccer ball, and volley ball plus a small mitt with grippers and ball for young catchers. 4 & up. For novelty appeal, **Fun Gripper Thumb Ball** ($16.99). Players press a thumb over a suction cup handle to capture the big 9" ball. Toss the ball, lift a thumb—and ball is released. 7 & up. (800) 653-2719. Also: **BLUE CHIP Nerf Balls** (Hasbro $7 & up), lighter than the real thing and safer for beginners. (800) 327-8764.

■ Vortex Power Bat **2000**

(OddzOn $19.99) Endorsed by homerun slugger Mark McGwire, the big hollow Power Bat has an extra-large sweet spot. Comes with a soft orange vinyl ball. Perfect for the 5 & up crowd getting ready for spring training. (800) 755-6674.

■ Turbo Hoops

(Hedstrom $89.99) Forget the arcade—now they can play hoops at home! Scaled for kids, this hoops game has an electronic scorer, comes with three balls, and folds against the wall when not in use. Takes patience to assemble, and 4 AA batteries. 5 & up. PLATINUM AWARD '98. (800) 765-9665. For plastic basketball hoops, see Preschool Chapter.

Sand and Water Toys

■ Beachbowl

(Do things $14.95) Press the numbered cups into the sand, put the backer board in place, and get ready to bowl! A fun game for mixed ages when kids need something to do out of the water. 4 & up. (888) 726-3869.

■ Giant Castle Building Set 2000

(Battat $29) A 14-piece set that comes in an oversized bucket will do the trick for a crew of sand castle builders. With forms for making watchtowers, battlements, and towers, this is an open-ended kit for beach buddies of all ages. 6 & up. (800) 247-6144.

■ Soakasaurus 2000

(Kidpower $7.99 each) We've loved these noodle-shaped floaters to stretch out and float on or use for kick-boarding. Now they come with heads that squirt for playful games, or straddle them and have your own "races" across the pool. (800) 545-7529.

■ Zome System Bubbles 2000

(Zometool $9.99 & up) We were fascinated with the bubbles within bubbles that you could create with this building system. Construct your own geometric shape and then dip it in bubble solution and be amazed with the shapes the bubbles take on within the shape. The manufacturer tells us it has to do with the 4th dimension and shadows. Whatever the scientific principle, this 72-piece set is great fun for 6 & up. (888) 966-3386.

Wheel Toys

 Shopping Checklist

⊛ Fives will continue to enjoy many of the wheel toys in the Preschool section.

⊛ By six or seven, most kids are ready and eager for a two-wheeler with training wheels. Steer clear of bikes with gears or hand brakes. Learning to balance is a big enough deal.

⊛ Tempting as it may be to surprise your child, your best bet is to take your child to the store.

⊛ Buy a bike that fits, rather than one to "grow into." When kids straddle a bike they should be able to put a foot on the ground for balance.

⊛ Budget and size will dictate the choices. Schwinn ($100 & up) and Huffy ($100 & up) offer solidly built 16" bikes with adjustable training wheels and an assortment of accessories.

⊛ Helmets do help! According to the Consumer Product Safety Commission, one in seven children suffers head injuries in bike-related accidents. While studies show that wearing helmets reduces the risk of injury by 85 percent, the sad fact is that only 5 percent of bike-riding kids actually wear helmets. See Safety Guidelines for new helmet standards.

Science Toys and Equipment

Science is still best understood with hands-on materials. Favorite equipment: magnifiers, magnets, gyroscopes, kaleidoscopes, prisms, and a compass.

■ Activity Rock Kit

(GeoCentral $18.95) If you have a budding rock collector in your family, this kit is a sure fire hit. Comes with activity book and 12 minerals that have special attributes sure to wow friends and family.

For example, there's optical calcite, floating pumice, and magnetic lodestone. Specialty stores.

Comparison Shopper—Archeological Dig Kits

We thought this kind of kit was pretty mindless, but our testers loved playing archeologist, chipping away at a clay block to unearth hidden treasures. For younger diggers, we found **Buried Treasure Kits** (Educational Insights $17.95 each), with **Castle, Egyptian,** or **Mayan Treasure** themes. Facts about the period they are digging into are included with age-appropriate tools. 7 & up. (800) 933-3277. **National Geographic Expedition Series** (Kristal $24 each) includes a splendid Chinese Terra-Cotta Figure or a Dinosaur Egg, is more delicate and requires careful handling in order not to break the hidden treasures. (888) 896-1625.

■Build-a-Bank *2000* PLATINUM AWARD

(Magnif $9.95 each) School-aged kids love amassing coins. Here's the perfect bank kit for kids to build, with gears that propel coins up through the bank, and a sorter at the end of the line. At only $9.95, this is an inexpensive building toy with a fun application. Pick up some coin wrappers at the bank—a hands-on lesson in money. The **Coin Coaster** and **Money Mixer** were our favorite models and they can be hooked together for a Rube Goldberg creation!

The **Treasure Twister** was harder to operate. Marked 6 & up, our 9 year olds needed help. (800) 869-5463.

■Volcano Kit *2000*

(Curiosity Kits $8) Use plaster casting gauze to shape a small-scale volcano. Add your own baking soda and vinegar and have a blast. Much smaller than most previous volcano kits. Adult assistance. 6 & up. (800) 584-5487.

∎Wild Wrecker Motorized Gears Building Set
2000 PLATINUM AWARD

(Learning Resources $37) By far the best gear sets this year come from Learning Resources. Testers loved both the **Wild Wrecker** that builds motorized trucks and the zany **Oogly Googly** ($37) kit for making alien-like creatures, which is the PLATINUM AWARD winner. Directions for both sets were less than great, but still got great reviews. 7 & up.

Both are great solo toys that develop problem solving skills as kids make moving "machines." Still top-rated: **Gears! Gears! Gears!,** the original sets with one size gear ($20/$40). Or add **Gears Power Motor Accessory Set** ($15) to motorize a set you own. 6 & up. (800) 222-3909.

Nature Houses & Lodges

∎ Hanging Bird Feeder & Bird Houses Kits *2000*

(TWC of America $16) While there are more bird kits around than ever, many were splintery and hard to put together. The best kits we found were from this company. We think kids will be more invested in watching if they have a hand in constructing the kits to attract the birds. We've looked at lots of kits over the years and these are beautifully crafted pine with rounded edges and pre-drilled holes for easier hammering. Younger kids can help with the decoration or hammering, but even older kids will need adult assistance. Also great: **Feeder** with plexi-glass windows ($20); **Bird house** ($16). 8 & up. (800) 301-7592.

∎ Butterfly Garden & Ladybug Lodge

(Insect Lore $21.95) These kits match kids' fascination with bugs—front-row seats to the metamorphosis of a caterpillar. Have kids keep a journal of the wonderful transformation from caterpillar to Painted Lady butterfly. Comes with butterfly box, instructions on their care, and a certificate to mail in for 3–5 butterflies. Also fascinating, a **Ladybug Lodge** ($14.95), with a log book and experiments to study the 75 ladybugs that you send for, keep for a week, and release to feast on your garden's aphids. (800) LIVE-BUG.

■Nature House 2000

(TWC of America $11/$15) With a big plastic cap side "door," screened sides, and fabric handle, this sturdy hut-shaped wooden house makes a perfect temporary habitat for captured bugs and other specimens from outdoors. Test families tell us kids are fascinated with trapping and observing their captives before they release them and start trapping again! Available in two sizes. Also top-rated, **Soil Dweller Nature House Kit** 2000 ($20). Kids can make their own earthworm or ant farm with this kit (approx. 8" x 11") with wooden frame and plexiglass windows. Captive creatures can be returned to the wild with ease after kids have had time to observe their specimens. Adult assistance. 8 & up. (800) 301-7592.

The Scoop on Scopes : Telescopes, Microscopes, Gyroscopes, Periscopes, Kaleidoscopes

■ Hydro Gyro 2000

(Rainbow Products $10) Feed the teeth of the launcher cord into this gyroscope and the inner fluid chamber that holds colored H_2O creates a whirlpool! It's easier than most gyros to activate and could be used with a stopwatch for races at a party. 5 & up. Still top-rated, **Odyssey Scope** ($15), a kaleidoscope that looks like a microscope with rotating disc and 50 holographic magnetic shapes that stick to the disc to arrange in ever-changing patterns. PLATINUM AWARD '96. 7 & up. (541) 826-9007. .

■ Giant Periscope

(Tasco $15) For exploring around corners, this sturdy plastic double-handled periscope is just right. This company also makes a full line of microscopes and telescopes. (888) 438-8272.

Microscopes 50x

Testers report that both Uncle Milton's **Super GeoScope** ($33.50) and Educational Insights' **Deluxe Magniscope** ($34.95) vie feature-for-feature for best scope. Though optics were a bit better in the GeoScope, testers liked Magniscope's tilting base and multiple ways of holding specimens. Removed from the stand for field use, testers found the built-in spacer on the GeoScope made it easier to focus. Both companies offer hand-held 30x models, of which our testers gave higher marks to GeoScope, because it's easier to focus. 6 & up. Uncle Milton (818) 707-0800 / Educational Insights (800) 933-3277.

■ Galactic Explorer

(Educational Insights $39.95) This is not a high-powered telescope, but unlike all too many kids' scopes, this one works pretty well. It has interchangeable 50x and 100x eyepieces, comes on a full-sized adjustable tripod, and includes a wide-field 3x finder scope and a guide with tips on viewing the moon. 8 & up. (800) 933-3277.

■ I Made My Microscope
& I Made My Telescope

(Kahoot $13 each) Our testers have consistently loved this series of hands-on science kits. **I Made My Telescope** (in ten easy steps, really!); **I Made My Kaleidoscope** with unbreakable Mylar mirrors and an end piece that can be loaded with ever-changing contents. A great parent/child project for 5s–7s or solo for 8 & up. Also top-rated, **I Made My Periscope** ($15). (770) 985-5460.

PREVIOUSLY RECOMMENDED: **Magnet Mania Kit** (Dowling $10) Two magnetic wands, colorful disks and marbles for open-ended exploration. (800) 624-6381. 5 & up.
Marvelous Magnets (Alex $20) A hands-on kit with experiments for ten types of magnets. 7 & up. (800) 666-2539.
Nature Station (HSP $20) A mini ecosystem. Kit has soil, seeds, trays, pyramid-shaped covers, plus a 40-page booklet. (619) 423-9399.

Best Travel Toys and Games

As kids get older they enjoy traditional games such as **I Spy, Twenty Questions, Geography,** or **Facts of Five.** They are also ready for word games and travel books. Be sure to bring along some story tapes (see Audio Chapter). Aside from classics such as **Slide Puzzles** (DaMert), **Scrabble** (Milton Bradley), and **Etch-a-Sketch** (Ohio Arts), here are some other neat take-alongs:

■ Block Puzzles *2000*

(International Playthings $9 & $15) Six different pictures can be made from these 12- or 24-block sets. To start, have kids match blocks to enclosed pictures. As they become more puzzle savvy, they can do the puzzles without the guide. Packed in their own case (we wish it had a better latch). Chose either **Maisy** or **Madeline** sets. They say 3 & up, we'd say more like older 4s with help, and 5s can solo once they discover how they work. 4–6. (800) 445-8347.

■ Crayola Compact White Board Drawing Set & Flip-Top Doodler *2000*

(Crayola $10) A vinyl zippered portfolio comes with a white board surface to use with six wipe-off markers. Crayola has improved this product's "wipeability." Perfect for doodling, serious artists, or playing hangman! (800) 272-9652. Also top-rated, **Flip-Top Doodler** (Fisher-Price $14.99). A magical two-sided white board that you pull to erase. Great for hangman, tic-tac-toe, messages, or spelling words. (888) 892-6123.

■ Electronic Hand-Held Yahtzee & Simon *2000*

(Milton Bradley $7.99 each) The classic game has made the leap to an electronic version that's fun but different. This is not your childhood game of Yahtzee. The machine rolls the dice. There's less adding and more emphasis on seeing patterns. Both kid and adult testers vied to play this game of chance. A smaller version of your old Simon game challenges visual and auditory memory. Both of these can be played sans sound! 8 & up.

■ Hoberman Pocket Flight Ring

(Hoberman $7) A new twist on a frisbee type of toss-and-catch

toy. This one has interlocking pieces that allow it to expand and contract from pocket size to a full sized ring. (888) 229-3653.

■Markers to Go

(Alex $15) An art supply dream! 50 assorted colorful markers come in a neat yellow fold-up case. (800) 666-2539.

■ Madeline Dollcase PLATINUM AWARD

(Eden $19) A perfect present for a Madeline fan. A 12" carrying case decorated as Madeline's house, with enough room for the adorable 8" pose-able Madeline and a friend, plus storage for outfits and shoes. Dolls sold separately ($14). (800) 443-4275.

■ Mrs. Grossman's Fun & Games/Travel Kits

(Mrs. Grossman $8 each) The sticker queen has put together a traveler's delight of game boards that reverse to sticker activity board scene—all right on the mark for 4–7s. There's **Dog & Cat Checkers, Leap Frog, Penguin Party, Bug Races,** or **Space Case.** Flat and easy to take along for airplane or restaurant. Also top-rated, **Travel Kit** (with blank postcards to decorate) and **School Kit** (with bookmarks) both come with small journals and scads of stickers cleverly packed in video cases! (800) 457-4570.

■ Polaroid Cameras
PLATINUM AWARD

(Polaroid $24.99 & up) Our testers enjoyed the novelty of the new **Polaroid Taz** (you know, as in manian) and **Barbie** cameras that can be used with spe-

cial film that frames the picture with Looney Tunes or Barbie-styled flowers. Great for special occasions! Older testers also raved about the new **I-Zone Instant Pocket Camera** that is ultra-compact and comes with flash and focus-free lens. It takes 12 sharp but extra tiny color photos (1" x 1½"). Film $5.99/$6.99 with sticker backing for decorating notebooks or cards. (800) 343-5000.

■ Pop Zolo *2000*

(Wild Planet $10) Fans of this funky Memphis-styled construction system will be happy with this miniature set that comes in a green carrying case and an attachment for making Zolo keychains that can be redesigned over and over again. 5 & up. (800) 247-6570.

■ Radio Watch

(Wild Planet $14) A very cool watch with small earphones that pick up both AM and FM stations. We were impressed with the sound quality of the radio. A great gift that both Mom and Dad will want to borrow. (800) 247-6570.

■ Rubber Neckers *2000*

(Candlewick $12.98) Guaranteed to keep passengers' eyes alert! Players score points by spotting objects on their playing cards. You get points for spotting trains, bird on a wire, a driver talking on the phone or eating, and extra points for making someone in another car wave back. The 68-card set is colorful and easy to read. Remember—the driver may not play! 5 & up. Bookstores.

Best Birthday Gifts for Every Budget

Big Ticket $100 plus	**Rokenbok Expandable RC Building System** (Rokenbok) or **Odyssey Globe** (Explore Tech) or **Chaos** (Chaos)
Under $100	**GeoSafari Talking Globe Jr.** (Educational Insights) or **American Girls Collection Doll** (Pleasant Co.) or **Muffy**

(Educational Insights) or **American Girls Collection Doll** (Pleasant Co.) or **Muffy Combo Trunk/Bunk Beds** (North American Bear)

Under $75   **Air Cushion Hockey** (Hedstrom) or **Music Maker Harp** (Peeleman-McLaughlin)

Under $50   **Expandagon Hoberman Kit** (Hoberman)

Under $40   **Oogly Googly Motorized Gear Set** (Learning Resources) or **Finger Puppet Theater** (Manhattan Toy)

Under $30   **Taz/Barbie Polaroid Camera** (Polaroid), or **Medieval Castle Theater** (Creative Ed. Of Canada), or **Les Mini Corolline** (Corolle)

Under $25   **X-V Racers Scorcher Chamber Stunt Set** (Mattel) or **MiniChimalong** (Woodstock Percussion)

Under $20   **Naboo Fighter** (LEGO Systems) or **Splash'n'Sparkle Umbrella** (Alex) or **Hand Painted Ceramic Treat Jar** (Creativity for Kids)

Under $15   **Ice Blocks** (Gamewright) or **Mummy Floor Puzzle** (Frank Schaffer) or **Pop Zolo** (Wild Planet)

Under $10   **My Size Puzzles** (Mattel) or **Lacing Puppets** (Lauri) or **Hydro Gyro** (Rainbow Products) or **I Scream, Dog Pound** games (M.J. Moran)

II • Books

Reading to children is more than a great way to entertain them. Studies show that young children who are read to every day learn to read earlier and with greater ease. But quite aside from the academic benefits, sharing books with children is one of the pleasurable ways of being together. With books we can share the thrill of adventure, the excitement of suspense, and the warm satisfaction of happily ever afters. Through books we can help children find answers to their questions about real things and how they work. Books give grown-ups and children a ticket that transports them from everyday events to a world of faraway, long ago, and once upon a time.

You'll find useful lists of Blue Chip Classics for each age group as well as reviews of the best new and recent award winners. Many classic picturebooks can also be found in the audio and video chapters.

Books are primarily arranged by age groups. "Coping with Life" and holiday book sections include books for mixed ages. You'll also find recommended reference books, encyclopedias, and magazines for mixed ages at the end of the section.

An "also" after a review indicates other recommended titles by that author, or other related books.

Babies and Young Toddlers

At this stage, books are not merely for looking at. Babies and toddlers tend to taste, toss, and tear their books. Even sturdy cardboard books may not survive this search-and-destroy stage. Cloth and vinyl make good chewable choices. The mechanics of turning pages, pointing to pictures, and even listening make books among baby's favorite playthings and a key to language development.

TEN BLUE CHIP BOOKS EVERY BABY AND YOUNG TODDLER SHOULD KNOW

* **Baby Animal Friends,** by Phoebe Dunn
* **Baby's First Words,** by Lars Wik
* **I See,** by Rachel Isadora
* **Spot's Toys,** by Eric Hill
* **This Is Me,** by Lenore Blegvad
* **Pat-A-Cake,** by Tony Kenyon
* **Tom and Pippo series,** by Helen Oxenbury
* **What Do Babies Do?** by Debby Slier
* **What Is It?** by Tana Hoban
* **My Very First Mother Goose,** edited by Iona Opie

Cloth, Vinyl, and Board Books for Babies and Toddlers

There are loads of wonderful, sturdy books for the very young—but don't be fooled. Many publishers have begun to issue preschool books in cardboard formats that look like baby books. Read before you buy! Choose books with round corners and clear pictures of familiar things to know, name, and talk about. For the littlest reader, single images on a page are easier to "read." Little stories that center on the child's world are most appropriate for young toddlers. Here are some favorites.

■ Peek-A-Boo Baby *2000*
PLATINUM AWARD

(by Emily Bolam, Price, Stern, Sloan $12.95)
There's a tethered baby in the kangaroo's pouch and baby critters under textured wings and paws.

This beautifully crafted fabric book has no hidden flaws! Also, **Peek-A-Boo Sleepy, Sleepy!** With critter under blankets with satin bindings. 6 months & up.

■ Bath Books

(FunFax/DK $4.95) Smooth edges, soft tubbable vinyl, and clear pictures make these a safe, interesting bet for early book tasters and page turners. Titles include: **Colors, Sea Animals,** and **1,2,3.** 6 mos. & up.

■ Baby Animals—Black and White

(by Phyllis Limbacher Tildes, Charlesbridge $4.95) Bold black-and-white faces of a panda, seal, bunny, puppy, kitten, and other animals make for interesting looking for babies. 6 mos. & up.

■ Hey Diddle Diddle 2000

(illus. by Jeanette Winter, Harcourt Brace $4.95) Charming illustrations accompany this traditional rhyme. Also good to sing: **Twinkle Twinkle Little Star.** 1 & up.

■ Old MacDonald Had a Farm 2000

(by Siobhan Dodds, Candlewick $3.99) You can sing this one to your baby instead of just reading it. Flip the flaps to discover who Old MacDonald has on his farm! 2 & up.

■ Show Me 2000

(by Tom Tracy/illus. by Darcia Labrosse, HarperCollins $5.95) Where is baby's nose? A chin under a grin? A fun book for interacting with baby. 1 & up. Also, **Pots and Pans.**

Resources for Parents

■ Baby Story 2000 PLATINUM AWARD

(Chimeric $29.95) Create your own story about your baby with favorite photos and captions. Decorate the pages with over 100 stickers, choose color, and the book will be returned professionally typeset and bound. Kit price includes one copy, but you can order additional copies. A great shower present. (800) 706-8697.

■ Here Comes Mother Goose 2000

(edited by Iona Opie/illus. by Rosemary Wells, Candlewick $21.99)
Like their PLATINUM AWARD-winning *My Very First Mother Goose*,
this sequel abounds with glorious art that makes these old rhymes
fresh again. You'll use both collections and boardbooks ($8 each) as
a resource for rhymes to recite aloud and share
through the years.

■ Knock at the Door 2000

(by Kay Chorao, Dutton $16) Just in case you
don't remember all the words to old finger
rhymes, this beautifully illustrated collection will give you both the words and the
actions to play with the baby.

■ Lullabies

(Metropolitan Museum/Harcourt Brace
$23) Words and music for 35 memorable lullabies are illustrated with
works of art from the Met's collection. A great baby shower gift.
PLATINUM AWARD '98.

■ Pat-a-Cake and Other Play Rhymes

(by Joanna Cole and Stephanie Calmenson, Morrow $14) 30 hand-
clapping and knee-bouncing rhymes to say and play almost any time
of day, each with "how-to" drawings.

Older Toddlers

By age two, toddlers are ready for new kinds of books. Just as
they can understand almost anything you say, they can also
follow books with small stories.

They like playful language with rhythm, rhyme, and repetitive lines they can chime in on. They enjoy stories about children like themselves. Toddlers also love books about real things
like colors, caterpillars, and cars. Choose books you really like
because toddlers like to hear their favorites again and again!

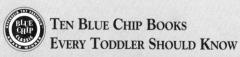

**TEN BLUE CHIP BOOKS
EVERY TODDLER SHOULD KNOW**

✳**Goodnight Moon,** by Margaret Wise Brown
✳**Jamberry,** by Bruce Degen

***Wheels on the Bus,** adapted by Paul Zelinsky
***Polar Bear, Polar Bear, What Do You Hear?**
  & Brown Bear, Brown Bear, What Do You See?
  by Bill Martin Jr.
***Sheep in a Jeep,** by Nancy Shaw
***Where's Spot?** by Eric Hill
***The Little Red Hen/The Three Bears,** by Byron Barton
***You Go Away,** by Dorothy Corey
***When You Were a Baby,** by Ann Jonas
***The Very Hungry Caterpillar,** by Eric Carle

First Little Stories, Adventures, & Mysteries

■ **Guess Who's On the Farm** 2000 PLATINUM AWARD

(by Naomi Russell, Candlewick $4) Split pages turn this clever flap book into a peek-a-boo game with obvious clues peeking out so tots can guess the names of the farm animals. Also in the same series: **Whose Socks are These?** by Jez Alborough. 2½ & up.

■ **On My Own** 2000

(by Miela Ford, Greenwillow $5.95) Older toddlers will love the independent polar bear who likes to play. Ford's close-up photos of the roly-poly baby bear wiggling, stretching, climbing, and rolling are sure to please toddlers. A sturdy cardboard format for independent reading. 2½ & up.

■ **Where Did Josie Go?** 2000

(by Helen E. Buckley/illus. by Jan Ormerod, Lothrop $16) Mommy (who is mightily pregnant), Daddy, brother, and the family cat and dog all join in on Josie's little game of hide and seek. Throughout this tot-sized mystery young listeners will be able to discover Josie's feet. 2½ & up.

■ **Arnold** 2000 PLATINUM AWARD

(by Mick Inkpen, Harcourt Brace $4.95) Kipper is a clever puppy who manages to deliver small, thoughtful toddler-sized stories. We're hoping the TV show will do the same. In **Arnold,** Kipper tries to get

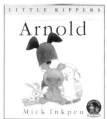

Arnold to play with one toy after another, but it's the empty box that most appeals to Arnold. In **Sandcastle,** Kipper is looking for the right topping for his creation. 1½ & up.

Rhythm & Rhyme & Repetitive Lines

■ Cows in the Kitchen

(by June Crebbin/illus. by Katherine McEwen, Candlewick $15.99) Using the rhythm of "Skip to My Lou," this bouncy nonsense song is illustrated with cows prancing in the kitchen, pigs munching in the pantry, and sheep bouncing on the sofa while Tom Farmer sleeps. PLATINUM AWARD '99. 2 & up.

■ Mrs. Wishy-Washy *2000*

(by Joy Cowley, Philomel $5.99) e.e. cummings would have called this a mud-luscious board book! Mrs. Wishy-Washy gets each of the muddy animals clean, but the moment they go out—they dive back into the mud. A short repetitive tale that will tickle the funny button of puddle lovers everywhere! 2½ & up.

■ Over in the Meadow *2000*

(illus. by Ezra Jack Keats, Viking $15.99) You'll be singing and counting the animals with this classic for years to come. For now, just enjoy the rhythm and rhyme. 2 & up.

NOTABLE PREVIOUS WINNERS: You're Just What I Need (by Ruth Krauss/illus. by Julia Noonan, HarperCollins) PLATINUM AWARD '99; **Row, Row, Row Your Goat** & **Peek-a-Moo** (by Bernard Most, Harcourt Brace) PLATINUM AWARD '99.

Slice-of-Life Books

■ Bertie and Small & the Fast Bike Ride *2000*

(by Vanessa Cabban, Candlewick $12.99) Bertie and his toy bunny, Small, go everywhere together. In this little adventure they take a pretend trip looking for treasure for Mommy. Short but sweet. 2½ & up.

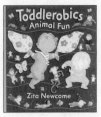

■ Five Little Kittens *2000* PLATINUM AWARD

(by Nancy Jewell/illus. by Elizabeth Sayles, Clarion $9.95) From wake-up porridge to five sleepy time kisses, the sensory language and cadence of this gentle little rhyme is simply purrrr-fect! 2 & up.

■ I Love You Just the Way You Are

(by Virginia Miller, Candlewick $15.99) George reassures Bartholomew that he loves him even when he's having a rough day. A comforting book for both toddlers and their parents. PLATINUM AWARD '99. 2½ & up.

■ My Day *2000*

(by Debbie MacKinnon/illus. by Anthea Sieveking, Little Brown $7.95) Pull the tabs to pull on a t-shirt, empty a juice bottle, close bear's eyes. This and a companion book, **Let's Play**, are sturdy and playful looks at typical events of a toddler's day. 2 & up.

■ Oh! *2000*

(by Kevin Henkes/illus. by Laura Dronzek, Greenwillow $15) After a night fall of snow the world is white and all the creatures large and small want to play. A celebration of snow that's scaled for young listeners. 2½ & up.

■ Toddlerobics Animal Fun *2000*

(by Zita Newcome, Candlewick $15.99) Toddlers will enjoy hearing, looking, chanting, and doing what the tots in this bouncy book are doing. Told in rhythmic verse and with lively illustrations, it will be hard not to get up and wiggle, wriggle, and giggle! 2½ & up.

Coping With Life's Little Ups & Downs

■ Baby Bird's First Nest *2000*

(by Frank Asch, Harcourt Brace $14) When Baby Bird falls out of her nest, she thinks she cannot get back. It's her friend Frog who helps her understand that although she can't fly yet, she can do it one hop at a time. 3 & up.

■ Bunny Bungalow *2000*

(by Cynthia Rylant/illus. by Nancy Hayashi, Harcourt Brace $14) Here's a honey of a bunny tale about moving to a new home. Told in sweet, easy couplets, this is just the right kind of reassurance young movers need. 2½ & up.

■ Good Job, Little Bear *2000*

(by Martin Waddell/illus. by Barbara Firth, Candlewick $15.99) Little Bear wants an audience as he tries new things. That's just what Big Bear provides. It's Big Bear's being there that gives Little Bear the courage to try new things. 2 & up. Also, **Just You and Me** (by Sam McBratney/illus. by Ivan Bates, Candlewick $15.99). 2½ & up.

■ When Mama Comes Home Tonight

(by Eileen Spinelli/illus. by Jane Dyer, Simon & Schuster $14) With tender illustrations and lyrical rhymes, this celebrates day's end when Mama comes home. Working mamas and their tots will enjoy this again and again. PLATINUM AWARD '99. 2 & up.

■ When Will Sarah Come? *2000*

(by Elizabeth F. Howard/photos by Nina Crews, Greenwillow $16) When his big sister goes off to school a small boy spends the day with his Grandmother. He plays with his toys, but all day long he is watching for his big sister's return. 2½ & up.

Potty Corner (Results not Guaranteed!)

■ Going to the Potty

(by Fred Rogers/photos by Jim Judkis, Putnam $5.95) In his usual reassuring way, Mr. Rogers talks with children about using the potty. This photo essay reinforces the idea that using a potty is another step toward growing up. Also excellent: **Your New Potty,** by J. Cole, Morrow. 2 & up.

■ Koko Bear's New Potty

(by Vicki Lansky, Bantam $3.95) Koko is a little bear who is learning how to become more independent by using the potty. Each page also includes a few of Lansky's tips for parents on their role. 2 & up.

Sweet Dreams—Bedtime Books

■ Good Night, Baby Bear

(by Frank Asch, Harcourt Brace $14) Every child who has ever stalled about going to sleep will relate to Baby Bear, who wants a snack, a drink, and even the moon. Mama Bear is not only patient— she even delivers the moon! A snuggle-up kind of bedtime tale. PLATINUM AWARD '99. 2–5.

■ Maisy's Bedtime 2000

(by Lucy Cousins, Candlewick $10.99) In the world of mice, Maisy, who is now on TV, is almost as well-known these days as Mickey. Not all Maisy books are equal—in fact, we're sorry to say that a few of her lift-the-flap books have some pretty sharp corners. We liked the simplicity of this getting-ready-for-bed book, which includes going to the potty, and the humor of **Maisy's Pool.** 2 & up.

■ Sleepytime Rhyme 2000 PLATINUM AWARD

(by Remy Charlip, Greenwillow $16) You'll soon know this lyrical love poem by heart and before long, your tot will be reciting it with you! This is one of those poems that feels like it has always been here waiting to be shared! All ages.

NOTABLE PREVIOUS WINNERS: **Goodnight Moon** (by M. W. Brown, HarperCollins); **Time For Bed** (by Mem Fox, Harcourt Brace); **Guess How Much I Love You** (by Sam McBratney, Candlewick); **Ten Play Hide-and-Seek** (by Penny Dale, Candlewick).

Early Concept Books

■ The Baby's Word Book 2000

(by Sam Williams, Greenwillow $9.95) There are lots of babies and toddlers doing what babies and toddlers do on the big busy pages of this oversized board book. Good for looking at and talking. 1 & up.

■ Do Monkeys Tweet? 2000

(by Melanie Walsh, Houghton Mifflin $15) Do dogs oink? Do horses bark? Older toddlers will giggle smugly at the totally ridiculous questions and gloat at how smart they are because they know the name of the animal that tweets, cheeps, barks, oinks, or... whatever, on the turn page. From the author of **Do Pigs Have Stripes?** 2½ & up.

■ Eyes, Nose, Fingers & Toes 2000

(by Judy Hindley/illus. by Brita Granstrom, Candlewick $16) Though the rhymes are sometimes uneven, this bouncy book celebrates the playful ways they can use their bodies. It's a giant leap beyond simply knowing and naming noses and toes, with lots of tot-size appeal. 2 & up.

■ Flappy Waggy Wiggly 2000

(by Amanda Leslie, Dutton $12.99) Who has a "flappy yellow tail and a sticky licky tongue?" Part of the answer to each riddle is peeking out of the illustrations under the flaps. Eye-appealing, bold illustrations. 2½ & up.

■ I Love Trucks! 2000

(by Philemon Sturges/illus. by Shari Halpern, HarperCollins $12.95) A jaunty verse celebrates the many kinds of trucks toddlers are beginning to know and name. 2½ & up. Still top-rated, **Boats; Planes; Trains; Trucks** (by Byron Barton, HarperCollins).

■ What Can You Do in the Rain? 2000

(by Anna G. Hines/illus. by Thea Kliros, Greenwillow $5.95) This and **What Can You Do in the Snow?** capture the typical things toddlers can begin to note and do in terms of the weather—which is often surprisingly fascinating to young children. Adorable multi-ethnic children. Sturdy cardboard format. 2 & up.

NOTABLE PREVIOUS WINNERS: Freight Train (by Donald Crews, Greenwillow); **From Head to Toe** (by Eric Carle, HarperCollins); **Let's Go Visiting** (by Sue Williams/illus. by Julie Vivas, Harcourt Brace); **Eye Spy Colors** (by Debbie MacKinnon/illus. by Anthea Sieveking, Charlesbridge); **Where's My Baby?** (by H. A. Rey $4.95).

Preschool Books for Threes and Fours

Preschoolers delight in books of all kinds. They enjoy longer stories about real kids like themselves and animal stories that are really about "kids in fur" with whom they can identify. Folktales and fantasy are fine as long as they're not too scary. They like the rhythm and rhyme of verse as well as prose that touches their hearts and funny bones. Eager to learn, they like playful counting and alphabet books. Kids are also interested in true facts about real things that match their curiosity about the world.

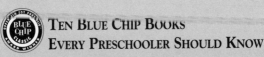

TEN BLUE CHIP BOOKS EVERY PRESCHOOLER SHOULD KNOW

* **The Runaway Bunny,** by Margaret Wise Brown
* **The Tale of Peter Rabbit,** by Beatrix Potter
* **The Little Engine That Could,** by Watty Piper
* **Curious George,** by H. A. Rey
* **Caps for Sale,** by Esphyr Slobodkina
* **Millions of Cats,** by Wanda Gag
* **If You Give a Mouse a Cookie,** by Laura J. Numeroff
* **A Snowy Day,** by Ezra Jack Keats
* **The Nutshell Library,** by Maurice Sendak
* **Make Way for Ducklings,** by Robert McCloskey

Great New Read-Alouds for Preschoolers

■ **The Best Place** 🏆 *2000* **PLATINUM AWARD**

(by Susan Meddaugh, Houghton Mifflin $15) Wolf takes off to see the world but soon longs for his old home. But Wolf sold his old house to the Rabbit family and they don't want to sell it back! After a temper tantrum which frightens his old friends, Wolf discovers that change can be unsettling but good—a giant concept for kids! As always, Meddaugh delivers with wit and meaning! 4 & up.

■ Don't Make Me Laugh
2000 PLATINUM AWARD

(by James Stevenson, Farrar, Straus $16) There are days when a good laugh is just what's needed and, as always, you can depend on Stevenson to provide the grist for the funny bone. In this silly romp an alligator orders young listeners not to laugh and then proceeds to make them do exactly that! 4 & up.

■ Mouse Practice *2000*

(by Emily Arnold McCully, Scholastic $15.95) Monk, a small mouse, loves to play baseball, but he's not too good at it. His parents are musicians, not athletes, but they do what they can to give Monk what he needs—practice! 4–8.

■ Snow Bear *2000* PLATINUM AWARD

(by Jean Craighead George, paintings by Wendell Minor, Hyperion $15.99) Young Bessie goes off to explore a huge block of ice that looks like a ship. Remember *Blueberries for Sal*? This is an Arctic variation. 4 & up.

Folktales

■ Gingerbread Baby *2000*

(by Jan Brett, Putnam $16.99) A lively retelling of the classic Gingerbread Boy with decorative pages full of details to discover with each reading. Kids love the repetitive refrain of "Catch me if you can!" Unlike the classic Gingerbread Boy, who gets gobbled up, Baby has a happier ending. 3 & up

■ Leola and the Honeybears *2000* PLATINUM AWARD

(by Melodye Benson Rosales, Scholastic $15.95) Forget the porridge—in this delicious African-American retelling, the Three Bears

go out while their pies are cooling. Who can fault little Leola who has lost her way in the woods and been frightened by sly Ol' Mister Weasel? You'll love reading this aloud! 4 & up.

NOTABLE PREVIOUS WINNERS: If You Give a Pig a Pancake (by Laura Numeroff/illus. by Felicia Bond, HarperCollins $14.95) PLATINUM AWARD '99; **Toot & Puddle** (by Holly Hobbie, Little Brown $16); **Bearsie Bear & the Surprise Sleepover Party** (by Bernard Waber, Houghton Mifflin); **When I Was Little** (by Jamie Lee Curtis/illus. by Laura Cornell, HarperCollins) PLATINUM AWARD '94.

All in the Family

■ Jacob's Tree 2000

(by Holly Keller, Greenwillow $15) Jacob is the littlest one in his family and can't wait to grow taller. Watching the height markings on the tree is slow going. A reassuring book. 3 & up.

■ About Twins 2000

(by Shelley Rotner/photos by Sheila Kelly, DK $16.95) What's it like to be a twin? With utterly simple language and delightful photos of twins of various ages, this is sure to delight twins as well as those who know a pair. 3 & up.

■ Oonga Boonga 2000

(by Frieda Wishinsky/illus. by Carol Thompson, Dutton $15.99) Only Daniel seems to know what to say to make his baby sister stop crying. Preschoolers will appreciate this all-powerful older sibling that knows just what to do! Along the same theme, **Baby Talk** (by Fred Hiatt/illus. by Mark Graham, Simon & Schuster $14) 3 & up.

■ If I Were Your Mother 2000

(by Margaret Park Bridges/illus. by Kady Macdonald Denton, Morrow $16) There's sheer delicious delight as a small girl pretends how she would care for her mom if she were the mother. A playful yet tender exchange. Also, **If I Were Your Father.** 3 & up.

NOTABLE PREVIOUS WINNERS: **What Mommies Do Best/What Daddies Do Best** (by Laura Numeroff/illus. by Lynn Munsinger, Simon & Schuster $16) PLATINUM AWARD '99; **Mama, Do You Love Me?** (by Barbara Joosse/illus. by Barbara Lavallee, Chronicle) 3 & up.

Separation

■ Baby Lemur 2000

(by Susan Hellard, Holt $14.95) A reassuring story about Liam, a baby lemur who is anxious about leaving his mother and going off to play with other lemurs. All's well that ends well since Mama is there at the end of the day. 3 & up.

■ Where's Bunny's Mommy?

(by Charlotte Doyle/illus. by Rick Brown, Simon & Schuster $14) A reassuring little story that shows what Bunny does at the daycare center and what Mommy does at the office. PLATINUM AWARD '96. 3–5.

Bedtime

■ Copy Me, Copycub 2000 PLATINUM AWARD

(by Richard Edwards/illus. by Susan Winter, HarperCollins $14.95) Through all the seasons a baby cub follows his Mama like a good little "copycub" as she calls him. But as winter approaches the little cub can hardly do what copycubs need to do. A nice bedtime tale. 3 & up.

■ Sweet Dreams: How Animals Sleep 2000

(by Kimiko Kajikawa, Henry Holt $15.95) In simple couplets and with close-up photos, this lyrical book captures the many ways that animals sleep. Hanging upside down, standing on one leg, piled in a heap—this is a perfect bedtime book. 3 & up.

■ What! Cried Granny
2000 PLATINUM AWARD

(by Kate Lum/illus. by Adrian Johnson, Dial $14.99) It's time for bed, but according to her grandson, there is no bed. Not to worry! Granny cuts down a tree, builds a bed, and paints it. But, oh-oh! There's no pillow! A funny tall tale that every child who has ever stalled about going to bed will relate to. 4 & up.

NOTABLE PREVIOUS WINNERS: I Love You, Little One (by Nancy Tafuri, Scholastic); **What Baby Wants** (by Phyllis Root/illus. by Jill Barton, Candlewick) PLATINUM AWARD '99.

Concept Books—Numbers, Letters, Words, and More

■ **Arf! Beg! Catch! Dogs From A to Z** *2000*

(by Henry Horenstein, Scholastic $12.95) Photographs capture a huge cast of dogs doing all the things dogs do in alphabetical order. Simple action words or phrases make this easy enough for beginners to figure out. 4–8.

■ **I Spy Little Numbers** *2000*

(by Jean Marzollo/photos by Walter Wick, Scholastic $6.99) Another simplified version of the well loved *I Spy* series, but here, objects are shown in isolation and are embedded in a big scene on the facing page. An amusing visual perception game that's fun for developing language, too. 2 & up.

■ **Five Trucks** *2000*

(by Brian Floca, DK $15.95) Both men and women drive the trucks that turn out to be at the airport, delivering luggage, food, and fuel to

a plane about to leave. A simple story with emphasis on ordinals, from first to last. 4 & up.

■ **Look-Alikes Jr.** *2000* **PLATINUM AWARD**

(by Joan Steiner, Little Brown $12.95) A sequel to last year's PLATINUM winner, this inspires young "readers" to look at the surprising details that make up the mini-world settings Steiner has composed and photographed with pretzels, crayons, and other familiar objects. 4 & up.

■ **My Favorite Word Book** *2000*

(by Selina Young, Doubleday $17.95) Here's a huge book with hundreds of words and pictures that preschoolers will love to "read." This is the kind of book that expands vocabulary and cements the big idea that the words we say can be written. It's like a picture dictionary, sans alphabetical order, with multiple story lines. 3 & up.

■ Teamwork *2000*

(by Ann Morris, Lothrop $16) Leave it to Morris to look at a theme with universal meaning. In this case she examines the nature of teamwork around the world. Like her books on bread, hats, and other familiar subjects, Morris inspires kids to think anew about a concept. 4 & up.

Young Science

■ Animal Homes *2000*

(by Debbie Martin/illus. Jane Rigby & Alan Baker, Usborne $8.95) This is one of the best lift-the-flap books we've seen, with painterly illustrations of the homes of polar bears, birds, chimps, and otters. Nuggets of information whet the appetite to know more. 4 & up.

■ First Discovery Books *2000*

(Scholastic $12.95) This consistently excellent series of small but captivating books give young children a close-up look at animals, plants, and other natural phenomena. Lift-up transparent pages magically change the images and introduce basic concepts. New for *2000* : **Fire Fighting** and **Atlas of Island.** Also new and interesting, **First Discovery/Hidden World** ($12.95) uses a paper "flashlight" to highlight hidden images. Our favorites: **Under the Sea** and **Under the Ground.** 4–7.

■ Guess Who's In the Jungle *2000*

(by Naomi Russell, Candlewick $3.99) Split pages with flaps to turn reveal amazing pictures of jungle creatures. Young listeners can guess from the clue and habitat who's likely to be under the next flap. 3 & up.

■ Safe, Warm, and Snug *2000*

(by Stephen R. Swinburne/illus. by Jose Aruego and Ariane Dewey, Harcourt, Brace $16) Using playful verse and watercolors, this lively collection shows the variety of ways that unusual creatures large and small care for their young. 4–8.

■ Snowy Flowy Blowy *2000*

(by Nancy Tafuri, Scholastic $15.95) A single word describes each month of the year, but each of

Tafuri's illustrations will inspire the flow of words. There's a small black dog to find on every spread and children doing what children do through the seasons. 3 & up.

■ The Very Clumsy Click Beetle
2000 PLATINUM AWARD

(by Eric Carle, Philomel $21.99) Everyone knows *The Very Hungry Caterpillar*—or they should—and now here's another bug tale with an important lesson about if at first you don't succeed, try, try again! This is a book that's sure to click with little listeners! 2½ & up.

Starting to School

■ At Preschool with Teddy Bear 2000

(by Jacqueline McQuade, Dial $5.99) A small slice-of-life book about a Teddy Bear who is a little anxious about starting preschool. 2½ & up.

■ Day Care Days 2000

(by Mary B. Barrett/illus. Patti B. Murphy, Little, Brown $12.95) From the alarm clock's first *Brrrring* to the last kiss goodnight, this romp in rhyme follows a child through a busy day at daycare. How refreshing that Dad helps dress the kids, takes them to and from daycare, and even cooks! 3 & up.

■ Off to School, Baby Duck 2000

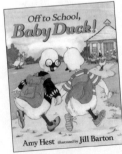

(by Amy Hest/illus. by Jill Barton, Candlewick $16.99) Baby Duck is excited about starting to school, but still a bit nervous. Once again, it's Grampa who knows just the right thing to say. Newest in a gem of a series that's right on target for preschoolers. 3 & up.

NOTABLE PREVIOUS WINNERS: Busy at Day Care Head to Toe (by Patricia B. Demuth/photos by Jack Demuth, Dutton); **Going to Daycare** (by Fred Rogers, Putnam); **Show & Tell Day** (by Anne Rockwell/illus. by Lizzy Rockwell, HarperCollins); **When You Go to Kindergarten** (by James Howe/photos by Betsy Imershein, Morrow $15).

Early School-Age Children

During the early school years, as kids become readers and not just listeners, keeping them "in books" is a challenge. Reading is something they should do for pleasure, not because it's "good for them." By bringing home a rich variety of books—fact and fantasy, science and history, humor and adventure, read-alouds and read-alones—you will be building that link to a lifetime of the pleasures found in books.

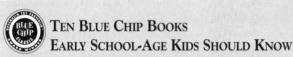

TEN BLUE CHIP BOOKS
EARLY SCHOOL-AGE KIDS SHOULD KNOW

* **Alexander and the Terrible, Horrible, No Good, Very Bad Day,** by Judith Viorst
* **Amazing Grace,** by Mary Hoffman
* **Amos and Boris / Sylvester and the Magic Pebble,** by William Steig
* **Martha** series, by Susan Meddaugh
* **Jolly Postman** books, by Janet and Allan Ahlberg
* **Magic Schoolbus** series, by Joanna Cole
* **Ramona** series, by Beverly Cleary
* **Tar Beach,** by Faith Ringgold
* **The True Story of the Three Little Pigs,** by Jon Scieszka
* **Where the Wild Things Are,** by Maurice Sendak

Great New Read-Alouds for Older Listeners

■ Harry and Lulu **2000**

(by Arthur Yorinks/illus. by Martin Matje, Hyperion $15.99) An amusing fantasy featuring a delightfully and highly opinionated girl who rejects a toy dog as an unacceptable substitute for the real thing. But, when Harry takes off on a Parisian adventure, Lulu goes along and discovers her imagination. 4–8.

■ Hitty, Her First Hundred Years
2000 PLATINUM AWARD

(by Rachel Field/illus. by Rosemary Wells & Susan Jeffers, Simon & Schuster $22) We usually don't like our favorite classics tampered with, but this version of Hitty is shorter and more accessible, and she's positively more beautiful! The adventures of a small wooden doll begin on a whaling boat and follow her through her first 100 years. 7 & up.

■ Swine Lake *2000* PLATINUM AWARD

(by James Marshall/illus. by Maurice Sendak, HarperCollins $15.95)

Two masters are brought together in this deliciously droll tale of a big bad wolf who sets out to feast on swine and ends up feasting on the beauty of the ballet. Small witty details in the subtext of the art add humor to the written word—both are to be savored! Kids and parents are going to wolf this down! The swine are divine! 5 & up.

Families Then and Now

Kids love stories about families like their own as well as those that are totally different. We've chosen family stories about kids today and those who lived in the past. The historic settings and figures offer kids a glimpse into another time and place. Past or present, good stories speak to kids about human experiences.

■ The Babe & I *2000*

(by David Adler/illus. by Terry Wiener, Harcourt Brace $16) Despite all the new records, Babe Ruth continues to hold a legendary place in baseball. Kids who have had a parent out of work will relate to this beautifully told story set in the Great Depression. This is not so much about the Babe as it is about a boy who helps his family by selling newspapers and sells one to Babe Ruth himself! 6 & up.

■ Mama and Me and the Model T
2000

(by Faye Gibbons/illus. by Ted Rand, Morrow $16) It may be hard to imagine a time when cars were so new that getting one was an event, but what about who was going to

drive them? In this lively picture book the assumption was that boys and men drove cars—not women. But Mama had other ideas. 5 & up.

■ Mimmy & Sophie *2000*

(by Miriam Cohen/illus. by Thomas Yezerski, Farrar Straus $16) Four tender stories set in Brooklyn during the Depression capture a time and place that many of today's grandparents remember. Yet the stories of a big bossy sister and her pesty, but always optimistic, little sister are warm and timeless. 4–8.

■ Raising Sweetness *2000*

(by Diane Stanley/illus. by G. Brian Karas, Putnam $15.99) A kind-hearted but none-too-bright sheriff has adopted eight orphans. His idea of good food, housekeeping, and other basics provide the chuckles in this tall tale with a twang. 6 & up.

■ Tea with Milk *2000* PLATINUM AWARD

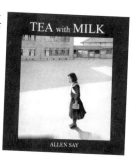

(by Allen Say, Houghton Mifflin $17) A young Japanese woman who spent part of her girlhood in the United States has difficulty living in the traditional ways when her family returns to Japan. Taking tea with milk is the least of her problems. As always, Say's illustrations are exquisite and this story about his grandmother speaks to the courage of a young woman who dared to be different. 7 & up.

■ Wilhe'mina Miles After the Stork Night *2000*

(by Dorothy Carter/illus. by Harvey Stevenson, Farrar, Straus $16) Eight-year-old Wilhe'mina has to run past the scary things of the night to fetch Mis' Hattie when the "stork" is on its way and her daddy is away. A beautifully crafted story about growing up and courage. 6 & up.

Fantasies Old and New

■ I Spy Treasure Hunt *2000*

(by Jean Marzollo/illus. by Walter Wick, Scholastic $12.95) Newest in the award-winning series, this year's settings have more of a fantasy edge, with treasure maps and settings that have a sense of mystery and adventure. 6 & up.

■ Rainy Morning 🏆 *2000*

(by Daniel Pinkwater/illus. by Jill Pinkwater, Atheneum $16) It's a rainy day and the hospitable Mr. & Mrs. Submarine welcome one guest after another into their cozy house for tea. The Pinkwaters' tall tale grows bigger and bigger as they welcome a wild coyote, a wandering wildebeest, Ludwig van Beethoven, the United States Marine Band! Rollicking good fun! 5–8.

■ Raising Dragons

(by Jerdine Nolen/illus. by Elise Primavera, Harcourt Brace $16) Pa & Ma didn't really approve of having a dragon around when daughter finds a giant egg. But, in this delightful fantasy, that dragon manages to do more good than harm. PLATINUM AWARD '99. 5–9.

■ Sector 7 🏆 *2000* PLATINUM AWARD

(by David Wiesner, Clarion $16) A class trip to the Empire State Building turns into a wordless adventure for a school boy who gets whisked away by a friendly cloud. In that faraway place, called Sector 7, something fishy happens to the clouds. As always, Wiesner gives us a memorable flight of fancy! 6 & up.

Friendship

■ Fishing for Methuselah

(by Roger Roth, HarperCollins $14.95) Ivan and Olaf have been vying with each other since they were no bigger than bear cubs. Now, each of them is bound and determined to outdo the other by catching the giant fish, Methuselah. An amusing story about friendship. PLATINUM AWARD '99. 5 & up.

■ Horace and Morris but Mostly Dolores
🏆 *2000* PLATINUM AWARD

(by James Howe/illus. by Amy Walrod, Atheneum $16) Mirroring the typical split between boys and girls in the early school years, this little tale talks to liking people because of who they are, not because of stereotyping by gender. A small but big message. 4–8.

NOTABLE PREVIOUS WINNERS: Bubba and Trixie (by Lisa Campbell Ernst, Simon & Schuster $16) 4–8; **Wanted Best Friend** (by A. M. Monson/illus. by Lynn Munsinger, Dial $15). 5 & up.

Legends, Bible Stories, and Folktales

■ The Crystal Mountain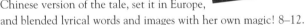

(retold & illustrated by Ruth Sanderson, Little, Brown $15.95) When her beautiful tapestry is carried away on the wind, a weaver's three sons vow to bring it back. Two sons are overcome by greed, but the youngest son has the courage to use the magic he is given to bring home more than his mother's tapestry. Sanderson has taken a Chinese version of the tale, set it in Europe, and blended lyrical words and images with her own magic! 8–12.

■ King Midas and the Golden Touch

(retold by Charlotte Craft/illus. by K.Y. Craft, Morrow $16) Children will pore over the small details and fantasy world that come alive through K.Y. Craft's painterly illustrations. This classic tale of greed is one every child should know. 6 & up.

■ Koi and the Kola Nuts   PLATINUM AWARD

(by Verna Aardema/illus. by Joe Cepeda. Atheneum $16.95) Koi (unlike his greedy brothers) receives nothing as an inheritance but the nuts of kola tree. Still, he sets out into the world and gives what he has to those in need and, in time, his generosity is returned to him. A gem of a story from West Africa told in the rhythmic prose of a master storyteller! 6 & up.

■ Raisel's Riddle

(by Erica Silverman/illus. by Susan Gaber, Farrar Straus $16) "What is more precious than rubies, more lasting than gold?" It is a riddle about learning, rather than a glass slipper, that sets this Jewish Cinderella story apart from the usual. When poor Raisel goes to the Purim Ball she wins the heart of the Rabbi's son with a clever riddle. 5 & up.

NOTABLE PREVIOUS WINNERS: Cinderella's Rat (by Susan Meddaugh, Houghton Mifflin); **The Cricket's Cage** (retold by Stefan Czernecki, Hyperion); **The Dragon Prince** (retold by Laurence Yep, HarperCollins); **The Bunyans** (by Audrey Wood, Scholastic); **King Long Shanks** (by Jane Yolen/illus. by Victoria Chess, Harcourt Brace).

Alphabet Books

■ ABC Discovery

(by Izhar Cohen, Dial $17.99) It's fun simply to try and find all the objects listed for each letter in the playful illustrations. But after an initial search there are challenging puzzles at the end of the book to make repeat readings rewarding. 5 & up.

■ ABC POP! *2000*

(by Rachel Isadora, Viking $15.99) In an homage to Pop Artists of the '60s, Isadora plays with the images and style of Lichtenstein, Warhol, and Oldenburg. Isadora uses witty quotes while adding sequential "stories" that are ideal for pre-readers. Our favorite—an ice cream sundae from three scoops, two dollops of syrup and a cherry on top! Delicious! 4–8

■ Miss Bindergarten Celebrates the 100th Day

(by Joseph Slate/illus. by Ashley Wolff, Dutton $15.99) The class prepares to celebrate the 100th day of kindergarten by bringing "100 of some wonderful, one-hundredful thing!" Done in ABC order, this should inspire some original collections. 5 & up.

Math Books

■ Bats on Parade *2000*

(by Kathi Appelt/illus. by Melissa Sweet, Morrow $16) Strike up the band—the big bat band, that is. Marching in twos, threes, fours and more, here's a batty way to reinforce some basic multiplication concepts. 6 & up.

■ If You Hopped Like a Frog *2000*

(by David Schwartz/illus. by James Warhola, Scholastic $15.95) If you could jump like a flea or were as strong as an ant you'd be able to do amazing feats. Using these kinds of comparisons, this collection shows what people could do if they could lift an object 50 times their own weight or jump 20 times their height. 6 & up.

■ **Let's Count** *2000*

(by Tana Hoban $16) Bold color photos of familiar objects are good for counting and talking about in this handsome counting book that goes from one to one hundred. 4–7.

Manners

■ **Never Take a Pig to Lunch**

(selected and illus. by Nadine Bernard Westcott, Orchard $18.95) A witty collection of poems about the fun of eating for kids who may have some reluctance about poetry; these delightful morsels will whet the appetite for more, please! 6 & up.

Tales out of School

■ **A. Lincoln and Me** *2000*

(by Louise Borden/illus. by Ted Lewin, Scholastic $15.95) Being teased at school for being very tall and skinny can be tough going. Finding that he shares not only physical traits but a birthday with the famous president gives comfort to the young narrator. Gives kids the sometimes elusive "big picture" that goes beyond the often hurtful bantering of school kids. 7 & up.

■ **Arthur Writes a Story** *2000*

(by Marc Brown, Little, Brown $15.95) In many classrooms, kids are often urged to edit and rewrite their stories. This Arthur book talks to an equally important idea. Arthur changes his story again and again to try to suit other people and almost loses the real story he set out to tell. New for *2000*, **Arthur and the Poetry Contest.** 5 & up.

■ **Happy Birthday to You, You Belong in a Zoo** *2000*

(by Diane deGroat, Morrow $15) Gilbert doesn't want to go to mean Lewis' birthday party. He buys himself a great toy and a frying pan for Lewis. Mom saves the day by switching the presents. A good book for talking about a typical school-aged problem. 6 & up.

NOTABLE PREVIOUS WINNERS: **Lilly's Purple Plastic Purse** (by Kevin Henkes, Greenwillow); **The Lost and Found** (by Mark

Teague, Scholastic) PLATINUM AWARD '99; **Yoko** (by Rosemary Wells, Hyperion).

Information, Please:
Science, History, Art, & More

School-age kids have an appetite for information about the real world. They want to know where things come from, how they are made, and how they work. Though they live very much in the present, they are curious about the past and how things were. Such information used to be found only in encyclopedias or dull textbooks. Today there are gloriously beautiful and lively nonfiction books for young readers.

■ Children's Guide to Insects and Spiders

(by Jinny Johnson, Simon & Schuster $20) A well-organized introduction to 100+ bugs with fascinating facts and clear illustrations. 6 & up.

■ The Art of Science   2000   PLATINUM AWARD

(by Jay Young, Candlewick $27.99) Imagine a pop-up camera oscura, a pendulum, a stereoscope, and electronic maze game built into one amazing book that explores how science and art go hand in hand. Stunningly crafted! 9 & up.

■ Tornadoes   2000

(by Seymour Simon, Morrow $16) For kids who want to know more about one of nature's powerful phenomenons Simon combines clear text and amazing photos. Also in this series, **Earthquakes, Lightning,** and **Volcanoes.** 8 & up.

■ Wild, Wet and Windy

(by Claire Llewellyn, Candlewick $12) When you need answers to weather-related questions about hurricanes, tornadoes, monsoons, and such, this is the book to share! 7 & up.

Animals

■ The Emperor's Egg
   2000   PLATINUM AWARD

(by Martin Jenkins/illus. by Jane Chapman, Candlewick $16.99) Did you know an Emperor penguin is almost four feet tall and eats nothing for two full months while he waits for his chick to hatch? Totally cool! 7 & up.

■ Ice Bear and Little Fox
2000 PLATINUM AWARD

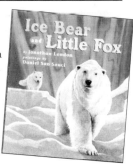

by Jonathan London/illus. by Daniel San
Souci, Dutton $15.99) Handsome paint-
ings capture the cold Arctic wilderness
where a young polar bear makes it through
his first year without his mother, followed
by a clever white fox who eats what bear
leaves. 7 & up.

■ How Whales
Walked Into the Sea **2000**

(by Faith McNulty/illus. by Ted Rand, Scholastic $16.95) Kids are
fascinated by whales generally, but this book shows how whales
evolved over millions of years from four-footed creatures who walked
on land to the whale as we know it today. 8 & up.

NOTABLE PREVIOUS WINNERS: Big Blue Whale (by Nicola
Davies/illus. by Nick Maland, Candlewick); **The Snow Whale** (by
Caroline Pitcher/illus. by Jackie Morris, Sierra Club); **Prairie Dogs
Kiss and Lobsters Wave** (by Marilyn Singer/illus. by Normand
Chartier, Holt); **Informania Sharks** (by Christopher Maynard,
Candlewick $14.99).

The Human Body and Reproduction

■ Big Head!

(by Dr. Pete Rowan/illus. by John Temperton, Knopf $20) A tour of
the human brain with lift-up vinyl pages that show how the brain
looks and functions, from the author of *Some Body!* 10 & up.

■ How Are Babies Made?

(by Alastair Smith/illus. by Maria Wheatley, Usborne $7.95) Simple,
clear text and illustrations on flap pages give children an intro to the
facts of life. 5 & up.

■ Magic School Bus Explores the Senses **2000**

(by Joanna Cole and Bruce Degen,
Scholastic $15.95) Fasten your seat belt for
a sense-sational journey that will fascinate
kids. Fans of the series will be delighted
with this latest adventure. 6 & up.

Notable Previous Winners: **Egg!** (by A. J. Wood/illus. by Stella Stilwell, Little, Brown $12.95) 5–8; **How You Were Born** (by Joanna Cole/photos by Margaret Miller, Morrow) 4–9.

Dinosaurs

■ Gigantic! *2000*

(by Patrick O'Brien, Holt $15.95) While the cover is pretty scary, the information is just right for young dinosaur enthusiasts. Dinosaurs are compared to modern-day objects like planes and firetrucks in order to give a sense of size. Also a good choice for 5 & up, **Dinosaurs Everywhere!** (by Carol Harrison/illus. by Richard Courtney, Scholastic).

■ Great Dinosaur Atlas

(by William Lindsay/illus. by Giuliano Formari, Simon & Schuster $14.95) An oversized dream book for dinoholics. Solid information, stunning illustrations, and maps. 5 & up.

■ Supergiants!

(by Don Lessem/illus. by David Peters, Little Brown $14.95) Subtitled *The Biggest Dinosaurs*, this big picturebook is brimming over with information about the giant dinosaurs and how they were found. 8 & up.

Looking Skyward

■ First On The Moon *2000*

(by Barbara Hehner/illus. by Greg Ruhl, Hyperion $17) Documenting the launch of Apollo 11, this book has more immediacy than most by telling part of the story as recalled by Armstrong's daughter Jan, who was eleven at the time. Combining actual photos and illustrations, this chapter book uses a picture book format. 9 & up.

■ The History News In Space *2000*

(by Michael Johnstone, Candlewick $16.99) Newest in an informative series that presents history in the format of newspaper stories. Here accounts of space begin with the ancient Greeks and follow news highlights of probing space. Also see, **Aztec, Egyptian, Greek, Viking History News.** 7 & up.

■ One Giant Leap

(by Don Brown, Houghton Mifflin $16) From his boyhood days in

Ohio to the historic moment when he became the first person to walk on the moon, this is an inspiring story of Neil Armstrong, an American hero who lived his dreams. 6–9.

PREVIOUSLY RECOMMENDED: **Out of This World** and **Seeing Stars** (by Carole Stott/by James Muirden, Candlewick) PLATINUM AWARD '99; **The Universe** (by Seymour Simon, Morrow).

People, Places, Things, and How They Work

People and Places

■ Amelia and Eleanor Go for a Ride
_2000_ PLATINUM AWARD

(by Pam Muñoz Ryan/illus. by Brian Selznick, Scholastic $16.95) Based on a true story, this superbly illustrated book conveys the independence and spirit of two of the most inspiring women of the 20th century. 7 & up.

■ Bedtime! **_2000_** PLATINUM AWARD

(by Ruth Freeman Swain/illus. by Cat B. Smith, Holiday $15.95) Who would have dreamed that the way people have gone to bed in the past or do so even today could make up such a witty, yet informative book? From outer space to underground, this informative book gives kids a look at bedtime and how fascinating non-fiction can be! 5–8.

■ A Big Cheese for the White House **_2000_**

(by Candace Fleming/illus. S.D. Schindler, DK Ink $16.95) Citizens in Cheshire, Massachusetts liked to claim their cheese was the best of all. When they learn that President Thomas Jefferson is serving cheese from Norton, Connecticut they are determined to change that! Based on historic fact, a story about community effort. 7 & up.

■ The Boy Who Loved to Draw **_2000_**

(by Barbara Brenner/illus. by Olivier Dunrea, Houghton Mifflin $15) There was nothing young Benjamin liked more than drawing or

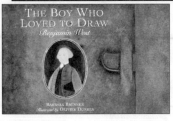

painting. He even borrowed fur from the family cat's tail to make a "hair pencil." A first rate young reader's biography about the boy who grew up to be America's first world-famous artist, Benjamin West. 6 & up.

■ Discoveries Series *2000*

(DK $14.95 each) For young people who have any interest in history, these books should help make the past come alive. The volumes give both the context of their period and graphic details. They are lively explorations of both everyday life and the overall picture. Choose from **Castle at War, Polar Exploration** & **Pompei.** 9 & up.

■ If a Bus Could Talk *2000* PLATINUM AWARD

(by Faith Ringgold, Simon & Schuster $16) Magic buses are not new to children's books, but this one talks and tells a young rider about another girl who changed history when she refused to ride in the back of the bus. Ringgold mixes fantasy with fact in a lively book that not only retells the Rosa Parks story, but paints a picture of segregation and those who led the Civil Rights movement. 5–9.

■ Rushmore *2000* PLATINUM AWARD

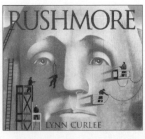

(by Lynn Curlee, Scholastic $17.95) If you are planning a trip or have already been there, this is a handsome picture-book history of the making of Rushmore. Curlee's narrative and paintings give a sense of the struggle and determination that went into this colossal undertaking—the making of a majestic American landmark. 8 & up.

■ Through My Eyes *2000*

(by Ruby Bridges, Scholastic $16.96) In November of 1960 a brave six-year old girl walked into an all-white segregated school and the history books. This is her story, told in her own words, punctuated with news stories and photos from the archives of newspapers and magazines. A story all of our children should know. 8 & up.

■ William Shakespeare & the Globe 2000

(by Aliki, HarperCollins $15.95) In five acts and sixteen scenes Aliki tells the histories of William Shakespeare and the reconstructed Globe Theater as resurrected by the late Sam Wanamaker. 9 & up.

Things and How They Work
■ Bridges Are To Cross

(by Philemon Sturges/illus. by Giles Laroche, Putnam $15.99) Brilliant cut-paper art makes this book a visual feast for the eyes. It takes you across bridges of steel, wood, stone, and bricks on crossings for llamas, trains, horses, cars, and people all over the world. 6 & up.

■ Dig a Tunnel 2000

(by Ryan Ann Hunter/illus. by Edward Miller, Holiday House $15.95) Clear illustrations and little text manage to convey much about the variety of tunnels, from moles and ants to castles and chunnels. 4–8.

■ The New Way Things Work

(by David Macaulay, Houghton Mifflin $35) This 10-year-old bestseller has been updated to include the digital revolution with 70 new pages and a dozen new machines. PLATINUM AWARD '99. 8 & up.

■ Special Effects

(by Jake Hamilton, DK $17.95) If you've ever wondered about the special effects in movies, here's a behind-the-scenes look at the tricks of the trade in such movies as "Star Wars," "Superman," "Jurassic Park," and many more. 7 & up.

Sports

To get reluctant readers to pick up a book, try a topic they have a lively interest in. Reading about sports is a key for some kids. Older readers will enjoy Matt Christopher's many sports-centered chapter books.

■ Froggy Plays Soccer 2000

(by Jonathan London/illus. by Frank Remkiewicz, Viking $15.99) Our friend Froggy is back and this time he's on the soccer team—but hardly a star player. As always, there's a lot of vitality here, and kids who are playing soccer will find a kindred soul. Also fun, **Froggy's Halloween.** 5 & up.

■ The Jungle Baseball Game 2000

(by Tom Paxton/illus. by Karen Lee Schmidt, Morrow $16) Based on a Paxton song, this romp pits the underdog Hippos against the smug Monkey team. The littlest Little Leaguer can take a lesson from this tale. 5 & up.

■ The NBA Book of BIG and little

(by James Preller, Scholastic $3.50) How big do you need to be to be an NBA star? Using photos of real players and objects, Preller gives readers another way of thinking about relative sizes. The big message

here is to have fun playing basketball—whatever your size. 4–8.

■ Sophie Skates 2000

(by Rachel Isadora, Putnam $15.99) Sophie's dream is to become a skating champion. With spare text and delicate watercolors, Isadora captures the dedication and lyrical movements of a young skater. 5 & up. Older skaters would enjoy **Michelle Kwan: Heart of a Champion** (by Michelle Kwan, Scholastic $14.95). 8 & up.

■ The Story of Baseball 2000

(by Lawrence Ritter, Morrow $16) Baseball buffs will love dipping into this updated classic. Here's a great way to meet the stars of the past and present in a book that's loaded with photos, anecdotes, and the history of the game. 10 & up.

■ Starting Soccer 2000

(by Helen Edom & Mike Osborne, Usborne $4.95) Young soccer players will find the illustrations and photographs of girls and boys performing various soccer moves instructive. An easy-to-use reference to use as your own skills develop. 5 & up.

NOTABLE PREVIOUS WINNERS: **Ballpark** (by Elisha Cooper, Greenwillow); **Take Me Out to the Bat & Ball Factory** (by Peggy Thomson/illus. by Gloria Kamen, Whitman); **Wilma Unlimited** (by Kathleen Krull/illus. by David Diaz, Harcourt Brace); **The Young Swimmer** (by Jeff Rouse, DK).

Art & Art History

■ Adventures in Art *2000*

(Prestel $14.95) Now you see it—now you don't. **Rene Magritte** is the newest addition to this excellent series that introduces kids to artists and their work. These are not cookie-cutter books; each approaches its subject differently. Also new for *2000*, **CHAGALL**. 8 & up.

■ A Child's Book of Play in Art

(by Lucy Micklethwait, DK $16.95) In this collection of great paintings, readers must find animals and birds in exquisitely reproduced art by such masters as Renoir, Holbein, Rousseau, and Picasso. A game you can play in the museum, too. 4–8.

■ Katie and the Mona Lisa *2000*

(by James Mayhew, Orchard $15.95) Katie wonders why Mona Lisa is not smiling. She steps into the famous painting to find out and off she goes with one of art's most famous subjects—visiting other works of art including Botticelli's *Primavera* and Carpaccio's *The Lion of St. Mark*. 5 & up.

■ Magpie Magic *2000*

(by April Wilson, Dial $14.99) A bird drawn by a child magically comes to life in a delightful wordless adventure. A colorful tale to inspire imagination as well as children's own drawing and storytelling. 5–8.

Easy-to-Read Books

Many of the books in this section are from series designed especially for young readers and are available in paperback. Keep in mind that many regular trade books listed elsewhere may also be easy to read.

TEN BLUE CHIP BOOKS
EVERY BEGINNING READER SHOULD KNOW

✱**Amelia Bedelia,** by Peggy Parish

✱**Are You My Mother?** by P. D. Eastman

✱**Frog and Toad,** by Arnold Lobel

✱**Go, Dog, Go! by P. D. Eastman**

✱**Green Eggs and Ham,** by Dr. Seuss

✱**Henry and Mudge** series, by Cynthia Rylant

✱**Little Bear,** by Else H. Minarik

✱**My Father's Dragon,** by Ruth S. Gannett

✱**Polk Street series,** by Patricia R. Giff

✱**The Stories Julian Tells,** by Ann Cameron

To help your beginner:

   📖 Choose books that are not a struggle. Easy does it!

   📖 If every other word is too hard, you've got the wrong book for now.

   📖 If your child gets stuck on a word, say the word. Some words can't be sounded out.

   📖 A bookmark under the line they are reading can help them keep their place.

Just Beginning Books: Easy to Read

■ What I See *2000*

(by Holly Keller, Harcourt Brace $3.95) Every sentence in this truly simple text begins with "I see a..." and the word that finishes each sentence rhymes with the word on the facing page. With pictures to serve as clues, this little book will give true beginners a sense of success. Also super easy in the same new series, **Down on the Farm** & **Brown Bear.**

■ Splish, Splash! *2000*

(by Sarah Weeks/illus. by Ashley Wolff, HarperCollins $12.95) Beginners will find the rhyming words and repeated pattern in this everybody-in-the-tub tale funny and easy enough to decode—with a bit of help.

■ Clifford Makes a Friend 🌟2000🌟

(by Norman Bridwell, Scholastic $3.50) Perfect for beginners, each page echoes the previous page with just one word added or the same words simply repositioned—for example: "The boy jumps." "The dog jumps." Clifford the big red dog imitates his friend and gives new readers a romp they can "read."

■ Tiny's Bath 🌟2000🌟

(by Cari Meister/illus. by Rich Davis, Viking $13.89) Beginning readers will see the humor of a huge dog named Tiny who can't fit in a tub. An entertaining romp with language that's simple and repetitive and visual clues that help beginners with new words.

■ Popcorn 🌟2000🌟

(by Alex Moran/illus. by Betsy Everitt, Harcourt Brace $3.95) A pot of hot popcorn gets out of control in this bouncy rhyme that beginners will like to read and reread as a chant.

■ The Red Hen 🌟2000🌟

(by Judith Bauer Stamper/illus. by Wiley Blevins, Scholastic $3.50) Here's a new twist on the Little Red Hen. In this version she's asking Fox and Duck to help her fix lunch, but they are much too busy.

■ Ted in a Red Bed 🌟2000🌟

(by Phil Cox/illus. by Stephen Cartwright, Usborne $7.95) One of several phonics-style readers with foldout pages. Emphasis here is on short "e" but not exclusively.

Moderately Easy Books

■ Class Picture Day 🌟2000🌟

(by Andrea Buckless/illus. by Patti Goodnow, Scholastic $3.50) When the class pictures were taken Amy told everyone to stick out their tongues. Only one girl did and she's miserable with the pictures! But she finds a funny and creative solution.

■ The Very Boastful Kangaroo 🌟2000🌟

(by Bernard Most, Harcourt Brace $3.95) A little kangaroo takes on a boastful jumper and plays a word trick that beats the big boaster. Also, **Catch Me If You Can!** All the dinosaurs are afraid of the great big dinosaur—all except for one small dinosaur that looks amazingly like her—grandpa!

■ Henry & Mudge and the Snowman Plan *2000*

(by Cynthia Rylant/illus.by Suçie Stevenson, Simon & Schuster $14)
Henry's dad turns his messy paint habits into a snowman-building
contest. A whimsical story.

■ Let's Read & Find Out Series *2000*

(HarperCollins $4.85) This excellent series provides underwhelming
information and includes activities children can do to bring abstract
ideas down to earth. New for *2000* , **Dinosaur Babies** & **Is
There Life in Outer Space?**

■ Rain, Rain *2000*

(by Maryann Kovalski, Fitzhenry & Whiteside
$5.95) Grandma promised the girls a picnic and a
day at the beach and nothing—not even rain—
keeps Jenny and Joanna's Grandma from delivering.
This lively trio always tickles the funny bone!

Intermediate Readers

■ Buster, A Very Shy Dog *2000*

(by Lisze Bechtold, Houghton Mifflin $15) Buster is not just a shy
dog, he's not too good at catching balls. He tries to catch the garbage
thief and ends up catching a skunk! Kids will relate to Buster in these
three small stories.

■ Gus and Grandpa and the Two-Wheeled Bike *2000*

(by Claudia Mills/illus. by Catherine Stock, Farrar
Straus $13) Giving up your training wheels and
learning to ride a two-wheeler can be daunting.
Gus's dad gets him a big new bike, but it's Grandpa
who gets Gus riding. Another gem from a
thoughtful series.

■ One Dark and Scary Night *2000*

(by Bill Cosby/illus. by Varnette P. Honeywood,
Scholastic, $3.99) Newest in the on-the-mark
Little Bill series, this time there's something scary
that's keeping Little Bill awake all night. Mom
and Dad send him back to bed, but Great grandma helps Bill with some "magic" other kids can
borrow. Also in the same excellent series, **Money
Troubles.**

■ Poppleton in Fall 2000

(by Cynthia Rylant/illus. by Mark Teague, Scholastic $14.95) It's fall and the geese are on the wing, but Poppleton knows about sharing and caring. This charming trio of stories speaks to how friends and neighbors care for one another. Also, **Poppleton in Spring.**

Transition Chapter Books for Advanced Beginners and Beyond

Kids at this stage often love reading books in series with continuing characters and familiar settings. Reading every book in a series may seem boring to adults, but satisfies young readers and helps them gain fluidity in their reading. Among our top-rated series to consider are: *Polk Street* series by Patricia R. Giff; sports series by Matt Christopher; *Boxcar Children* by Gertrude C. Warner; *Arthur* chapter books by Marc Brown; *Amber Brown* series by Paula Danziger; *Song Lee* series by Suzy Kline; and *The Zack Files* by Dan Greenburg.

■ Captain Underpants & the Attack of the Talking Toilets 2000

(by Dav Pilkey, Scholastic $16.95) For reluctant readers with a taste for slapstick humor, the second Captain Underpants adventure returns with enough lowdown bathroom humor and sci-fi comic book tricks to satisfy 8s & 9s.

■ Not My Dog 2000

(by Colby Rodowsky/illus. by Thomas Yezerski, Farrar Straus $15) Ellie has always wanted a puppy, but when Great Aunt Margaret moves from a house to an apartment her dog Preston cannot go. Ellie rejects Preston as "her dog" but he gradually wins her over. A tender, short, and easy read for beginning chapter book readers.

■ Ramona's World 2000

(by Beverly Cleary, Morrow $15) Ramona is now in fourth grade, Beezus is a teenager old enough to babysit, and they have a baby sister! It's been 15 years since the last Ramona book, so the newest generation of readers has one extra story to look forward to. Cleary hasn't lost her touch in capturing the small but meaningful moments in the lives of school aged kids. 8 & up.

■ **The Scrappers** *2000*

(by Dean Hughes, Aladdin/S&S paper $3.99) The Scrappers are hoping for a shot at the championship in their league. Each book in this new series features a different player with particular baseball related problems. Easy chapter books for 8–12.

True Readers

■ **Chronicles of Prydain** *2000*

(by Lloyd Alexander, Holt $17.95 each vol.) Looking for a memorable gift for your fourth or fifth grader? Alexander's five-volume chronicle, published in the 1960s, has become a classic. This re-issue with the original art also includes a Prydain pronunciation guide. 9 & up.

■ **Dear America Series** *2000*

(Scholastic $10.95 each) This series of historic journals holds great appeal to kids in the intermediate grades, many of whom keep their own journals. Written by both girls and boys, they capture details of everyday life in another time while reflecting major historic events. Our favorites for *2000*: **The Journal of Ben Uchida,** a Japanese-American who was sent to an internment camp during WWII, and **The Diary of Margaret Brady** and her voyage on the Titanic. 8 & up.

■ **Thomas in Danger** *2000*

(by Bonnie Pryor, Morrow $15) After surviving a Revolutionary War massacre, Thomas is captured by a Tory and handed over to the Iroquois. Pryor serves up a well-paced blend of adventure and history. An exciting sequel to **Thomas**, first of an action-packed series of historic fiction. Also, **Joseph**, who must stand with or against his stepfather, who is an abolitionist during the Civil War. 8 & up.

■ **Harry Potter series** *2000* **PLATINUM AWARD**

(by J.K. Rowling, Scholastic $17.95 each) If you have 9s & up in your midst, they will be able to navigate the fantasy world where Harry, an orphaned wizard, leads anything but a charmed life. Try these as a read-aloud family story time for 7s & up—an alternative to so-called family programming. But don't be surprised if some kids try to read ahead. Start with **Harry Potter and the Sorcerer's Stone.** Enjoy! 9 & up.

Read-Aloud Chapter Books

Long before school-age kids can tackle big chapter books on their own, they enjoy the more fully drawn characters, richer language, and multi-layered plots found in storybooks. These first novels, with more words than pictures, push children to imagine with the mind's eye—something they will need to do as they grow into reading. In time these books may be reread independently. For now, the best way to motivate the next level of readership is to continue reading good books to your child. Among the most beautiful and collectible for the family library are the Books of Wonder editions. After seeing films such as "The Borrowers" and "Charlotte's Web," try reading the originals and do a little comparative lit with young listeners.

- **The Black Stallion,** by Walter Farley
- **The Borrowers,** by Mary Norton
- **Catwings,** by Ursula LeGuin
- **Charlie and the Chocolate Factory,** by Roald Dahl
- **Charlotte's Web, Stuart Little** by E. B. White
- **Harry Potter** series by J. K. Rowling
- **The House at Pooh Corner,** by A. A. Milne
- **James and the Giant Peach,** by Roald Dahl
- **Lassie Come-Home,** by Eric Knight
- **Little House** series, by Laura Ingalls Wilder
- **The Littles,** by John Peterson
- **Mary Poppins,** by P. L. Travers
- **My Father's Dragon,** by Ruth S. Gannett
- **Ramona** series, by Beverly Cleary
- **The Real Thief,** by William Steig
- **Sarah Plain and Tall** and **Skylark,** by Patricia MacLachlan
- **Wizard of Oz** series, by L. Frank Baum

Resource/Activity Books

■ Blue Moon Soup 2000

(by Gary Ross/illus. by Jane Dyer, Little, Brown $16.95) A "souper-dooper" collection of soups from many cultures and for all seasons. Chef Gary Ross shares appealing recipes for hot and cold soups that the family can chop, cook, stir and eat together. Dyer's fine hand adds visual charm to the mix. Also, for bread making around the world, **Knead It! Punch It! Bake It!** 2000 (by Judith and Evan Jones, Houghton Mifflin $16).

■ An American Girls' Family Album 2000

(American Girl $7.95) Here's a guided family history kids can record by interviewing their moms and grandmothers and themselves. Generations get to share experiences from their own girlhood and how it was to celebrate a birthday, holiday or summer vacation. 8 & up.

■ Create Anything with Clay 2000

(by Sherri Haab & Laura Torres, Klutz $19.95) Sequels are often disappointing, but this is the exception! From the authors of the award winning **Incredible Clay Book,** this includes new techniques for making vehicles, dollhouse furniture, beads, jewelry and even snow globes. A good supply of bakable clay in bright colors comes with the book and inspiring ideas. Adult assistance with oven. 7 & up.

■ Summer Fun 2000

(Williamson $12.95) For those "what can I do now?" moments, here are 60 activities that are on the mark—from making pretzels to yo-yos and a whole lot more! Also, **Cut-Paper Play!** & **Super Science Concoctions.** 5 & up.

NOTABLE PREVIOUS WINNERS: **Kids' Paper Airplane Book** (Workman); **You Can Make a Collage** (by Eric Carle, Klutz) PLATINUM AWARD '99.

Coping with Life's Ups and Downs: Books for Mixed Ages

Many of the books in this section are what we call bridge books— they span two age groups. Some are on the young side, others are for older kids, and many will do for both. Included are books that address problems that families often need to cope with.

Feelings

■ A to Z Do You Ever Feel Like Me? *2000*

(by Bonnie Hausman/photos by Sandi Fellman, Dutton $16.99) Letters of the alphabet give a clue to the word that describes a "feeling" word that's missing on each page. But it's the pithy description and expressive photo of each child that provides the clues for a clever guessing game. What a fun way to put kids in touch with their feelings! 5 & up.

■ How Are You Peeling? *2000* PLATINUM AWARD

(by Saxton Freymann and Joost Elffers, Scholastic $15.95) Whatever your mood, **How Are You Peeling?** is a tasty treat that's sure to add a smile to your day. Amusing "sculptures" of fruit and veggies are accompanied with small rhymes that invite kids to express their feelings. From the creators of **Play With Your Food.** All ages.

■ Why Do You Love Me? *2000*

(by Dr. Laura Schlessinger & Martha Lambert/illus. by Daniel McFeeley, HarperCollins $15.95) This story reassures kids that they are loved, not because they are good at karate or even if they are not perfect in all things. Use this for talking about the bigger ideas. 4–7.

BOOKS

A New Baby

■ Hannah's Baby Sister

(by Marisabina Russo, Greenwillow $15) Hannah decides that the new baby will be a sister with red hair, named Patsy. Despite her parents' attempts to prepare her for a brother, Hannah holds to her fantasy until she gets a reality check named Benjamin. 4–8.

■ Just Like a Baby ⟨2000⟩

(by Rebecca Bond, Little, Brown $16) Each member of the family adds a unique talent to making a cradle ready for the new baby they are waiting to welcome. A joyful celebration. 4 & up.

■ Rosie and Tortoise ⟨2000⟩

(by Margaret Wild & Ron Brooks, DK Ink $14.95) Many books deal with the new baby in the family, but this one is about a super-little baby and an older sib's reluctance to even hold him. This might be just the right book when a preemie comes into the family. 3 & up.

■ When I Am A Sister

(by Robin Ballard, Greenwillow $15) Like all big sisters-to-be, the narrator wants to know how things will be when the new baby comes. But here, there's an extra tension, since this is a child in a stepfamily where her dad lives and she visits. A tender and reassuring book. 4–8.

NOTABLE PREVIOUS WINNERS: McDuff and the Baby (by Rosemary Wells/illus. by Susan Jeffers, Hyperion); **The New Baby At Your House** (by Joanna Cole/photos by Margaret Miller, Morrow); **Waiting for Baby** (by Harriet Ziefert/illus. Emily Bolam, Holt).

Adoption

■ Our Baby from China

(by Nancy D'Antonio, Whitman $14.95) Families who have adopted a child from China may have their own photo journal to share. This tender account chronicles the journey there and back and the joy of becoming a family. 3 & up.

■ Over the Moon

(by Karen Katz, Holt $15.95) Exuberant illustrations and a joyful text recount the happy story of anticipating an adoptive baby's birth, the excitement of getting everything ready, and the happiness everyone shares when the baby finally comes home! 3 & up.

Notable Previous Winners: Happy Adoption Day! (by John McCutcheon/illus. by Julie Paschkis, Little, Brown) PLATINUM AWARD '97, 2 & up; **Tell Me a Real Adoption Story** (by Betty J. Lifton/illus. by Claire Nivola, Knopf) 4–9; **Tell Me Again About the Night I Was Born** (by Jamie Lee Curtis/illus. by Laura Cornell, HarperCollins) 4–8.

Moving

■ **Absolutely Positively Alexander** BLUE CHIP

(by Judith Viorst/illus. by Robin P. Glasser, Atheneum $20) Now in one volume, three loved stories about Alexander, including **Alexander, Who's Not (Do you hear me? I mean it!) Going to Move.** 5 & up.

■ **Good-Bye, House**

(by Robin Ballard, Greenwillow $14) Room by room, a child says good-bye to the house she has always lived in. A tender book with an upbeat ending. 3 & up.

■ **Goodbye Hello Kit** *2000*

(ParentingPacks $19.95) This kit includes a countdown calendar, a book that kids can write or dictate and illustrate. Comes with postcards for sending new address to friends plus a booklet of great ideas for kids of varying ages. (888) 277-2257. For a less expensive variation, look at **Goodbye, House: A Kids' Guide to Moving** (by Ann Banks & Nancy Evans/illus. by True Kelley, Crow $9.95) A journal style book with lots of activities kids can do before and after the move. 6–10.

Divorce, Separation, & New Families

■ **A Girl's Guide to Divorce and Stepfamilies** *2000*

(American Girl Library $8.95) While we're usually not fans of "for girls only" books, here's a helpful book for the 8 & up crowd. Identifying many of the hot issues, this is a good book for getting the conversation going. 8 & up.

■ As the Crow Flies

(by Elizabeth Winthrop/illus. Joan Sandin, Clarion $15) Second-grader Michael's parents are divorced and his dad lives seven states away—as the crow flies. But his dad comes to visit for a week and in this gentle tale Michael learns things about himself and his dad that he never knew. 5–9.

■ Mama and Daddy Bear's Divorce

(by Cornelia M. Spelman/illus. by Kathy Parkinson, Whitman $13.95) Dinah Bear is frightened when she learns that the two people she loves best are getting divorced. A reassuring story that says important things stay the same. 3–6.

■ The Un-Wedding

(by Babette Cole, Knopf $17) With tongue-in-cheek humor Cole empowers the children of two quarrelsome parents to get them un-married. While few kids would choose that solution, this book will give parents and other caring adults a chance to talk about the positive sides of a breakup. 7 & up.

NOTABLE PREVIOUS WINNERS: **Amber Brown Series** (by Paula Danziger, Putnam) 7 & up; **I Live With Daddy** (by Judith Vigna, Whitman); 7 & up; **Living with My Stepfather Is Like Living with a Moose** (by Lynea Bowdisch. Farrar, Straus), 7 & up; **Stepfamilies** (by Fred Rogers, Putnam), 5–8; **Priscilla Twice** (by Judith Caseley, Greenwillow) 4–8.

Staying Healthy

■ Going To The Doctor & Going To The Dentist

(by Fred Rogers, Putnam $5.95 each) With photos of preschoolers doing what must be done, Mister Rogers gives kids a preview of routine trips to the doctor and dentist. 3–7.

■ The Paper Chain

(by Claire Blake et al., Health Press $8.98) Few books for young children have dealt with the fears and problems they face when a parent is ill with cancer. This sensitive and reassuring book fills that void and will be a welcome tool for families as they cope. 5 & up.

■ Sam's Science Series *2000*

(by Kate Rowan et al., Candlewick $9.99) Meet Sam, a boy with a sense of humor who knows plenty about how his body works. In both **I Know How We Fight Germs** and **I**

Know Why I Brush My Teeth Sam gives readers the facts. 4–7.

NOTABLE PREVIOUS WINNERS: **Great-Uncle Alfred Forgets** (by Ben Shecter, HarperCollins $14.95); **When Someone in the Family Drinks Too Much** (by Richard C. Langsen/illus. by Nicole Rubel, Dial $14.99)

Death
■ Rudi's Pond *2000*

(by Eve Bunting/illus. by Ronald Himler, Clarion $14) A school-aged girl's best friend, Rudi, dies. In simple prose Bunting manages to convey the shared grief, of the child, their friends and family. Rather than avoiding or denying her sense of grief, the adults help her find meaningful ways of remembering. 5 & up.

■ Thanksgiving Wish *2000*

(by Michael J. Rosen/illus. by John Thompson, Scholastic $16.95) A first holiday after the death of a loved one is difficult. Amanda's grandmother has died and despite everyone's efforts to make Thanksgiving right, a series of mishaps almost make matters even worse. By keeping grandmother's traditions alive the family finds comfort. 6 & up.

PREVIOUSLY RECOMMENDED: **Bye, Mis' Lela** (by Dorothy Carter/illus. by Harvey Stevenson, Farrar Straus $16) 4 & up; **Pearl's Marigolds for Grandpa** (by Jane B. Zalben, Simon & Schuster $15) 5 & up; **Annie and the Old One** (by Miska Miles/illus. by Peter Parnall, Little, Brown $13.95) 6 & up.

Death of a Pet
■ A Dog Like Jack *2000*

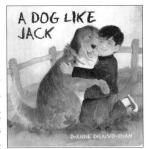

(by Dyanne DiSalvo-Ryan, Holiday House $15.95) Lovingly and tenderly told, this chronicles the joy of adopting an older dog and captures the happiness as well as the sadness of his inevitable loss. For any family struggling with the loss of a beloved pet, this may help with the healing. 5 & up.

■ The Tenth Good Thing About Barney

(by Judith Viorst/illus. by Eric Blegvad, Atheneum $12.95) When his cat, Barney, dies, a young boy deals with his loss by remembering the good things about him. This bittersweet classic says it all. 4–8.

■ When a Pet Dies

(by Fred Rogers, Putnam paper $5.95) Mister Rogers talks in clear language about what happens when a pet dies because it is hurt or ill. 4–8.

Holiday Books

Thanksgiving

■ The Can-Do Thanksgiving

(by Marion H. Pomeranc/illus. by Nancy Cole, Whitman $16) Lots of kids participate in can drives during the holidays, but they don't always understand where their donations go. This story provides a good starting place for that conversation and may inspire some to do more than bring a can. 6 & up.

■ Thanksgiving Day   *2000*

(by Anne Rockwell/illus. by Lizzy Rockwell, HarperCollins $14.95) Using a Thanksgiving play in school each child takes a part in explaining the important people who made the first Thanksgiving possible. 4 & up.

■ Molly's Pilgrim   BLUE CHIP

(by Barbara Cohen/illus. by Michael Deraney, Lothrop $3.99) A young Russian/Jewish immigrant is taunted by her classmates because of her clothes and accent. She brings an unusual pilgrim doll for her third-grade Thanksgiving project. A modern-day story brings rich meaning to the religious freedom we celebrate. A gem now available in paper. 6 & up.

Kwanzaa

■ The Children's Book of Kwanzaa

(by Dolores Johnson, Atheneum $16) A guide book for celebrating the holiday. An excellent resource book with wonderful crafts, recipes, and the story of how Kwanzaa came to be and its meaning. A resource book for the family. Also: **It's Kwanzaa Time!** (by Linda Clay Gross, Putnam $19.95).

Christmas

■ Auntie Claus *2000*

(by Elise Primavera, Harcourt Brace $16) Sophie knows her eccentric great aunt is special, but it's only when she stows away in her luggage for her annual business trip right around the holidays that she discovers her aunt's secret!

■ I Spy Little Christmas *2000*

(by Jean Marzollo/photos by Walter Wick, Scholastic $6.99) Just like others in this delightful little series, the I Spy "riddles" are shown on the left page along with the objects in isolation and "hidden" in the facing page. 4 & up.

■ The Tub People's Christmas *2000*

(by Pam Conrad/illus. by Richard Egielski, HarperCollins $15.95) A charming story with equally pleasing illustrations about a family of Christmas ornaments known as the Tub People. In the wee hours before Christmas Day we witness their encounter with Santa as he places them on a tree. 5 & up.

■ Where Does Joe Go? *2000*

(by Tracey C. Pearson, Farrar, Straus $16) What happens to the ice cream man when summer ends? Where does he go? A playful variety of answers told in rhyming couplets are sure to amuse young listeners as they dream up some places of their own. 3 & up.

■ The 12 Bugs of Christmas *2000*

(by David A. Carter, Little Simon $14.95) You've heard of the 12 days of Christmas? Now there are 12 sparkling, dancing, yodeling, and popping Christmas bugs from the master of pop-ups. 4 & up.

Our Favorite Classic Christmas Picturebooks

🍬 **Carl's Christmas** (by Alexandra Day, Farrar, Straus & Giroux) 4 & up.

🍬 **Jingle Bugs** (by David Carter, Simon & Schuster) 3 & up.

🍬 **The Jolly Christmas Postman** (by Janet & Allan Ahlberg, Little, Brown) 4 & up.

🍬 **The Night Before Christmas** (illus. by Anita Lobel, Knopf).

🍬 **The Nutcracker** (retold by Jenni Fleetwood/illus. by Phillida Gili, HarperCollins) 4–8.

🍬 **The Polar Express** (by Chris Van Allsburg, Houghton Mifflin) 5 & up.

🍬 **Santa Calls** (by William Joyce, HarperCollins) 6–10.

🍬 **A Taxi Dog Christmas** (by Debra & Sal Barracca/illus. by Alan Ayers, Dial) 4–8.

🍬 **Twelve Days of Christmas** (by Robert Sabuda, Simon & Schuster) 6 & up.

Hanukkah

■ Chanukah in Chelm

(by David A. Adler/Kevin O'Malley, Lothrop $16) Folks in Chelm have never been too bright and Mendel the caretaker is no exception. When the rabbi sends him to find a table for the menorah Mendel goes to great lengths to make the four-legged table follow him. 5 & up.

■ Eight Days of Hanukkah

(by Harriet Ziefert/illus. by Melinda Levine, Viking $10.99) A simple counting book with all the symbols of the holiday from dreidels to latkes. 3 & up.

■ Latkes, Latkes Good to Eat 2000

(by Naomi Howland, Clarion $15) Borrowing an old folktale device of a bountiful pot that won't stop giving,

Howland has spun a tale that's as delicious as a plate full of latkes with sugar on top! 4 & up

Easter

■ The Dumb Bunnies' Easter

(by Sue Denim/illus. by Dav Pilkey, Scholastic $12.95) These funny bunnies have got all the holidays of the year completely mixed up. A celebration of unadulterated nonsense! 4–8.

■ Rechenka's Eggs

(by Patricia Polacco, Philomel $14.95) When old Babushka rescues a wounded goose, the bird accidentally breaks the old woman's beautiful, hand-painted Ukrainian eggs. But all is not lost! Rechenka, the goose, gives the old woman more than a dozen miraculous gifts. A beauty! 4–8.

Passover

■ The Matzah That Papa Brought Home

(by Fran Manushkin/illus. by Ned Bittinger, Scholastic $14.95) A rhythmic cumulative verse recaptures familiar traditions of the Passover Seder from the matzah that Papa brought home to opening the door for Elijah. Bittinger's illustrations are memorable. A glossary of foods and traditions is tucked in for good measure. 4–8.

Bilingual Books

Some of these are written in two languages. Others are done chiefly in English with a fair sprinkling of words and phrases in another language.

■ Can You Count Ten Toes? *2000*

(by Lezlie Evans/illus. by Denis Roche, Houghton Mifflin $15) We all have toes, but how we count them is quite another matter. Using hats, boats, fish, and other universal items, children are introduced to counting from 1–10 in French, Russian, Japanese, Hebrew, Chinese, Hindi, Korean, Spanish, Tagalog, and Zulu!

CAN YOU COUNT TEN TOES?
Count to 10 in 10 Different Languages

by Lezlie Evans
Illustrated by Denis Roche

■ My Day/Mi Día

(by Rebecca Emberley, Little, Brown $14.95) Bright paper cut-outs of
familiar objects are labeled in both English and Spanish. One of a
handsome series for young children who are bilingual or learning a
second language. Also **Let's Go/Vamos** & **My House/Mi Casa.**
4–8.

PREVIOUSLY RECOMMENDED: **Tortillas and Lullabies/Tortillas y
Cancioncitas**, and **Margaret and Margarita** (by Lynn Reiser,
Greenwillow); **My Family/Mi Familia** (by Neil Ricklen, Simon &
Schuster)

Reference Books for Mixed Ages

Dictionaries

Preschool: Very young children don't
really need a dictionary, but their love of
words and their exploding vocabulary
make books with tons of pictures and
labels great for looking at. Most are
arranged in categories rather than
alphabetical order. Any of these would
be a good choice:

My Big Dictionary (by the Editors of the American
Heritage Dictionaries/illus. by Pamela Cole, Houghton Mifflin
$18.95) A giant "pictionary" with words and pictures in alpha-
betical order. Some pages can be used like a game to find other
objects that start with the same letter. Fun for browsing for
prereaders as well as beginners. 4–7.

My First 100 Words in Spanish and English (also
French and English) (Simon & Schuster $12) 4–7.

Macmillan Picture Wordbook (Macmillan $8.95)
5–8.

Early School Years—First to Third Grades: Beginning
readers and writers start to use dictionaries with A-to-Z list-
ings and pictures to find words they need. Too big a book will
be hard to sift through, so less is best!

Words for New Readers (HarperCollins $12) 1,500 words with definitions, used in sentences. A mix of cartoons, photos, and illustrations. 5–7.

Scholastic First Dictionary (Scholastic $14.95) Easy-to-read definitions with pictures and the words used in sentences. A good choice for second and third graders. 6–9.

American Heritage First Dictionary (Houghton Mifflin $14) Definitions are numbered when a word has several meanings. Illustrations and verb tenses. 6–9.

Macmillan First Dictionary (Macmillan $14) Illustrated with photos and drawings. Gives plurals of nouns, past tenses of verbs, and numbers definitions for words with multiple meanings. 6–9.

Later School Years—Fourth Grade and Up These dictionaries are more complex, with syllabification, pronunciation, and often word histories. They have fewer illustrations and many more words. Both also include maps and biographical and other historical data. For 9 & up.

Macmillan Dictionary for Children (Macmillan $16.95) updated for 2000 with more color photos. 8-12

Scholastic Children's Dictionary (Scholastic $16.95) Uses phonetic pronunciation instead of traditional symbols; includes Braille and American Sign Language alphabets and 100 high-tech terms. Photos, illustrations, and diagrams. Also, **Scholastic Children's Thesaurus** ($15.95). 9–13.

Encyclopedias

Before making a big investment in an encyclopedia, go to the public library or your child's school. Look at several sets without pressure from a salesperson. Keep in mind:

> Most kids won't regularly use an encyclopedia before fourth grade, so don't rush.

> Look up the same entry in each set—for example, look at the presentation for "dogs" or "dinosaurs" in each encyclopedia and compare content, style, and illustrations.

📖 Visuals such as photos, charts, and drawings will be very important to your child.

📖 A used edition costs less, but statistics, maps, and other information will be dated.

Following are the best choices:

■ Compton's Encyclopedia or World Book

(Compton's/World Book $420 & up) Both of these sets will be used by students from fourth grade through high school. The entries are not super-easy to read, but they are clear and well written, with attractive, colorful illustrations and photos. Both sets are of equal value and the choice is one of personal preference. See Computer chapter for multimedia encyclopedias.

■ New Book of Knowledge

(Grolier $995) This 21-volume set is written strictly for elementary school students. Entries are printed in fairly large type. It is illustrated with colorful pictures and focuses on subjects that interest younger students.

Song Books

■ From a Distance *2000*

(by Julie Gold/illus. Jan Ray, Dutton $17.99) Shimmering with glints of gold, Ray's folk art paintings contrast in fine detail the horrific images of war with a world of peace and hope. You'll probably sing this book and hear Bette singing in your ear as you do. All ages.

■ This Land Is Your Land

(by Woody Guthrie/illus. by Kathy Jakobsen, Little Brown $16.95) The spirit and beauty of this song are captured with folk art paintings and quotes from other Guthrie songs. It's full of little details that span not just the country but events and people that were significant to Woody and this land of ours. All ages.

■ Miss Mary Mack

(adapted by Mary Ann Hoberman/illus. by Nadine B. Westcott, Little Brown $14.99) Remember this old clapping rhyme? Hoberman has taken the original and embroidered it into a comic fantasy that

Westcott has brought to life with great good humor. 5–8.

NOTABLE PREVIOUS WINNER: Gonna Sing My Head Off! American Folk Songs (collected by Kathleen Krull, Knopf $20); **Disney's My First Songbook** (Disney Press $16.95).

Single-Volume Resource Books
■ Animal Atlas
(by Barbara Taylor/illus. by Kenneth Lilly, Knopf $20) An oversized book illustrated with maps and full-color paintings of animals arranged by geographic locations. Filled with clear info, such as what animals eat and where and how they build their homes. 7 & up.

■ Eyewitness Living Earth
(by Miranda Smith, DK $30) This big coffee-table kind of book gives kids a wonderful introduction to plant and animal life. Smaller collectible field type books on all topics are also noteworthy. Most will not replace an encyclopedia for writing reports, but they are ideal for matching current interests. Also: **Eyewitness Books** (Knopf $19) This excellent series covers a great range of topics that match interests of school-aged readers. 8 & up.

■ Factastic Book of 1001 Lists *2000*
(by Russell Ash, DK $14.95) Looking for the biggest, fastest, worst, first, or last? Ash's lists cover history, science, people, and places. Great fun for browsing or finding factoids. 8 & up.

■ National Audubon Society First Field Guides *2000*
(Scholastic $11.95 each) Designed to be used in the field or as a resource at home, each of these handsome books has hundreds of photos, clear information, and a "spotter's card," a quick reference card to identify an animal or plant. Build a science library with titles that include: **Birds, Insects, Mammals, Reptiles, Rocks, Trees, and Wildflowers.**

■ National Geographic World Atlas for Young Explorers *2000*

(National Geographic Society $24.95) Stunning images from space, photos, and handsome physical maps introduce each continent and its people with political maps that zoom in on countries and states. This is a book that could not have existed when today's parents and grandparents were in school. It's a book that could turn young readers into map lovers instead of map phobics! 7–70.

■ Random House Children's Encyclopedia

(Random House $60) A huge one-volume encyclopedia that kids love to get lost in. Won't replace World Book or Compton's, but great for browsing. 7 & up.

■ Reader's Digest Children's World Atlas

(Reader's Digest $15) With 61 maps, plus hundreds of photos and illustrations, this is a resource book that older students will find useful. 8 & up.

■ Turning Point Inventions: The Lightbulb *2000*

(by Joseph Wallace, Atheneum $17.95) Both this and the book on **The Telephone** don't condescend to young readers hungry for information. Using a well-balanced mixed of text and photos, readers are taken through the history of these revolutionary inventions. 9 & up.

Recommended Magazines

Preschool

Highlights for Children. Stories, puzzles, science articles, crafts, and thinking games. Dept. CA, P.O. Box 269, Columbus, OH 43216-0269.

Ladybug. Stories, poems, and art from well-known children's authors and illustrators. P.O. Box 58343, Boulder, CO 80321-8343.

Sesame Street Magazine. Kids' issue is designed to be cut up for active play with skills like numbers, letters, and colors. A parents' guide has informative articles. P.O. Box 55518, Boulder, CO 80322-5518.

Your Big Backyard. (National Wildlife Federation) Big, colorful photos and short features plus simple activities. (800) 432-6564.

Early School Years
Literature, Art, & Writing

American Girl. Crafts, cooking, travel, human interest stories, history. Pleasant Co., 8400 Fairway Place, Middleton, WI 53562.

Cricket. A literary magazine with book excerpts and adaptations from well-known writers of fact and fiction. P.O. Box 51144, Boulder, CO 80321-1144.

Nickelodeon. Games, humor, puzzles, contests, and feature stories. P.O. Box 37214, Boone, IA 50037-2214.

Stone Soup. For aspiring young writers, this magazine publishes original stories, poems, and art by children. P.O. Box 83, Santa Cruz, CA 95063.

Sports, Scouts, and Shopping

Boy's Life. The magazine of the Boy Scouts of America. Articles on scouting and sports, prose fiction, and cartoons. 1325 W. Walnut Hill Lane, P.O. Box 152079, Irving, TX 75015-2079.

Sports Illustrated for Kids. Stories about athletes. Features for girls as well as boys. P.O. Box 83069, Birmingham, AL 35283-0609.

Zillions—Consumer Reports for Kids. Preteens test, rate, and report on products directed to them. P.O. Box 54861, Boulder, CO 80322-4861.

Science

World (National Geographic Society). Environmental features, high-quality photos, science activities, stories about kids, plus contests, puzzles, and handsome pull-out maps. P.O. Box 2330, Washington, DC 20078-9955.

Ranger Rick (National Wildlife Federation). Features on animals and plants, and people who are involved with both. Also games, activities, and puzzles. 8925 Leesburg Pike, Vienna, VA 22184-0001.

3-2-1 Contact (Children's Television Workshop). Features on science and scientists, computers, ecology, animals, and other info. Includes games, cartoons, stories, science, and math activities. P.O. Box 51177, Boulder, CO 80322.

Click (Cricket/Smithsonian). Features on the real world, science, art, and history. **Muse** for younger kids. 4–7. P.O. Box 7468, Red Oak, IA 51591-2468.

III • Videos

Trends. On the whole we were disappointed with the quality of videos aimed at children. Even series we have recommended in the past have had taken some serious missteps. For example, why did *Blue's Clues*, that had until now made young children feel very smart, now become a reading readiness program that will make most preschoolers feel inadequate? Why did *Little Bear's Halloween* adventures need to be a scary walk in the woods? Why did the newest *Thomas the Tank Engine* need to be as action-packed with disasters as a Bruce Willis film? The producers of children's videos seem to feel that in order to sell their films, they need to be nail-bitingly suspenseful and, in many cases, unnecessarily scary and violent. From our point of view, young children do not need to be frightened to be entertained. While many of us remember watching the Wicked Witch of the West from behind a blanket, most of us were school-aged, not three. These filmmakers seem to forget that young children are still working on the distinction between real and make-believe. Given that many parents use videos as a better alternative to television, it's important to know that videos are no longer a safe haven.

Baby Videos. Developmentally, babies learn from active, real-life experiences rather than being "plugged in" to passively watching others at such an early age. We believe a mirror would be more interactive and age-appropriate than a video screen. We are delighted that the American Pediatric Association has agreed with our position.

Positive Choices. What you will find in this chapter are quality music, story, information, and how-to videos that involve kids in active doing. These are arranged from choices for the very young to those for older viewers. Some videos span a broad age range, from preschool to early school years. If you have a child between four and eight, look at the choices in Toddlers, Preschoolers, and Early School Years.

A Word of Warning. Like many products directed at children, age labels are often marked too broadly. Parents who remember feature films fondly from their childhood often hurry home with classics—only to find that these are too scary for young children. Videos, like toys, are not "one size fits all."

Screen Your Videos. Whenever possible, take the time to preview videos or at least watch with your children the first time round. You may be surprised with the number of videos you choose not to watch to the end. Teaching kids to turn off a film because it's just not worth watching is also not a bad lesson to pass on.

Music

Don't Just Sit There!
Activities for Preschoolers and Early-School-Years Kids

■ **Blue's Clues Rhythm and Blue** *2000*
   PLATINUM AWARD

Play Along with Blue
Rhythm and Blue
Blue's Clues

What music does Blue want to play?

(Paramount $9.99) Preschoolers love being in the know by finding Blue's Clues before Steve the host finds them. In this latest video, Steve needs to find musical clues to know which song Blue wishes to sing. A good introduction to matching rhythm and sounds. Series introduces concepts like sequencing and size relationships. Still top-rated: **Blue's Clues Story Time** (PLATINUM AWARD '99); **Blue's Clues Arts & Crafts.** Thumbs down for **Blue's Big Treasure Hunt** and **ABC's and 123's**—which take a wrong-headed turn in the road. This is not the audience for reading or spelling lessons! (Closed-captioned.) 2–5.

■ Clap To It!

(Go Kid Productions $12.95) You and your kids will love learning these clapping games and rhymes to play with friends or family. We laughed out loud as we tried to keep up with the kids who demo and then teach you traditional clapping games that would be fun for a party. Thank goodness for the rewind button! 5–9. (888) 201-2006.

■ Fiesta!

(Sony $12.95) A lively Sesame Street video with many songs performed in both English and Spanish, introducing kids to counting, colors, and familiar music with a Latin beat. Also top-rated: **Get Up & Dance** (Sesame Street/Sony $12.98) It's Big Bird's little teddy bear's birthday and he's having a dance party—so everyone get up and boogie! Closed-captioned. Also, PLATINUM AWARD '97 winner, **Elmocize** (Sony Wonder $12.98). 2½ & up.

■ How To Be a Ballerina

(Sony Wonder $9.98) Young ballerinas can join along with a children's class at the Royal Academy of Dance. From warm-ups, to rehearsing, to a charming performance of scenes from "Sleeping Beauty," viewers are invited to dance along. A short telling of Sleeping Beauty is told as film clips show adult ballerinas dancing, but it is the children's performance of the story that will inspire viewers. 5–9.

Music to Sing By

■ Cathy & Marcy's Song Shop

(Community Music $14.95 each) If you're looking for music videos to actively engage kids, these are for you! On "Yodel-Ay-Hee-Hoo!!!" kids sing along, learn to yodel, and even sign along in American Sign Language. "Is Not, Is Too!" also has plenty of audience participation. Using a hammered dulcimer, banjo, and guitar with a blend of traditional and new songs, they make real music for the whole family! PLATINUM AWARD '97. 4 & up. (800) 669-3942.

■ Kids' Favorite Songs *2000*

(Sesame Street/Sony $12.95) Elmo is going to play kids' top ten favorite songs on his radio show. The problem is picking them. With hits like "Row, Row, Row Your Boat"; "John Jacob Jingleheimer Schmidt"; "Twinkle, Twinkle Little Star" in the line-up there's not a miss in the list. But what is

Elmo's favorite? A good choice of songs kids should know with lots of counting backwards mixed in. 2 & up. Still top-rated, Jim Henson singing **The Best of Kermit** ($12.98).

■ Raffi BLUE CHIP

(Rounder $19.95) A real musical experience with the "eco-troubadour" singing many old favorites such as "Baby Beluga." We could have done without the pessimism of "Will I Ever Grow Up?" but kids probably hear it as a song of longing rather than doubt. PLATINUM AWARD '95. 4 & up. Also classic: **Raffi in Concert.** (800) 443-4727.

■ Sing Along Songs

(Disney $12.99) Over the years we have found some of the Sing Along tapes a better alternative for preschoolers than the feature-length films which are too scary for young viewers. However, these are uneven and sometimes include clips that are not for all ages. We suggest renting and previewing before you buy. We do like the way the words to the songs bounce along the bottom of the screen so kids who can read can sing along. 4 & up. Closed-captioned.

■ Sing & Dance with Barney 2000

(Lyons Group $14.95) It's hard to believe that Barney is celebrating his tenth anniversary. Depending on where you stand, this 56-minute reunion tape featuring 27 Barney hits will either be a preschooler's dream come true, or your nine-year old's worst nightmare. Still top-rated, **Barney Live in New York City.** From Radio City Music Hall, here's Barney in the Big Apple! 2–6. (800) 791-8093.

Blue Chip Folk Music Videos

■ Ella Jenkins Live at the Smithsonian

(Smithsonian/Folkways $14.98) Without gimmicks, here's a master teacher involving kids in sing-, clap-, snap-, and tap-along fun! All ages. (800) 443-4727.

■ Pete Seeger's Family Concert

(Sony $14.98) An outdoor concert by one of our best-loved folk singers. All ages.

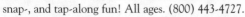

■ Peter, Paul, and Mommy, Too

(Warner $19.98) From the opening bars of "Puff," the magic is still here! All ages.

■ This Pretty Planet:
Tom Chapin Live in Concert

(Sony $14.98) Thirteen of his best-loved songs, such as "The Wheel of the Water," "Good Garbage," and others with an ecology theme. All ages.

About Music & Musicians for Older Audiences

■ Behind the Scenes with Max Roach
2000 PLATINUM AWARD

(First Run Features $14.95) This is the liveliest, most child-friendly and engaging of the "Behind the Scenes" video series, originally produced for PBS. Penn & Teller are the witty hosts of this entertaining introduction to jazz with composer and percussionist Max Roach and other performers including the funky Blue Men Group, sputtering out popcorn with a beat. 8 & up. (800) 229-8575.

■ Playing From the Heart

(Globalstage $27) Filmed by the BBC this is the story of Evelyn Glennie, the world famous percussionist and her determination to become a professional musician despite the fact that she lost her hearing at eight. In a stylish performance by the Polka Children's Theatre in England, this is not your typical TV dramatization. It is an inspiring story about determination and dreams and the family that supported her. Followed with a delightfully inspiring interview with Ms. Glennie. Closed captioned. 8 & up. (888) 324-5623.

Picturebook Videos

Many wonderful picturebooks have been brought to life as videos. Still other stories are being written and produced for video and then turned into picturebooks. Either way, video offers another way to connect kids with books and reading. To save space and avoid repeats, many BLUE CHIP picturebooks not reviewed in the book section appear here. Try them both ways!

Toddlers and Preschoolers

■ Count with Maisy *2000*
PLATINUM AWARD

(Universal $12.98) Maisy is the conductor of the train and picks up two giraffes, three peacocks... you get the idea. Includes four other slice-of-life Maisy stories. Very slow paced—just right for young video viewers. 2½ & up.

■ Kipper *2000*
PLATINUM AWARD

(Hallmark $9.98) Mark Inkpen's storybook dog, Kipper, has made his television and video debut this year. Like the storybooks, each little vignette has a small adventure without the all-too-typical terrifying drama that has marked so much of today's video for the very young. 2 & up.

■ Weston Woods Video Library Collection *2000*

Some of our favorite story videos for preschoolers have come from CC Studios, no longer sold in stores. Here are some recent past winners that have been repackaged chiefly for libraries. These are a must for building a video library and bringing to life some of the best storybooks every child should know. Many are not animated and move at a slower pace than Disney-type productions. (800) 243-5020.

▣I◉ The Snowy Day & Other Caldecott Classics. Many parents will recognize these now-classic stories—*The Snowy Day*, *Owen*, *Blueberries for Sal*, and *Goldilocks and the Three Bears*. 3 & up.

▣I◉ Owl Moon and Other Caldecott Classics. Jane Yolen's beautiful story plus *Strega Nonna*, *Make Way for Ducklings*, and *In the Night Kitchen*. 4–7.

■ Dr. Seuss's My Many Colored Days 2000

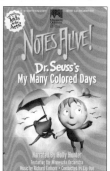

(Notes Alive! $19.95) Dr. Seuss's ode to color and feelings is narrated by Holly Hunter and orchestrated with an original music by Richard Einhorn. The camera shifts from close ups of the Minnesota Orchestra conducted by Eiji Oue to 3-D animated scenes that capture the tone and moods of the music. This is a quiet, reflective film—an imaginative trip that's far and above the usual video fare. It ends with a behind the scenes look at how the animation and video were made. 4 & up. (888) 666-6837.

■ Little Bear Summertime Tales
2000 PLATINUM AWARD

(Paramount $9.95) We continue to find good choices in this series. Summertime Tales features four adventures about Little Bear and his friends and the games they play in the garden and in the woods. Also new and entertaining, **Little Bear Friends.** However, forget **Little Goblin Bear,** a seasonal attempt at safe scare with several dream sequences that may be edgy for some viewers. Still top-rated, the charming **Little Bear Winter Tales, Family Tales,** and **Goodnight, Little Bear** (PLATINUM AWARD '99). 3 & up.

■ Madeline at the Ballet 2000 PLATINUM AWARD

(Sony $9.96) Once more they've come up with a new story based on the original characters in the Ludwig Bemelmans book series. This one will have special meaning to the many little ballerinas who long to get their first toe shoes and worry about living up to their dreams of becoming prima ballerinas. Narrated by Christopher Plummer, this one talks to the importance of practice and believing in oneself. Closed captioned. 4 & up.

■ Mama, Do You Love Me?
THUMBS DOWN

(Sony) Although the cover art looks like the well loved book by the same name, this video is not a replay of Barbara Joose's story of unconditional love. Instead, they've taken the character, added a few more, and spun a story that gets more than a bit edgy for young viewers. Not only does the little girl disobey her mama, she and a pal wander away from their village and end up getting lost on an ice floe. Sure, she gets rescued, but why turn this little classic into a cartoon? Happily, the music does not rise to the usual feverish pitch that signals the perils of Pauline, but that said, this was disappointing. We suspect it will disappoint many who are expecting to find a favorite book on film.

■ The Tale of Peter Rabbit and Benjamin Bunny

(Goodtimes $19.95) Even purists will be impressed by the artistry that brings Beatrix Potter's well-loved stories and watercolors to life with a technique called rendered art. Opening with a live-action scene portraying Potter at work, the film melts from her little drawings to animation. **The Tale of Samuel Whiskers** is a bit scarier and would be better for older kids. PLATINUM AWARD '94. 3 & up.

■ The Very Hungry Caterpillar

(Disney $12.99) The story of that very well-loved, hungry caterpillar has been transformed into a totally magical video! Animation and music have enhanced Eric Carle's beautiful illustrations and given them another dimension while retaining their original beauty. The title story is just one of five gems on this video, which includes: "Papa, Please Get the Moon For Me," "The Mixed-up Chameleon," "The Very Quiet Cricket," and "I See a Song." A delicate blend of imagination and information illuminated with great artistry. PLATINUM AWARD '96. (Closed-captioned.) 2–6.

■ Winnie the Pooh Series

(Disney $12.99) In the past, we have recommended this series as "a kinder and gentler animated cartoon than most of Saturday morning fare." Unfortunately, all recent Pooh videos have gone in another direction with story lines that are too intense for young viewers. For example, in Tigger-ific Tales, Tigger's so-called friends give him a bath and his stripes disappear—for preschoolers who typically worry about body integrity, this video is developmentally inappropriate.

Ditto *Pooh's Grand Adventure*. We suggest you rent and preview newer titles. We still recommend the original videos: **A Blustery Day** and **The Honey Tree.** (Closed-captioned.) 2 & up.

NOTABLE PREVIOUS WINNERS: Are You My Mother? (Sony Wonder) 2 & up. **Jay Jay the Jet Plane: Old Oscar Leads the Parade** (Kidquest) 3–6. (800) 687-2177; **Sweet Dreams, Spot** (Disney) 2–6.

Early School Years

Some of the videos in this section have pieces that may be enjoyed by older preschoolers, but for the most part these are stories for 5 and up.

■ The Bear 🏷️*2000*

(Miramax/Buena Vista $12.99) From the author of the classic The Snowman, this charming story begins when Tilly accidentally drops her toy teddy bear at the zoo. She cries herself to sleep, but "wakes up" to find a giant polar bear who not only brings home her bear—he brings her friendship, adventure, and love. Like the Snowman, this tale is told without dialogue, so viewers must follow the action to interpret as the story unfolds through the art. 6 & up. Still top-rated, **The Snowman,** an enchanting fantasy of a snowman who takes a small boy on a flying adventure. A word of warning: One three-year-old dissolved in tears when the snowman melted. A better choice for 4 & up.

■ The Fool of the World & the Flying Ship

(WGBH $14.95) An animated version of a well-loved Russian folktale. Narrated by David Suchet, the clay sculpted figures look nothing like Saturday morning animation and the pace is also slower. Still, there's plenty of magic as a poor woodcutter sets off to find his greedy brothers and ends up with a flying ship and a princess. 6 & up. (800) 949-8670.

■ Kristen's Fairy House

(Great White Dog $19.95) Vacationing with her aunt, who is writing a book about Fairy Houses, Kristen and others begin to build their own fairy houses from twigs, shells, moss, and the like. Set on an island off the New England coast, this enchanting film is sure to put some children in touch with their imagination as well as nature. A perfect follow-up to **Fairy Tale** (see feature films) for those who believe and want to do more than clap their hands. 5 & up. (800) 397-7641.

■ On the Day You Were Born

(Notes Alive $19.95) The Minnesota Orchestra, conducted by Bill Eddins, debuts its Notes Alive series with a stunning animated version of Debra Frasier's picturebook, *On the Day You Were Born*. The story weaves the animation and the orchestra's performance of Steve Heitzeg's original score and is followed by the author and composer discussing where they found their inspiration. Truly a gem! PLATINUM AWARD '97. 4 & up. (888) 666-6837.

■ Saturday Sancocho 2000

(Reading Rainbow/GPN $23.95 each) We recently discovered this charming book about a girl and her grandmother who trade a basketful of fresh eggs for all the ingrediaents they need for a special stew. The book (available in paperback) includes the recipe for Sancocho. Reading Rainbow uses the story as a jumping off place for trading and a segment on knowing the value of things from baseball cards to auctions is interesting and informative. 5 & up. (800) 228-4630.

■ The Storycrafters

(Galler West $14.95 each) Imagine two master storytellers with no props but a few instruments, the words of stories, and their dramatic tellings holding the interest and participation of listeners of all ages! Here is interaction of the human kind! **Ladder to the Moon** includes several unfamiliar nighttime stories from Brazil, China, and the Arctic North. **Apples, Corn & Pumpkin Seeds** features harvest/Halloween tales from all over the world. 5–9. PLATINUM AWARD '98.

■ The William Steig Library

(Weston Woods $19.95) What could be better than one Steig storybook? How about four of his best, plus an interview with the master himself! There's the unforgettable "Sylvester and the Magic Pebble," "The Amazing Bone," "Doctor De Soto," and "Brave Irene." PLATINUM AWARD '96. 4–8. (800) 243-5020.

Folktales, Legends, Heroes, and Heroines from Many Cultures

The stories in this section are good choices for school-aged children, who more clearly understand the difference between real and make-believe.

■ Annie Oakley

(Lyrick $9.99) Jamie Lee Curtis plays that sharpshooting legend of the west, Annie Oakley. Combining live action with footage from old archival films, this video manages to be both informative and amusing with cameo appearances by such luminaries as Sitting Bull, Thomas Edison, and Queen Victoria. Originally produced in the '80s, this video from *Shelley Duvall's American Tall Tales & Legends* series is a welcome rerelease! 6 & up.

■ Rabbit Ears Folktales Series BLUE CHIP

(Rabbit Ears $9.95 each) Many of the best-loved folktales and legends of heroes and heroines were found in this distinguished series. Most of our favorite titles, however, are no longer available. We suggest you rent and preview before you buy. Although done by well-known performers, these artful films have little or no animation and may be somewhat slow for kids who are accustomed to Disneyesque production values. 6 & up.

Our top choices are **Brer Rabbit and the Wonderful Tar Baby,** Platinum Award '93, and **How the Leopard Lost His Spots,** both narrated by Danny Glover.

■ Why Mosquitoes Buzz in People's Ears and Other Caldecott Classics BLUE CHIP

(Weston Woods $19.95) This classic is narrated by James Earl Jones. The brilliant artwork is enhanced by limited animation. Video also includes "Goggles," "Mufaro's Beautiful Daughters," and "The Village of Round and Square Houses." PLATINUM AWARD '94. 5 & up. (800) 243-5020.

■ Zin! Zin! Zin! A Violin

(Reading Rainbow/GPN $23.95) In addition to the award-winning picturebook, Zin! Zin! Zin! A Violin, a musical counting book that introduces kids to musical groups, this video moves on to rehearsals and thoughts of young musicians at Juilliard and from there to a rhythmic percussive performance by Stomp. 5 & up. PLATINUM AWARD '98. (800) 228-4630.

Feature-Length Films

■ Air Bud Golden Receiver
2000 PLATINUM AWARD

(Disney $19.99) Buddy, once a star canine slam dunker, now uses his considerable talents to help his pal Josh score as a quarterback on his school's football team. Break out the popcorn—this is one the whole family will enjoy watching together. 5 & up.

■ The Borrowers

(Polygram $19.95) Based on the classic Borrowers books, this updated version stars John Goodman as a villain/lawyer who tries to rob a family of its home and, with them, the family of little people who inhabit the walls of their house. The whole family will enjoy this. Why not read the original book together and use the book and video as an exercise in comparative literature. PLATINUM AWARD '99. 8 & up.

■ Charlotte's Web
2000 PLATINUM AWARD

(Paramount $9.99) Few characters in literature are as memorable as dear Charlotte the spider who teaches young Wilbur the pig about friendship, trust, and life and death. This re-issued animated version (1972) of E.B. White's classic features the voices of Debbie Reynolds, Paul Lynde, Agnes Moorehead and Henry Gibson. Bring home the book for the complete experience! 6 & up.

■ Fairy Tale

(Paramount $19.95) During World War I when so many lost loved ones, seances and a belief in spiritualism was not at all unusual. In fact, famous people such as Houdini and Sir Arthur Conan Doyle were well known for their beliefs in the supernatural. Set against that time and place, two girls, who have also suffered losses, discover real fairies in the garden. Their photos cause quite a stir among both believers and others. Not for small children. A beauty! PLATINUM AWARD '99. 8–80s.

■ Flubber

(Disney $26.95) Robin Williams stars in this remake of the '50s film. Our viewers enjoyed the special effects, his high tech robot, and the drama of a very poor basketball team that gets a little extra bounce thanks to the wonders of flubber. 6 & up.

■ Fly Away Home

(Columbia Tristar $19.95) A flock of geese lose their mother and that is where the adventure begins for 14-year-old Amy (Anna Pacquin) who goes to live with her father (Jeff Daniels) in Canada after her mother has been killed in a car accident in Australia. The flock will not fly or migrate until Amy shows them the way. A story of courage, commitment, and new-found bonds of love. A beauty. (Does includes one "holy s...!")

■ Harriet the Spy

(Paramount $19.95) We had mixed feelings about seeing this favorite book brought to life on the big screen. Somehow the meanness of Harriet's world seemed larger than life when it was translated from words on a page to action on the big screen. It certainly leaves a lot to talk about when the film is over and done.

■ The Indian in the Cupboard

(Columbia TriStar Video $19.95) Lynne Reid Banks' well-loved fantasy is a story about a three-inch-tall toy Indian who comes to life and fills the imagination of the boy who owns him. An action-packed adventure with a sense of humor, at its heart it speaks to some deeper issues about life, growing up, and taking responsibility. There are some tense, suspenseful moments here that make this a better choice for 8 & up. Bring home the book, too!

■ Madeline

(Columbia TriStar $19.95) Blending pieces of several of the well-loved Madeline books, this live-action film captures much of the flavor of the original Bemelman picturebooks. Miss Clavel is played with great good humor by Frances McDormand, and the entire cast of twelve little girls in two straight lines is exceedingly fine—most especially Madeline! PLATINUM AWARD '99. 5 & up.

■ Madeline Lost In Paris
THUMBS DOWN!

(Buena Vista) This starts out looking like all the other Madeline animated videos but when an "uncle" arrives to claim Madeline (and her inheritance) the trouble begins. He takes her to a squalid place where Madame La Crock runs a sweat shop where children are forced to make lace out of their own hair. While there is a happy ending, there is nothing to recommend the beginning or middle.

■ **Mulan** 2000 **PLATINUM AWARD**

(Disney $24.99) Unlike a lot of recent Disney fare, Mulan is right on target for the six-and-up crowd. Featuring a strong and courageous girl who fights in her father's place and rejects the traditional female role won high marks from our viewers. The music and imagery of China are stunning for any age audience. Although this film is not without violence (it is about war after all), it is not here for its own sake. There is a bigger story here with clear lines of good and evil. Suspenseful without being overly violent, Disney should use this well-crafted film as a model for future films.

■ **The Lion King II: Simba's Pride**

(Disney $26.99) In this Romeo and Juliet tale (with a much happier ending), Simba's daughter and Scar's son meet, and their love story is the vehicle for making peace with the past and reuniting the two prides. The lines between good and evil are very clear and, therefore, scary scenes are more suspenseful than terrifying. Smaller in scale than the original, it is visually beautiful and clearly conveys that prejudices and grudges need not be passed from one generation to the next. Not for preschoolers. PLATINUM AWARD '99. 6 & up.

Blue Chip Feature-Length Films

These are widely available films that you'll find in the video store or library. They also are shown frequently on TV, but the video versions lack interrupting commercials—a real plus! Most of these are for early school years and beyond.

     Anne of Green Gables

     Apollo 13

     Babe

     Beauty and the Beast

     Beethoven Lives Upstairs

     Cinderella

     Chitty Chitty Bang Bang

- ET
- Gulliver's Travels
- Homeward Bound & Homeward Bound II
- Honey, We Shrunk Ourselves
- The Little Mermaid
- Mary Poppins
- The Nutcracker (with Baryshnikov)
- Peter Pan (Mary Martin version)
- The Red Balloon
- Sarah, Plain and Tall
- The Secret Garden
- The Sound of Music
- Snow White
- Sounder
- To Kill a Mockingbird
- Willy Wonka and the Chocolate Factory
- The Wizard of Oz

Information, Please

Toddlers & Preschoolers

■ The Alphabet Jungle Game

(Sony $12.95) Kids who are learning the names of the letters may enjoy this whirlwind tour. This is more like a video alphabet book than a sound and letter association game. It concentrates on learning upper and lower case letter names. Also, **The Great Numbers Game** is equally speedy. 4 & up.

■ At the Zoo: 2

(Goldsholl $14.95) Like the original **At the Zoo,** this is one trip to the zoo you'll enjoy hearing as well as seeing. Beautiful film footage from the Brookfield Zoo outside of Chicago gives kids unobstructed views of animals from Africa, Asia, and North America with refreshingly uncute music that's easy to listen to while it tells young listeners a lot about the animals. 2–7. PLATINUM AWARD '98.

■ Barney Safety Video

(Lyons $14.95) Barney and friends have managed to produce a safety tape that is instructive without being preachy or scary. Covers diverse but important issues such as seatbelts, wearing helmets, rules for crossing the street, and safety tips for around the house, in the bathtub, and in the kitchen. Also top-rated: **1-2-3 Seasons** and **Sharing** are the best. 2 & up. (800) 791-8093.

■ Big Bird Gets Lost

(Sony $12.95) In the newest of Sesame Street's Kids Guide to Life series, Maria takes Big Bird shopping. The bad news is that Big Bird gets lost; the good news is that Maria has taught Big Bird & viewers a catchy song for remembering their phone number as well as how to find help in the store. A non-threatening but valuable video with guest star Frances MacDermot. PLATINUM AWARD '99. 3–7.

■ Choo Choo Trains

(Stage Fright $15.98) All aboard! Train buffs will adore this almost wordless journey with spectacular views of trains in the city, country, and mountains, racing over trestles, through snow, under bridges, and onto turntables. A full half-hour of trains—from steam engines chugging and tooting to modern diesels wheeling on steel. Also fun from the same maker, **Big Rigs.** 2 & up.

■ Cleared For Takeoff

(Fred Levine Productions $14.95) Fasten your seat belt and get ready for a fast-paced look at commercial aviation that follows a mother and three kids on a trip from start to finish. Interesting information and film footage takes kids behind the scenes at the airport. From the maker of the granddaddy of construction videos, **Road and House Construction Ahead.** PLATINUM AWARD '96. 2½ & up. (800) 843-3686.

■ Doing Things BLUE CHIP

(Bo-Peep Productions $14.95) Every video library should have **Doing Things!** With almost no talking or cutesy narrative, we watch kids and familiar barnyard animals go through the routines of the day—eating, washing, and playing. There's something new to see each time you watch. The cast of kids is multiethnic and the music is fun but not intrusive. **Doing Things** leaves the talking to you and your kids. 2 & up. Also recommended, **Moving Machines.** 2 & up. (800) 532-0420.

■ Sesame Street Let's Eat! *2000*

(Sony $12.95) Billed as "Funny Food Songs," Grover the waiter (who works at Planet Storybook) and his pals serve up a lot of good advice about the most important meal of the day with a ditty called "Cereal Girl." That's just for openers. There's a trip to a pasta factory, foods that we like that animals eat, and a visit with a picky eater. As always, Sesame Street manages to deliver information wrapped in good humor instead of the typical food pyramid preachment. 3 & up.

■ Let's Go To the Farm

(Vermont Story Works $14.95) Our viewers were captivated with this visit to a working farm and seeing how cows are milked, hay is baled, trees are tapped, and honey and other crops are harvested. The film is better than the title! An engaging trip through the seasons. 3–7. ßPlatinum Award '96. (800) 206-8383.

Early School

■ The Adventures of Monty the Moose

(Alaska Video Postcards $19.95) Breathtaking footage of Alaskan wildlife is presented with lively music by Monty the Moose, an animated tour guide with a sense of humor. Parents and kids who liked GeoKids will love this even more! Platinum Award '97. **Tundra Tails,** which focuses on spring & summer in Alaska with info about modern Eskimos, is interesting, but less compelling than the original. 3 & up. (907) 349-8002.

■ Behind the Scenes with Carrie Mae Weems *2000* Platinum Award

(First Run Features $14.95) Hosted by the witty duo Penn & Teller, these videos introduce young viewers to ideas about perspective, illusions and the unique ways artists like David Hockney and Carrie Mae Weems look at familiar objects with fresh eyes. Originally broadcast on PBS, this is a better choice for young viewers than the Julie Taymor video which goes behind the scenes with a production of The Tempest. The latter is more suited to older audiences. 8 & up. (800) 229-8575.

■ The Big Space Shuttle ★2000★

(Little Mammoth Media $14.95) This well-paced documentary combines information with splendid footage of the Shuttle, astronauts in training, and space camp. A wonderful way to explore the vast frontier of space. 5 & up. PLATINUM AWARD '99. New titles for ★2000★: **The Big Park** is a good choice if you are planning a trip to Yellowstone. Serious footage explains the source of "Old Faithful." Chances are you'll see more wildlife here than in person. **The Big Aquarium** took too long showing everything but fish in the opening. 5& up. (800)KID VIDEO.

■ Building Skyscrapers

(David Alpert Assoc. $19.95) Kaboom! Down with the old and up, up, up goes a new skyscraper in New York City. Step by step from implosions to raising the steel and concrete oozing out of hoses, here's a ringside seat for watching a building go from foundation to finish. Real construction people, both male and female, answer the questions of a seven-year-old child in a well-paced, clearly written film that was shot from many perspectives, including a helicopter. PLATINUM AWARD '95. (40 min.) (800) 265-7744.

■ Dare to Dance

(Grey Dawn Productions $19.95) This is not a how-to dance-along tape. It is an inspiring and beautifully crafted video with interviews and film of three young talented dancers from ten to seventeen that captures their feelings and love of dancing. PLATINUM AWARD '97. 8–17. (800) 400-2036.

■ I Want to be a Ballerina

(Big Kids Productions $14.95) Aspiring ballerinas will enjoy this behind-the-scenes look at the casting, rehearsing, fittings, and highlights of the performance of the Nutcracker by student dancers. (800) 700-8622.

■ The Magic School Bus Videos ★2000★

(Kid Vision $12.95) Wacky Ms. Frizzle (voice of Lily Tomlin) continues to lead her students on merry field trips. Entries for ★2000★ were less informative and more cartoonish than ever. We preferred **Butterflies!** which is about butterflies in the bog and how they adapt for survival. Spins a Web begins as Ms Frizzle drives the class into a giant drive-in movie screen and enters a black and white world—very Twilight Zone-ish—but how many kids know about drive-ins or black and white movies? We prefer prior winners: **Getting Energized,** gives kids a look at different types of energy; **Busasaurus,** a journey back into the time of dinosaurs (PLATINUM AWARD '98); **Gets Ants In Its Pants,** a trip into the social world of ants; **The Magic Schoolbus for Lunch,** a trip through the digestive system; and **Gets Lost in Space.** PLATINUM AWARD '96. 5 & up.

■ Math Curse **2000** PLATINUM AWARD

(Reading Rainbow/ GPN $23.95) Jon Scieszka's PLATINUM AWARD winning book, *Math Curse*, speaks to the big idea that math is a part of just about everything we do. For the math phobic that's a frightening thought, but not in the hands of the creators of Reading Rainbow! A trip to a giant Fed Ex center and the studio of an artist designing a giant mural, shows kids that whatever they do, math is a piece of the pie. Still top-rated, **How Much Is a Million?** ($23.95) helps kids conceptualize what a million represents plus a visit to a Crayola factory to see millions of crayons. PLATINUM AWARD '97. closed-captioned. 5–8. (800) 228-4630.

■ Really Wild Animals

(National Geographic/Columbia TriStar $14.95 each) A lively blend of splendid film footage, information, and music have made this series a hit with kids. Dudley Moore narrates all three videos: **Monkey Business** looks at animal families; **Dinosaurs and Other Creature Features** explores the mysteries and characteristics of some of the weirdest wildlife; **Polar Prowl** travels from North to South Pole. Closed-captioned. 5–11.

■ Here's My Question: Where Does My Garbage Go?

(Middlemarch $18.95) An informative video that held the attention of our testers (young and old). Kids "follow" the garbage as it leaves in a garbage truck from New York City to landfills and recycling centers. We preferred the pace, style, and humor of this video to **Where Garbage Goes** (Fred Levine Prod.) 4 & up. PLATINUM AWARD '99. (212) 645-2324.

■ Winter on the Farm

(Chris Fesko Enterprises $19.95) Just when we thought, "Who needs another farm video?" Chris Fesko, a farmer herself, narrates and directs a refreshing tour of her farm as winter arrives in upstate NY. Like a perfect field trip where everyone can see and hear, Fesko, a former teacher, answers the kinds of questions kids ask. This is our favorite in this three-part series. Spectacular footage of winter combine with solid information and a good-natured guide who clearly loves what she is doing. 4 & up. (800) 747-6470.

■The Making of Zoom
2000 PLATINUM AWARD

(WGBH $19.95) Fans of the new "Zoom" will love this behind-the-scenes look at what it takes to put on the popular PBS series. Cast members take you through their auditions, bloopers, and process of taping a television show. Also, **Party with Zoom** ("Zoom"-inspired party ideas and games). (800) 949-8670.

Coping with Real Life

New Baby in the House

■ A New Baby In My Family

(Sony Wonder $9.95) Who better than Mrs. Snuffelupagus to help Snuffy deal with some of his confusing feelings about sharing his space—in every sense—with his little sister? A good mix of songs, stories, and assurances about becoming a big brother or sister. (Closed-captioned.) 2–5.

■ Arthur's Baby

(Random House/Sony $12.95) When Arthur learns that he's about to become a big brother, he has mixed emotions about the changes in his life. A second story, "D.W.'s Baby," features the arrival of Baby Kate. PLATINUM AWARD '98. Note: Unfortunately, this series has not been consistently solid. In **Arthur's Tooth** there are monsters and spitting contests; **D.W. Picky Eater** includes vomiting and negative behavior; in **Arthur Makes the Team,** the second story, "Meek for a Week," has a fantasy sequence in which Francine "blows her top" and her head actually comes off and lands on a lawn (still talking). We find these images unnecessary for any age, but particularly inappropriate for Arthur's large preschool audience.

Going to School

■ I Love My Day School

(eaho productions $12.99) If you have a preschooler who needs a pre-view of preschool, this will give him a look at the day from good-bye to hello again—all told in 12 original songs. 2½ & up.

■ Franklin Goes to School ⭐2000⭐

(Polygram $12.95 each) Franklin is starting to school and worried that he should know how to read and write when he gets there. Many kids will identify with Franklin's fears about false expecta-tions and in the dilemma he gets into by telling his friends that he can eat 76 flies in the blink of an eye. Also, **Franklin Plays the Game** With help from his coach and forest friends, Franklin learns about team play. In true turtle fashion, Franklin has an unhurried pace that's right for young viewers. 4 & up.

■ Owen

(Reading Rainbow/GPN $23.95) Wherever Owen goes, so goes his blankie— until it's time to go to school. Mom comes up with a solu-tion, that gives him a small piece of home to take along. Narrated by Matthew Broderick, this video deals with separation, growing up, becoming a big sibling, and other changes—subjects many kids worry about as they begin school.4 & up. (800) 228-4630.

■ Spot Goes to School

(Disney $14.99) There are some real stories here that preschoolers will relate to. Spot's first day at preschool gives a reassuring glimpse of a typ-ical day of playing with friends and paw painting. On the same tape is **Spot at the Playground,** which reinforces ideas of taking turns and safety without preaching. Also recommended: **Where's Spot?, Spot Goes to a Party.** Platinum Award '95. 2 & up

Potty Videos

There are no magic bullets, but it may be a helpful reinforcement. Of course, our reluctant potty user left the room when either of these tapes were put on. Two to try: **It's Potty Time** (A

Vision $19.98) Developed by the Duke University Medical Center, this "story" features kids of many ages getting ready to go to a party. **Now I Can Potty** (K.I.D.S. $19.95) Kids show and tell kids through songs and action how they learned to stop what they are doing to go to the potty. (800) 282-3466.

Other Issues

■ Arthur's Eyes

(Random House/Sony $12.95) Arthur can't see the chalk board or make a basket. His eyeglasses solve those problems, but it's Arthur who must come to terms with being called four eyes. Also on the same video, "Francine's Bad Hair Day," deals with class picture day and Francine's longing to look like her "glamorous" friend, Muffy, while still wanting to be herself. Like other earlier videos in this series, these stay true to the well loved Arthur books. Also solid: **Arthur Writes a Story** and **Arthur's Pet Business.** 5 & up.

■ Telling the Truth

(Sesame Street/Sony $12.98) Telly makes the mistake of telling a lie to impress his friends and then has to live with the consequences. Dennis Quaid makes a guest appearance and helps Telly face up to the truth. An age-appropriate retelling of "The Boy Who Cried Wolf" parallels Telly's predicament. From the Kids' Guide to Life series. Also, **Learning to Share** with Katie Couric. Closed captioned 4–8.

■ Preschool Power #8

(Concept Videos $14.95) Self-help videos for preschoolers! The newest from this series shows easy ways to make musical instruments, fix a no-cooking banana snack, clean up spilled popcorn, dance, and make crowns with fall leaves. Many projects need adult assistance, but this is a good video to leave with a sitter who wants some ideas for easy-to-do fun for 3s & up. We still recommend **Preschool Power #1** & **#2.** (800) 333-8252.

■ Sesame Street Home Video Visits the Hospital

(Sony Wonder $9.95) Big Bird expresses a lot of the anxiety kids may have about hospitals, and discovers that the hospital is not so scary after all. A good starting point for discussing your child's fears about her own visit to the hospital or that of a family member or friend. closed-captioned. 3 & up.

Science and Ecology

■ Amazing Insect Warriors ★2000★

(Schlessinger Media $12.95) Once you get past the corny opening,there is some amazing close-up footage, plus interesting information about bugs. Hosted by Dr.Art Evans, Insect Zoo Director of the Natural History Museum of Los Angeles County and actress Christina Ricci—though we could have done without the puppet Bugsy Seagull. For kids who are still too young for National Geographic. (800) 843-3620.

■ Bill Nye, The Science Guy Videos

(Disney $12.99) **The Human Body—Inside Scoop, Reptiles and Insects: Leapin' Lizards!** and **Powerful Forces: All Pumped Up!** are informative, upbeat and sort of frenetic, uneven videos taken from Bill Nye's very popular science show. 8 & up.

■ Science, Discovery and Laughter

(The Science Club $19.95) Parents or teachers can use this video and guide book as a resource that turns them into the next best thing since Mr. Wizard! Simple hands-on science experiments that are guaranteed to delight your 5- to 10-year-old are demonstrated on the video. No special gear needed—just time and a willingness to explore sounds, gases, rocks, seeds, and matter. (800) 391-6939.

■ The Amazing Panda Adventure

(Warner $19.98) Shot in the Himalaya mountains, this film has its Perils-of-Pauline moments that kept testers at the edge of their seats. A moving blend of adventure, ecology, friendship, and family ties all bound together in a memorable film. 8 & up. Closed-captioned.

■ Free Willy

(Warner $24) Eleven-year-old Jesse finds new meaning in his life when he meets Willy, an orca whale, who is being held in captivity. His concern and friendship grow and so does he.

Holidays

Thanksgiving

■ Giving Thanks

(Reading Rainbow/GPN $23.95) Opening with a Native American's

Good Morning Message written by Chief Jake Swamp, this handsome video celebrates the beauty and bounty of earth. It moves on to fascinating footage that shows how cranberries are harvested as well as a segment featuring city kids planting trees on a city street, followed by a Native-American woman making clay for pottery. 5 & up. (800) 228-4630.

Christmas, Chanukah, & Kwanzaa

■ The Country Mouse and the City Mouse

(Sony Wonder $9.95) Young Emily, a country mouse (who happens to sing country music), takes off for the city for a Christmas visit with her sophisticated cousin, Alexander, the city mouse. Based on the Aesop fable, this gem is performed by Crystal Gayle and John Lithgow. Closed-captioned 4–8.

■ How The Grinch Stole Christmas

(Sony Wonder $9.95) Who better than Walter Matthau to narrate the tale of the grumpy, cold-hearted curmudgeon whose ways are changed by the spirit of giving and love in the Christmas season? 4–8.

■ The Santa Clause

(Disney $22.99) Tim Allen stars as a divorced father who quite by accident becomes Santa and discovers a lot about himself and his relationships. 5 & up.

■ Sesame Street Celebrates Around the World

(Sony Wonder $14.95) If you live in Portugal, you would celebrate the New Year by making wishes and eating 12 grapes, one for every month of the year. With music and humor, Big Bird & friends introduce viewers to children and customs in many parts of the world. 4 & up.

■ Spot's Magical Christmas

(Disney $12.99) It's almost Christmas and Santa's sleigh is lost! Two of Santa's reindeer enlist Spot and his friends to help them find it. Lucky Spot not only spots the sleigh, he gets a magical ride to Santa's workshop! A charmer! Closed-captioned. 2–6.

■ Handel's Last Chance

(Sony Classical $19.98) When Handel arrives in Dublin, his career is faltering and the choir that will sing his newest oratorio is dreadful. By his helping a street urchin, the son of a washerwoman, Handel's "Messiah" has its first performance. Also recommended, **Rossini's Ghost.** 7 & up.

■ Shalom Sesame Chanukah

(Children's Television Workshop $19.95) From the Israeli version of Sesame Street, this lively video celebrates the Festival of Lights and includes a funny send-up of "Wheel of Fortune" called "Dreidel of Fortune," starring Lavana White. The Count is doing his thing in English and Hebrew. 3–8. Comet International. Also, for Passover: **Jerusalem Jones and the Lost Afikoman** and **The Aleph-Bet Telethon.**

■ Winter Holiday Stories 🌟2000

(Weston Woods $19.95) This ecumenical video includes Nina Jaffe's Chanukah story, *In the Month of Kislev; The Night Before Christmas* illustrated by Ruth Sanderson; and *Seven Candles for Kwanzaa* by Andrea & Brian Pinkney. (800) 243-5020.

SHOPPING TIP: Finding some of the videos listed in this chapter will be as simple as going to the nearest toy supermarket, video store, children's book/specialty shop, or on-line site. Unfortunately, big companies like Sony Wonder, Disney, and Warner no longer have 800 numbers. We've listed numbers for smaller companies that may be harder to locate.

Noteworthy Catalogs

Big Kids Productions (800) 477-7811.
Family Planet Music (800) 985-8894.
Music for Little People (800) 409-2457.

Noteworthy On-Line Sites

eToys.com
kidflix.com
rightstart.com
amazon.com
reel.com

IV • Audio
Great Music & Stories

Music Exploration. Audio tapes and CDs are a great way to introduce children to a broad range of music, folksongs, marches, classics, and show tunes that they might not hear on the radio. These musical explorations are opportunities for dancing, conducting, drawing by, and even daydreaming.

Story Power. Listening to stories told on tapes can help beginning readers as they follow along in a book. Simply listening provides food for the imagination—to make one's own pictures from the spoken word. Children enjoy and understand stories well beyond their reading level and do so when no adult is available to read with them. For quiet or sit-down travel time, few take alongs are as valuable as some well-selected tapes.

Criteria. In testing new products, we continue to reject "children's music" that is preachy, overproduced, and, in many cases, condescending to young listeners. Our ultimate test is still whether we can stand being in a car with it or whether someone in the driver's seat or car seat screams, "Turn it off!"

Shopping Tips. We also recommend that you share your favorite music, whether it be contemporary, folk, jazz, classical, or show tunes. If you're enjoying the music, chances are it will be contagious.

We have listed the prices for tapes first and then for CDs, if available. Large music stores carry major companies like Disney, CBS, Sony Wonder, etc. We have provided numbers to help you locate titles from smaller recording companies that sell directly or through catalogs.

Music

Lullabies and Songs for the Very Young

■ At Quiet O'Clock

(Sally Rogers, Round River $8.98) These lullabies are just the ticket for a quiet time—whatever the hour might be. Accompanied by guitar, dulcimer, or piano, this wonderful collection of traditional and original lullabies by award-winning vocalist Sally Rogers is still our favorite! PLATINUM AWARD '95. (800) 342-0295.

■ A Child's Celebration of Lullaby

(Music for Little People $9.98/$12.98) What an eclectic mix of artists to sing you to sleep: Lena Horne, Raffi, Jerry Garcia, Kathie Lee Gifford, and Linda Ronstadt. First rate! (800) 409-2457.

■ Childhood Memories & Lullabies On Guitar

(Michael Kolmstetter, Kolmstetter Musik $9.98/$14.98) You'll know these songs and be able to sing along to Kolmstetter's wonderful classical guitar recordings of familiar lullabies and nursery songs such as "Kum Ba Ya" and "Hush, Little Baby." PLATINUM AWARD '97. (800) 536-8409.

■ DreamSongs *2000*

(Pacific Rose $9.98/$15.98) Seductively soothing music to lull you and your baby to dreamland... just let the baby go first! Laurie Burke's voice is like the binding on a blankie—smooth and silky! (800) 862-7232.

■ 40 Winks

(Jessica Harper, Alacazam! $9.98) After a long day of reviewing, Jessica Harper's latest recording was a welcome treat! This lyrical, jazzy, and soothing collection of original songs by Ms. Harper is the perfect kind of bedtime music for all. PLATINUM AWARD '99.

■ Moondreamer

(Redwing $9.98/$15.98) Grab your blankie and get set for beautiful moondreams as Priscilla Herdman blends new and traditional lullabies and works her special silken magic. (800) 342-0295.

■ The Sun Upon the Lake is Low

(Mae Robertson & Don Jackson, Lyric Partners $10/$16) A sequel to PLATINUM AWARD '96 **All Through the Night,** this is a collection of glorious traditional and contemporary folk songs—a soothing way to end any day. Includes, among others, "Circle Game," "Michael Row Your Boat Ashore," and "Gaelic Lullaby." PLATINUM AWARD '98. (800) 490-8875.

NOTABLE PREVIOUS WINNERS: Goodnight Guitar (Ray Penny, Applewild Recordings $10.98/$14.98) PLATINUM AWARD '98. (888) 88-APPLE; **Nature Sounds** (Twin Sisters $8.99/$12.99) (800) 248-8946; **Night-Night Lullabies** (The Dream Factory, Baby Music Boom $9.98) (888) 470-1667.

Music for Moving, Singing, & Dancing

■ Animal Groove 2000

(Blue Vision $9.95/ $14.95) James Coffey's newest collection of songs is an invitiation to getup and waddle like a penguin, hippity hop like a kangaroo or boogie like a bear. There's a range of instruments and beats that invite kids to find new ways to move in creative ways.

■ Birthday Songs

(Disney $9.98/$15.98) If you have no memory of the basic childhood musical games you played, such as "Hokey Pokey," "London Bridge," "Head, Shoulders, Knees and Toes," this is a must for your first preschooler's birthday party. Still top-rated, **Friends Forever** (Disney $9.95/$15.95), a surprisingly solid and musical recording about friendship that features Pooh and friends. PLATINUM AWARD '99. 2 & up.

■ Color Me Singing ⭐2000 PLATINUM AWARD

(Susan Salidor $10/$14) What a worldly mix of music! From American folksongs to African chants to Hebrew prayers, this is a musical box of treats for the entire family. Salidor has added her own lyrics to some familiar songs as well as given us her own stylish spin to many traditional songs. Also top-rated, **Little Voices in My Head.** (773) 271-5568.

■ Elmopalooza

(Sony $9.95/$13.95) To celebrate 30 years of Sesame Street, Elmo and the gang are joined by such artists as Gloria Estefan, Jon Stewart, The Fugees, Rosie O'Donnell, and Kenny Loggins. If your family is in this zone, this will be a hit. We prefer this audio version to the video of the same name. PLATINUM AWARD '99. 21/2 & up.

■ Jazz-A-Ma-Tazz ⭐2000

(Baby Music Boom $10.98/$15.98) If you want to introduce your kids to hearing familiar tunes in new and less familiar ways this intro to jazz is one way to do it. Using such classics as "Skip To my Lou," "Oh, Susanna," (vocal by Richie Havens) and "The Muffin Man"—as you've never heard it sung. This is not for everyone and may not work in the confines of your car—but

that said, this is a novel blend of kid's music played by real jazz musicians with the accent on jazz. (888) 470-1667.

■ Kid'n Together: Singin' at the Swing Set

(Alex & Ben Meisel/Kid'n Together $9.98/$14.98) We loved the vitality of this recording that includes both upbeat toe-tapping tunes as well as sweet lullabies. Solid concepts, like shapes, rhyming, and please and thank you are reinforced without being teachy or preachy. A product of what seems to be the entire Meisel family—Alex & Ben provide the main vocals with their whole family getting into the act. (Of course, we look kindly on family ventures!).

PLATINUM AWARD '99. (800) 543-6386.

■ On the Good Ship Lollipop 2000 PLATINUM AWARD

(Music for Little People $9.98/$15.98) If you never heard the Persuasions you're in for a great treat! If you know them, you may be surprised to know that they have never before made an album for kids. But what a great a cappella treat this is! A disc that is by turns tender and rollicking, and always musical! (800) 409-2457.

■ Raffi: The Singable Songs Collection

(Rounder $20/$30) Not one, not two, but three CDs—"Singable Songs for the Very Young"; "More Singable Songs"; & "Corner Grocery Store" include more than 50 top Raffi hits. Put this in your car for enough Raffi to get young travelers there and back. 3 & up. PLATINUM AWARD '98. (800) 443-4727.

■ Run, Jump, Skip and Sing

(Barney, Lyrick Studios $14.95) A very Barney collection of 25 songs for singing and moving to that will be a hit with true Barney fans. Includes now Barney standards: "Boom Boom, Ain't It Great To Be Crazy" and "I Love You." Be forewarned: the older "I hate Barney" testers needed to retreat to another room. 2 & up. (800) 342-0295.

■ Singin' In the Bathtub 2000 PLATINUM AWARD

(Sony $9.95/$13.95) Bravo! That's what you'll want to shout when you hear the energy and joy packed into every song John Lithgow sings on this new release. Like a Danny Kaye for the '90s, he gives familiar songs a fresh spin and adds a special flavor to less well known but amusing songs. An instant classic! All ages.

■ Songs From a Parent to a Child

(Art Garfunkel, Sony $9.95/$13.95) Fans of Art Garfunkel will love this collection of songs including James Taylor's "Secret O' Life," The Beatles' "I Will," as well as traditional songs like "Now I Lay Me Down to Sleep." PLATINUM AWARD '99.

■ Sounds Familiar 🌟2000

(David Alpert, D&A Records $12/$18) We are great fans of Alpert's original collections of children's music that feature banjo, mandolin, guitar, harmonica, and dulcimer—giving his music a rich textured sound that makes you think of being on a porch with a gentle summer breeze. **My Front Porch, 2000** PLATINUM AWARD winner, is a quieter collection of down home fare. (203) 457-0855.

■ Teaching Hippopotami to Fly

(CanTOO $19.95/$15.95) When we talk about what makes a winning children's audio, this is how it sounds! Real music and witty lyrics, all harmoniously blended by the Chenille Sisters. PLATINUM AWARD '98. (800) 830-1919.

NOTABLE PREVIOUS WINNERS: Joanie Bartels' Adventures with Family and Friends (Youngheart Music $10.98/$13.98) 4 & up; (800) 444-4287; **Big Blues** (Kid Rhino $9.98/$15) (800) 342-0295; **Hello Everybody!** (Rachel Buchman, A Gentle Wind $8.95) (888) 386-7664. **Shakin' A Tailfeather** (Taj Majal et al., Music for Little People $8.98/$15.98) (800) 409-2457; **Timeless** (Cathy Block, Intuition Music $9.98/$15.98) (215) 794-8199.

Folk Tunes for All Ages

■ Bill Staines' One More River

(Red House Records $8.98/$17.98) If you are a folk music person, you'll need no introduction to Bill Staines. This isn't a collection of cutesie songs chosen for the kiddies. It's honest-to-goodness music—some somber, some classic, some less familiar, and all joyful. Accompanied by everything from banjoes to violins, congas to penny whistles, guitars to bass.

■ Ella Jenkins' Songs Children Love to Sing: A 40th Anniversary Collection

(Smithsonian Folkways $9.50) What a treat! Ella Jenkins, the ultimate songsmith for the young, has selected 17 of her favorite songs that she recorded during the last forty years, including "Miss Mary Mack" and "This Old Man." These are classic folksongs with plenty of repetition and easy sing, clap, and tap-along fun. 3 & up. (800) 342-0295.

■ Never Grow Up 2000 PLATINUM AWARD

(Flying Fish/Rounder Records $14.98) Tap your toes and get ready to enjoy a collection of less familiar but engaging folksongs sung by the talented Anne Hills & Cindy Mangsen. These are not just a cute little ditties made up for the kiddies—this is real music from the late 19th & 20th century—pieces of our musical heritage. Banjo, guitar, fiddle, harmonica, washboard, piano and even tuba accompany the many songs! (800) 443-4727.

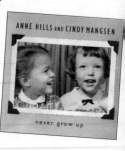

■ Pete Seeger For Kids & Just Plain Folks

(Sony $8.98/$17.98) An interesting mix of Seeger's classics such as "Michael Row Your Boat Ashore," "This Land Is Your Land," "Put Your Finger in the Air," plus a good many less familiar folksongs, many originally released in the '60s. All ages. Also recommended, **Pete Seeger's Family Concert.**

■ Peter, Paul & Mary Around the Campfire

(Warner Bros. $13.95/$17.95) This double CD collection is a treat and includes such favorites as: "If I Had a Hammer," "Blowin' In The Wind," and "Puff, The Magic Dragon." Celebrating their 38th year together, their music is truly multi-generational. PLATINUM AWARD '99.

■ Sweet Dreams of Home 2000 PLATINUM AWARD

(Magnolia Music/Lyric Partners $10/$16) Mae Robertson and Eric Garrison's eclectic collection of contemporary folk music celebrating the concept of "home" includes Graham Nash's "Our House" to David Byrne's "This Must Be the Place." (800) 490-8875.

■ This Land Is Your Land

(Rounder $9.50/$15) Introduce your kids to the music of Woody and Arlo Guthrie singing such classics as the title song, "So Long, It's Been Good to Know Yuh," and "Riding In My Car. " PLATINUM AWARD '98. (800) 443-4727.

■ Water Sign

(DKI Inc. $10/$15) An uplifting, thoughtful, and wonderful collection of new and old folk songs that makes great quiet-time listening, including the best mermaid song we've ever heard. (212) 721-9382.

Multicultural Music
■ Cada Nitura

(Tish Hinojosa, Rounder $11.95) A rare truly bilingual recording that celebrates Latino and American cultures with 11 songs sung in both English and Spanish. (800) 443-4727.

■ Cajun for Kids

(Papillion, Music for Little People $9.98/$15.98) Papillion, a Cajun musician, blends music and story in this get-up-and-move collection of Cajun music that includes such songs as "Down On the Bayou," "Jambalaya," and "You are My Sunshine." We could have done with less talking and even more music. (800) 409-2457.

■ Jumpin' Jack

(Jack Grunsky, BMG $8.98/$14.98) A wonderfully interesting mix of French, Spanish, English, Rajasthani, and Caribbean music. Songs include "Iko Iko" and "Songbirds." A treat!

■ Le Hoogie Boogie: Louisiana French Music for Children

(Michael "Beausoleil" Doucet et al., Rounder $9.98/$11.98) Looking for something different that will brighten everyone's spirits? Try a musical tour of Cajun country that will be sure to make you get up and dance. Wonderful! (800) 443-4727.

NOTABLE PREVIOUS WINNERS: Choo Choo Boogaloo (Music for Little People $9.98/$12.98) (800) 409-2457; **Harry Belafonte: His Greatest Hits** (Woodford Music $12.99); **More Reggae For Kids** (RAS $11/$15) (301) 588-5135; **I Got Shoes** (Sweet Honey in the Rock, Music for Little People $9.98/$12.98) (800) 409-2457.

Music from Broadway and Hollywood

■ A Child's Celebration of Show Tunes

(Music For Little People $9.98/$12.98) A wonderful intro to some of the best-known show tunes from "Oliver!," "The Sound of Music," "The King and I," "Peter Pan," and "Fiddler on the Roof," with the added bonus of having them sung by the original casts. A real treat! (800) 409-2457.

■ The Broadway Kids Back On Broadway 2000

(Lightyear $8.98/$15.98) If you have an aspiring Broadway singer in your midst this collection of show tunes sung by young Broadway veterans will hit the spot! Songs include "Anything You Can Do (I Can Do Better)," "Seasons of Love," "I Just Can't Wait to be King," and more. (800) 229-7867.

■ Disney's Greatest Top Hits 2000

(Disney $10.98/$15.98) A collection of the big songs from all of Disney's recent biggies! These are direct from the soundtrack with the original singer and orchestration.

■ The Lion King: Original Broadway Cast Recording

(Disney $9.98/$15.98) We get goose bumps every time we listen to the opening number. The Elton John and Tim Rice score is rich and magical! Short of a ticket to the hottest show on Broadway, bring this home for the whole family. PLATINUM AWARD '99.

■ Mary Poppins / Lion King / Aladdin / Beauty and the Beast / Pocahontas / Mulan / Tarzan

(Disney $9.98/$15.98) Our testers loved listening to the scores from Disney's latest run of mega box-office hits. Disney enthusiasts will also want to consider **The Music of Disney** ($35.98/$49.98), a three-part set of 78 classic Disney tunes dating back to 1928.

■ Peter Pan BLUE CHIP

(Mary Martin et al., RCA $9.95/$17) This is the original cast from the 1954 Broadway production and simply the best! No one sings "Never-Never Land" like Mary Martin!

■ Really Rosie
2000 PLATINUM AWARD

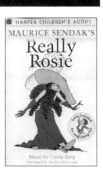

(Sony $5.98/$11.98) If you're a Carole King fan or you have a special place in your heart for Maurice Sendak's *Nutshell Library*, (remember *Pierre* & *Chicken Soup with Rice?*) you may even remember the original animated feature from 1975. Now the sound has been digitized and reissued for another generation to enjoy. Bring home the books, too!

Introducing the Classics

If you don't have a classical music collection, there are a number of new recordings that are responding to reports linking increased learning capacity with listening to classical music at an early age. Whether you put together your own collection of favorites or buy them pre-compiled, this is music to share with children of all ages. Children will enjoy dancing, drawing, conducting, or simply daydreaming to many of the selections here. If it builds brain power—that would be a plus.

■ Bernstein Favorites

(Sony $7.98/$14.98) Children's classics "The Carnival of the Animals," "The Young Person's Guide to the Orchestra," and "Peter and the Wolf" are all part of this wonderful introduction to classical music.

■ H.M.S. Pinafore

(London $14.96) Part of every child's musical experience should include the sparkling music of Gilbert and Sullivan. "H.M.S. Pinafore" is always a good place to start.

■ Kids Classics Series

(EMI $7.99/$10.99 each) Truly a hit parade of classical music. On Animals you'll hear "The Carnival of the Animals," Itzhak Perlman narrating "Peter and the Wolf," and "The Flight of the Bumble-Bee." Nature includes Vivaldi's "Winter," Beethoven's "Pastoral Symphony," and Debussy's "Gardens in the Rain." Also recommended, **Toys, Lullabies.** PLATINUM AWARD '98.

■ The Power of Classical Music
2000 PLATINUM AWARD

(Twin Sisters $8.99/$12.99) Music by Bach, Mozart, Schumann, and Grieg played by a 16-piece string ensemble. Beautiful arrangements are ideal for movement and dance time or for daydreaming. All ages. (800) 248-8946.

■ The Classical Kids Collection

(The Children's Group $9.98/$16.98 each) If you're looking for a way to introduce your kids to classical music through stories, this series fits the bill. In **Vivaldi's "Ring of Mystery,"** Katarina meets the great composer, who is the music director at the orphanage she is sent to in Venice. The exciting story is rich with suspense and Baroque music. Others in the series: **Beethoven Lives Upstairs, Mr. Bach Comes to Town,** and *Mozart's Magnificent Voyage.* (800) 668-0242.

■ The Mozart Effect, Vols.1–3

(BMG $8.98/$17.95) Responding to research that links the value of Mozart's music to learning, these three volumes offer a range of music performed by first class artists: **Vol. 1, Tune Up Your Mind; Vol. 2, Relax, Daydream & Draw; and Vol. 3, Mozart in Motion.** It couldn't hurt! All ages. PLATINUM AWARD '99.

■ Peter and the Wolf with Uncle Moose and the Kazoo-O-Phonic Jug Band

(Dave Van Ronk, Alacazar $8.98/$11.98) Van Ronk does a jug band version of "Peter and the Wolf" that's pure fun, as well as other favorites such as "Swing on a Star." (800) 342-295. Other "Peter and the Wolfs" of interest: Sting (Polygram $14.99 CD), David Bowie (RCA $9), and Itzhak Perlman (EMI $14.99 CD).

■ SmartPlay with Classical 2000

(Wee Are Young $11.98) You're probably not going to listen to all 45 minutes at once, but this is an elegant collection of piano music to dip into for listening or moving to. Heidi Brende plays Mozart (including all 12 variations of "Twinkle, Twinkle!"), Bach, Scarlatti, and Beethoven. Also, **SmartSleep,** a dreamy collection of familiar Chopin, Mozart, Debussy, Bach and Schumann piano music for bedtime. (800) 970-7801.

NOTABLE PREVIOUS WINNERS: Classics for Kids (BMG $8.98); **Hush** (Yo-Yo Ma & Bobby McFerrin, CBS $9.98/$17.98); **The Living Violin** (book by Barrie C. Turner/CD EMI, Knopf $25) 8 & up; **My Favorite Opera for Children** (Opera Made Easy: Pavarotti $7.95/$13.98) All ages.

Holiday Songs

■ Boogie Woogie Christmas

(College Street Pub. $9.95/$13.95) If you're looking for tradition with a little cha-cha-cha, here's a fun collection of the standards. (800) 246-8386.

■ A Child's Christmas Revels

(Revels Records $14.95) In more and more cities, Christmas Revels have become a tradition to celebrate the Winter Solstice. This collection of 29 songs is sung beautifully by the children (ages 6–13) of the Washington Revels.

Stories: Audio/Book Sets

Most storybooks published in audio form have already been well received as stand-alone books. Add music, sound effects, and a well-known narrator, and a good thing just gets better! These combined forms of media can do a lot to promote kids' positive attitudes and appetites for books and reading. Here are some of the best tickets to pleasurable and independent storytimes. Some are just audio, others are packaged with book and audio.

Preschool Stories

■ Blueberries for Sal

(by Robert McCloskey, Puffin $6.95) In this classic mix-up, a mother bear and cub get separated as do a mother-and-child duo. All's well that ends well. This no-frills paperback and audio set has no big-name stars, but beginning readers can follow the text or flip the tape for lively activity songs related to bears and berries. The Puffin series includes **The Story of Ping, Ferdinand,** and other classics. 3–7.

■ The Cat in the Hat (El Gato Ensombrerado)

(by Dr. Seuss, Random House $6.95) Now both book and tape of this classic beginner book are done in English and Spanish. Children can follow the word-for-word text in either language as they listen to the tape. PLATINUM AWARD '94. Also, **Are You My Mother?** 3–7.

■ If You Give a Moose a Muffin

(by Laura Joffe Numeroff/illus. by Felicia Bond, HarperFestival $10.95 book & tape) The amusing circular story of what happens when you give a moose a muffin is now available in a book and audio set. Narrated by Robbie Benson, the story is followed by a rap about making muffins and a lively song, "Doin' the Moose." 3–7. PLATINUM AWARD '98.

■ Tell Me a Story Series

(HarperChildren's Audio $7.95) Many best-loved classics are available in inexpensive paperback and audio sets. These make good take-along travel treats, great gifts and are an excellent way to build your child's love of books, listening ability, and personal library. We still suggest a mix of classics such as **Caps for Sale** by Esphyr Slobodkina, **A Baby Sister for Frances** by Russell Hoban, and **Dinner at the Panda Palace** by Stephanie Calmenson.

PREVIOUS NOTABLE WINNERS: Angelina Ballerina & Other Stories (HarperChildren's Audio $11.95) 4 & up; **On Mother's Lap** (by Ann Herbert Scott/illus. by Glo Coalson, Clarion $8.95 book & tape) 2 & up.

Early School Years

■ Arthur's New Puppy

(by Marc Brown, Little, Brown $8.95 book & tape) The trials and tribulations of having a new puppy provide the drama for this typical life experience. Read by Marc Brown. PLATINUM AWARD '99. 4–8. Also, **Arthur Meets the President.** PLATINUM AWARD '97. Bookstores.

■ The Chronicles of Narnia

(by C. S. Lewis, HarperChildren's Audio $11.95 each) There are seven tapes in this notable collection. Each can stand alone. Together, they tell the whole story of the magic land of Narnia. 9 & up.

■ A Christmas Carol

(Greathall Productions $9.95/$14.95) Jim Weiss gives young listeners a bit of historic background about Dickens's London before stepping into storytelling mode and dramatizing this classic. Also on the same tape is O. Henry's "Gift of the Magi." A nice stocking stuffer. 7 & up. (800) 477-6234.

■ Gather 'round the Fire

(Storycrafter $9.95/$14.95) Like their lively videos, this audio features five original retellings of international folktalks. Accompanied by music and repetitive refrain that listeners will enjoy chanting. 5 & up. (518) 672-7664.

■ The Illustrated Book of Ballet Stories

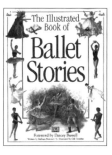

(by Barbara Newman/illus. by Gill Tomblin, DK $19.95) This handsomely illustrated book includes five ballet stories including "The Nutcracker," "Swan Lake," "Sleeping Beauty," "Giselle," and "Coppelia." Comes with CD that includes music from all five ballets. PLATINUM AWARD '99. Also recommended, **The Young Person's Guide to the Ballet** (by Anita Ganeri, Harcourt Brace $25) comes with a CD and a book about the ballet world. You can't go wrong with either.

■ Best Loved Stories

(Greathall Productions $9.95/$14.95) This collection includes "The Twelve Dancing Princesses," "The Sleeping Beauty," and "Snow White." Jim Weiss is a master storyteller who plays a whole cast of characters in every tale he tells. His selections from this classic are likely to excite young listeners enough so that they'll seek out the printed page. Also recommended, **The Jungle Book** (PLATINUM AWARD '96), and **Fairytale Favorites.** 5 & up. (800) 477-6234.

■ Let's Read & Find Out Series

(HarperCollins $7.95 each) For beginning readers, a book with an easy-to-read text accompanied by a word-for-word cassette provides an excellent way to reinforce reading skills. New tote carriers make these inexpensive book-and-tape combos ideal for travelers. Here are some of the best recent releases: **From Tadpole to Frog** by Wendy Pfeffer and **What Makes a Shadow?** by Clyde R. Bulla.

■ Listening Library 2000 Platinum Award

(Listening Library $9.95–$19.95) For young reader/listeners, this company has a wealth of unabridged story tapes that can be enjoyed with or without the print version in hand. New for 2000, we recommend: Mindy W. Skolsky's **Love from Your Friend, Hannah,** a story told largely through the pen pal letters of young Hannah who corresponds with Franklin & Eleanor Roosevelt, among others. This is a gem done with a cast of players, rather than a single story-teller reading. 8 & up. Previous award winners: Jack Prelutsky reading his **Monday's Troll,** Platinum Award '98; and Judy Blume reading her well-loved **Otherwise Known as Sheila the Great** and **Tales of a Fourth Grade Nothing.** 8 & up. Call for their catalog. (800) 243-4504.

■ Tarzan Read & Sing Along 2000 Platinum Award

(Disney $10.98) Kids who have seen the film will enjoy this capsulized version in a 33-page book with a word-for-word audio tape they can follow. Also top-rated, **Mulan Read Along.** 6 & up.

■ The Odyssey

(Odds Bodkin, Rivertree Prod. $35 four tapes or $49.95 four CDs) Our 11-year-old tester listened to this four-hour set of tapes at bedtime over a period of weeks. Told with many voices and accompanied by Celtic harp and 12-string guitar, this telling introduces kids to the adventures of Odysseus and returns Homer's written words to the oral tradition from which they came. Platinum Award '97. 10 & up. (800) 554-1333.

■ The People Could Fly

(told by Virginia Hamilton/illus. by Leo & Diane Dillon, Knopf $15) James Earl Jones and Virginia Hamilton narrate a dozen of the best American black folk tales from her prize-winning collection. A spellbinding mix of animals, fantasy, supernatural, and slave tales of freedom. A 75-min. tape with a paperback book. 7 & up.

■ Rabbit Ears Folktales Collection

(Rabbit Ears/Simon & Schuster $10.95–$19.95) Classic folktales narrated by well-known actors, and illustrated by marvelous artists, with accompaniment by well-known musicians, make these minibooks and full-sized books with audiocassettes outstanding gift choices. Be forewarned that these are not written in an easy-to-read format. These are just a few of the best choices:

- **Johnny Appleseed** told by Garrison Keillor
- **Goldilocks** told by Meg Ryan
- **Koi and the Kola Nuts** told by Whoopi Goldberg
- **The Emperor's New Clothes** told by Sir John Gielgud
- **Anansi** told by Denzel Washington

PREVIOUS NOTABLE WINNERS: Alexander and the Terrible, Horrible, No Good, Very Bad Day (by Judith Viorst, HarperChildren's Audio $11.95) 5 & up; **The Best Christmas Pageant Ever** (by Barbara Robinson, HarperChildren's Audio $11.95) PLATINUM AWARD '96. 6 & up; **Tell Me About the Night I Was Born** (by Jamie Lee Curtis, Harper Audio $15.95 book & tape) PLATINUM AWARD '99. 4 & up; **The True Story of the 3 Little Pigs** (Puffin $9.99 book & tape) PLATINUM AWARD '98. 5 & up.

Play Along Instruments

Some instruments are especially fun for kids to play as they listen and move to music. These late arrivals are more about rhythm than melody:

■ **Boomwhackers** 𝟚𝟘𝟘𝟘

(Whacky Music $19.98 a set & up) Whacky is the right word to describe these tuned percussion tubes—wonderfully whacky! Whack your head, hip, knee (we hope not your brother). These unique color-coded plastic tubes provide for a playful low-tech exploration of rhythm and harmony. Hand one or two out to each member of the family and have a happy whacky time! (888) 942-2536.

■Jamtown 2000

(Jamtown) We loved the sound quality and authentic folk beauty of a carved **Peruvian shaker** ($8), **Gourd Scraper** ($16), and rosewood **Clave Sticks** from Mexico ($12). You can buy a small drum, claves and shaker in a **Jamtown Jr.** kit with a tape ($35). These and other folk instruments from places like Africa and Indonesia make unusual gifts for the family. (888) 526-8696.

■ Lynn Kleiner Rhythm Sets 2000

(Remo $24.95 & up) Many instruments for young kids make noise instead of music and are basically unsafe. Strike up the rhythm band with these kits that are well crafted with sound and safety in mind. **Babies Make Music** includes jingle shaker, wrist jingle, and a small drum and scarf (safe enough for toddlers who still mouth their toys). 2 & up. **Kids Make Music** includes a 7" tambourine, triangle, wrist bell (with big jingles), rhythm sticks, and one maraca; **Kids Make Music, Too** has an 8" drum, scarf, finger cymbals, woodblock with mallet, and one egg shaker. 3 & up. (800) 397-9378.

Audio & Electronic Equipment

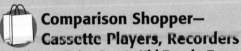

Comparison Shopper— Cassette Players, Recorders

For threes, Fisher-Price's **Kid-Tough Tape Recorder** ($45) player has better sound quality than in the past. Comes with nondetachable microphone, a safety hazard for kids under three. (800) 432-5437. Little Tikes **Tough Tike Tape Recorder** (Little Tikes/Play Tech $40) comes with a built-in holder for three cassettes and a sing-along nondetachable microphone. Boom-box shape will appeal to the 4 & up crowd. Also recommended, **Cassette Player** ($30), an oversized Walkman-styled player with adjustable headphones and a volume limiter. Takes 2 AA batteries. 3 & up. (800) 321-0183. Sony's **My First Radio/Cassette Recorder** ($54.95) is heavier and has a more grown-up design. #CFM-2300. 4 & up.

■ Time Blaster

(Long Hall/Nickelodeon $49.95) Wake up to either a bugle, a cuckoo, a boing-boing, or the Nick theme. Comes with an AM/FM clock radio. Also fun, **Rugrats Talking Alarm** ($24.99) with nightlight face and wake-up call from five different characters. (516) 293-6900.

■ Talk Blaster

(Long Hall/Nickelodeon $49.95) Short of a phone line of their very own, few gifts will be more welcome than this amusing multiringer phone that rings with a choice of a moo, honk, bell, laugh, or Nick theme. This has a power rod that lights up with incoming calls and hi/low ringer volume. This touch-tone phone is also hearing aid compatible so it might be multigenerational for seniors with a sense of humor who need a loud ring! Takes 3 C batteries. 6 & up. PLATINUM AWARD '98. (516) 293-6900.

Resources

Catalogs

- **Family Planet Music** (800) 985-8894.
- **Music for Little People** (800) 409-2457. This great catalog is back in business with a wide selection of music, videos, and instruments.
- **Listening Library** (800) 243-4504.

Online

- **eToys.com**
- **rightstart.com**
- **cdnow.com**
- **cdworld.com**
- **amazon.com**
- **musicblvd.com**

V • Computer Software/CD-ROM

In this chapter we have included the best software we have reviewed, plus titles marked **PREVIEW 2000** which were not ready to be tested in final form, but which look especially promising. Please consult our website (www.toyportfolio.com) for up-to-the-minute software reviews, plus the **2000** Platinum Software Award winners.

Trends

Violence

Video games and software came under attack this year for promoting a culture of violence. Parents should be aware that just because a game has an "all ages" rating does not mean the content is actually for children. Loopholes in the rating system allow games to get kid-friendly ratings if the violence is directed at non-human targets, or if the destruction is implied, but not depicted. Perhaps the most egregious insinuation of violence into kids' media comes from Sega DreamCast, which starts the newest version of Sonic with a horrific annihilation of a city. Parents need to personally check games for content, because industry standards are too lax.

They Would Be Giants

Chances are that the software you buy your kids this year will be manufactured by a toy company, and this is a huge change from just a year ago. Mattel, for instance, swallowed up Broderbund, The Learning Company, Creative Wonders, Mindscape, PrintPaks, American Girl Software, Comptons, and Purple Moon.

One result of this consolidation is reduced creativity in the field. The components used in KidPix might also get reused in programs bearing licenses from American Girl and Sesame Street. A playset designed to attach to a keyboard might be the Millenium Falcon in one package and a workbench in the next, depending on the plastic surfaces and license applied to it.

On the other hand, consolidation has also brought some heavy investment, the most notable example this year being the computerized microscope co-developed by Intel and Mattel.

Not Just PCs

Increasingly, computing is growing to involve more than traditional IBM clones. After several years of decline, the Apple Macintosh line of personal computers has made a strong comeback, particularly in the home/family market. Over the next several years we expect alternate platforms to become important competitors to the PC: notably in the rise of game platforms such as Sony's new Playstation set for release in late 2000. Even now, many children use their Nintendo Gameboys more than the PCs and a market is responding with games directed at a younger audience.

Computer play no longer is limited to those with a traditional PC. Smart toys with computer chips built in are the new rage. Last year's dolls that were programmed by a computer have been displaced by dolls with microchips. Lego's robotic Mindstorms set will now come in flavors that can be programmed on the toy, rather than through computer linkup. Kids too young to play with a keyboard can have computerized music and language fun with Neurosmith's computerized toys.

Cyberfriends

Today's dolls with computer brains and robotic limbs can interact with your child, almost realizing Pinocchio's dream. The trend this year is away from dolls that are programmed to work with PCs in favor of less capable dolls with self-contained microchips on board.

■ Actimates **2000**

(Microsoft $99 for Barney, $59.95 for computer transmitter and software) Barney, the first of the audio-animatronic dolls, is still the best to date. This plush purple dino can move his head and arms as he speaks and sings. Cover his eyes and he can even play peek-a-boo. PLATINUM AWARD '98. 18 mos.–3. Win. (800) 426-9400. **Buyer's Update:** First, pass on the doodads that connect the doll to the computer because Microsoft has offered no new software since the original titles were released two years ago. Further, avoid the follow-up dolls: the built-in games in **Arthur** & **D.W.** were too difficult for preschoolers. This year's **Actimates Teletubbies,** directed at an even younger audience, come with a light show on their "tummy screen" that is totally random and

for some reason includes letters but not the corresponding sound or name of the letter. Why put letters on a toddler toy, to begin with, and then make it worse by adding a confusing unrelated sound?

And More Cyber-Pals

Not all cyber-pals are dolls. Some of our favorite virtual playmates are:

■ Catz III and Dogz III **2000**

(PF Magic $29.95 each) These virtual cats and dogs that live on the computer screen are especially fun for kids who can't have pets because of allergies, domestic limitations, or special needs. **PREVIEW 2000**: This year the cyberpetz get voice recognition and will respond to your commands. Well, the cats will hear you, but only do what you ask if it suits their fancy! And, stop the presses, one of the most requested sequels: **Babyz!** virtual infants will finally crawl, cuddle and coo their way to your home. 4 & up. Win. (415) 495-0400.

■ Creatures 2 *2000*

(Mindscape $29.95) Taking a more scientific approach to cyberlife, the virtual animal life in Creatures learns language, breeds, and evolves. While exploring the artificial world players attempt to develop a self-sustaining population. ***PREVIEW 2000***: In addition to **Creatures 3, Creatures Adventure** will bring the franchise to younger players. 10 & up. Win. (800) 973-5111.

Robotics

Constructing and programming robots develops creativity and excellent logic skills. The news this year is that Lego is expanding its groundbreaking robotics kits with new models that don't require a computer.

■ The Robot Club *2000*

(South Peak $29.95) Although the Star Wars-based Droidworks got more hype, South Peak's strategy game has better graphics, and tested higher with our 'tweens. The object is to solve problems by building virtual robots to complete a series of missions. 10 & up. Win. (919) 677-4499.

■ Lego Mindstorms Robotics Invention System *2000*

(Lego Mindstorms $199) Lego's robot-building kit integrates computers, robotics and construction sets into one of the most creative toys in history. At the heart of the system is a brick of yellow Lego that contains a microprocessor into which kids can plug sensors that test for light and touch, infrared communications ports that allow the system to receive programs from the PC, and control motors which power wheels and gears. Optional add-ins include a camera, remote control, and theme sets; plus, the kits work with all standard Lego blocks. PLATINUM AWARD '99. Lego's two new kits, **Lego Mindstorms Droid Developer Kit** *2000* PLATINUM AWARD and **Mindstorms Robotics Discovery Set,** priced at $100 and $150 each, dispense with the personal computer and permit direct programming of the robot via a built-in keypad at a lower price. The less-expensive Star Wars-inspired kit creates R2D2 and other droids from the Phantom Menace. 9 & up. Win. (800) 510-5773.

Story Book Software

The trend away from book-based children's software accelerates this year. Fewer titles are adapted from books, and those that are have so many multimedia doodads that they seem almost embarrassed to admit their book-based roots. Disney still puts out what it calls "animated story books," but its latest foray, **Winnie the Pooh and Tigger, Too**, was less of a story than a contrived plot designed to hold together a series of simple games. Even the venerated Living Books series from Broderbund has announced no new book-based titles, instead moving toward drill-and-review activity titles. Still top-rated, BLUE CHIP titles in the Living Books collection from Broderbund (about $29.95 each) include: **The Cat in the Hat, Green Eggs and Ham, Grandma & Me, Arthur's Teacher Troubles,** and **Arthur's Computer Adventure.** 5 & up. Win/Mac. (800) 776-4724.

DiaperWare, ToddlerWare & Pre-K-Ware: Software for the Youngest Users

Infants need interaction with real people. They need to be sung to, reacted to, and nurtured. Baby-play should be with people and three-dimensional objects, not flat images. This is why we do not recommend baby videos or baby software. Unfortunately, manufacturers are marketing these products as must-haves for smart children. Relax, your kids will be plenty smart without them—in fact, smarter! These products encourage passivity and develop little more than a readiness to plug into Saturday morning cartoons.

Toddlerware is subject to the same sort of abuses. If you feel compelled to get a program for your toddler, limit usage or you may find your child tuning in and zoning out of more appropriate activities that develop interpersonal skills and active play. Among the most interactive toddlerware titles are **Jump Start Toddlers** (Knowledge Adventure $34.95) and **Fisher-Price Little People Discovery Farm** (Knowledge Adventure $20). (800) 457-8357.

The 3 Rs: Reading, Writing and RAM

Schoolhouse Grade-Based Software

A few years ago every software company was producing storybook titles. Now, they have moved on to schoolhouse software —essentially electronic workbooks.

Why? It is relatively easy to produce drill-and-review software. Take one of about ten standard workbook templates and slap on a licensed character (Tarzan, Winnie the Pooh, Ernie, or Madeline, for example), put it in a big, shiny box and— *voilá*—you're making children's software. Never mind that it might not have much real play or instructive value.

We are also concerned that kids will be confused if the school is using one methodology and the software is using another. Some schools, for instance, emphasize phonics, while others do not. For this reason we strongly recommend that you talk to your child's teacher before buying a lot of "educational" software that may be confusing.

While there is room for software that aims at skill mastery, unless you offer your children a balanced diet of more interesting software they will soon push away from the computer. Putting it simply, when the school day is over, kids want an alternative, not more of the same.

Math Software

■ Math Blaster: First & Second Grade *PREVIEW 2000*

(Knowledge Adventure $30) This classic line of arcade-based drill-and-review software will be getting a 3D makeover this year. Win/Mac. (800) 457-8357.

■ Mighty Math Series

(Edmark $39 each) Learning math is more than drill and review. Though lots of practice is important, getting the concepts is fundamental. This series' use of language, manipulatives, and traditional math exercises to explain concepts is unparalleled and highly recommended. **Mighty Math Carnival Countdown** and **Mighty Math Zoo Zillions** (ages 5–8); **Mighty Math Calculating Crew** and **Mighty Math Number Heroes** (ages 8–11); **Mighty Math Cosmic Geometry** (ages 12–14). PLATINUM AWARD '98. Win/Mac. (800) 691-2985.

■ Blue's 123 Time Activities *2000*

(Humongous $19.99) The snappy graphic style of the Blues Clues TV show translates well to the computer screen. Counting, patterns, and matching games reward kids with Blues Bucks that they can use to purchase things in the game's store. 4–6. Win/Mac. (800) 499-8386.

■ I Love Math *2000*

(DKI $59.95) In addition to the standard arithmetic drills, this British import covers measurement, fractions, and shapes, and has good word problems. 7–10. Win/Mac. (888) 342-5357.

NOTABLE PREVIOUS WINNERS: Disney's Math Quest, Disney Interactive, $35.00, 6–9, Mac/Win, (800) 900-9234. **Major League Math 2** & **NFL Math,** Sanctuary Woods, $39.95 each, 9 & up, Win/Mac. (415) 286-6000. **Math Heads** (Theatrix, $29.95, 9–13, Win. (800) 795-8749.

Reading, Spelling, & Grammar Software

■ Reader Rabbit's Complete Learn to Read System

(Learning Company $69.95) This impressive set aims at being a comprehensive, step-by-step course in reading. Inside you'll find two CD-ROMs, seven printed storybooks, flash cards, workbook, and poster. The system starts with letter and sound recognition and continues through phonics, sight words, and ultimately putting it all together with sentences. We think the scope of this package makes it more suited for classroom or home-schoolers, because after school most children will be better served by a diet of more captivating story and early-reading books. But, if your child needs extra help, this package will give plenty of exercises and books to practice with. 3–7. Win/Mac. (617) 761-3000.

■ JumpStart Reading for Second Graders

(Knowledge Adventure $19.95) This program doesn't attempt to recreate the total school experience, but instead gives exercises in alphabetization, vocabulary, contractions and compound words, reading comprehension, spelling, homophones, synonyms, antonyms, and rhymes. The "adventure" setting tries to sugar coat what are essentially electronic worksheets. 6–8. Win/Mac. (800) 457-8357.

■ Reading Blaster Ages 9–12

(Knowledge Adventure $30) The latest installment in the Reading Blaster series aims at improving reading comprehension and grammar skills for late elementary and early middle school students. Though at

Its core it is a drill-and-review program, the "work" is made lighter by a mystery setting which tests with games based on scrambled sentences, antonyms, word relationships, and parts of speech. 9–12. Win/Mac. (800) 457-8357.

■ My Personal Tutor 2: First and Second Grade

(Microsoft $34.95) Although this cross-curriculum three-disk set covers math and logic, it is really the reading disk that is special. It contains many mini-books, each illustrated and written in a unique style that makes going through the disk much more appealing. The program goes beyond being an electronic workbook by using artificial intelligence to track a child's progress. If problems arise, an animated professor provides proactive instruction. ***Buyer's Update:*** This second effort in the series is much improved over the "not recommended" Preschool & Kindergarten product. PLATINUM AWARD '99. 6–8. Win. (800) 426-9400.

Spelling

■ Spelling Blaster

(Knowledge Adventure $30) Spelling is one of the areas where drill and review really helps. Here you can use the word lists provided or customize the program to work with your child's class lists. As a bonus the computer can print word lists, crossword puzzles and word search games. 6–9. Win/Mac. (800) 457-8357.

Science

■ IntelPlay QX3 Microscope *2000* PLATINUM AWARD

(Mattel $80) This dazzling demonstration of how creative and empowering computer technology can be mates a computer-connected video camera to a microscope. The result: kids can take time-lapse movies of growing crystals, watch bugs scurry about inside little viewing bubbles, or take video snapshots of the microscopic world for inclusion in reports. The optics on the prototype units gave better images than any home microscope we've seen to date. 10 & up. (800) 524-TOYS.

■ I Love Science *2000*

(DKI $59.95) Less of a "game" and more like a visit to a hands-on science museum, this disk is packed with useful facts and hands-on experiments in chemistry, biology, and physics. 7–10. (888) 342-5357.

■ Magic School Bus Animals 2000 MIXED EMOTIONS

(Microsoft $19.95) There are good facts and a few amusing activities in this science title about animals and their habitats, but there are also some weird situations that might put kids in harm's way, like kids "playing" with raccoons. Like other titles in this series, science often takes a back seat to silliness—such as the morph machine that shows what people would look like if they were blended with animals. There are more factoids and videos in this than in previous Magic Schoolbus titles, but there is not enough information, variety, or replay-ability here. 6–10. Win. (800) 426-9400.

■ My First Amazing Science Explorer 2000

(DKI $29.95) Thirty learning activities center on answering the "why" questions of childhood like, "Why is the sky blue?" and, "Why are bubbles round?" A computerized scientific journal turns kids into observers of the world around them at the same time it develops verbal skills. 6–9. Win/Mac. (888) 342-5357.

■ Virtual Serengeti *PREVIEW 2000*

(Grolier Interactive $29.99) Over 150 videos featuring sixty exotic animals, plus 360-degree bubble views, make this a compelling science adventure on the African plain. 10 & up. Win. (203) 797-3530.

■ Zap 2000

(Edmark $29.95) Where many companies are content to recycle ubiquitous drill-and-review activities, Edmark consistently serves up fascinating, creative, challenging puzzles for kids to sink their teeth into. Zap explores sound, light, and electricity through activity centers that include simulated circuits, lasers, sound and light. PLATINUM AWARD '99. 8–12. Win/Mac. (800) 691-2985

Foreign Language

■ KidSpeak 10-in-1 Language Learning 2000

(Transparent Language $59.95) Rudimentary vocabulary including alphabet and number skills are taught in this multi-disk set that covers 10 languages: Spanish, French, Italian, German, Japanese, Indonesian, Korean, Hebrew, Chinese, and Portuguese. Each language gets its own set of lessons, but since each

works similarly, covering the same material, the children rapidly make connections from one language to the next. 6 & up. Win/Mac. (603) 465-2230.

■ Kaplan Spanish/French for the Real World 2000

(Knowledge Adventure $29.95 each) No language product has been so well received by our kid critics! Children with little inclination to learn a foreign language have been seen using this as a product of choice, in favor of conventional games. Stylish graphics and real-world situations make language study fun and relevant—this one never sounds like "school." 11 & up. Win/Mac. (800) 457-8357.

Geography, History, & Social Studies

■ My First Amazing World Explorer

(DK Multimedia $29.95) Many programs we review for elementary school kids use a lowest common denominator approach: saccharine sweet music, ugly cartoon characters, and dopey, surrealistic cartoon graphics. This one appeals to all of the best in your child. It depicts the world as full of wonderful places to think about, imagine, and visit. Its positive view of the world makes this a winner! PLATINUM AWARD '97. 4–9. Win/Mac. (888) 342-5357.

■ Carmen Sandiego Geography Series:
Where in the World is Carmen Sandiego?
Where in the USA is Carmen Sandiego?
Where in the World is Carmen Sandiego Jr.?
BLUE CHIP

(Broderbund $39 and up) Carmen Sandiego has become a conglomerate. Kids can search for her in America, Europe, time, and the world. Kids enjoy these games of geography and logic. To win, you must travel to gather clues that establish the identity of the crook. The newest versions of USA features video clips, Internet links, informative guides, mini-quizzes (a new way to gain clues), and an extensive on-disk library about the states. We'd like to see some more activities added including some based on the TV series, such as race-against-the-clock capitals and state locating. 9 & up. Win/Mac. (800) 716-8503.

■ Oregon Trail 3 BLUE CHIP 2000

(Learning Company $39.95) What makes the Oregon Trail series so remarkable is the way it personalizes the determination, courage and danger of the road west. Children have always responded well to the chance at making difficult adult decisions that this program empowers them to make. The attention to detail, and new multimedia additions keep attention high and make this much more than a "game." 9 & up. Win/Mac. (617) 761-3000. Also recommended: **Amazon Trail.** *PREVIEW 2000*: The next installment in this series will be **Road Adventure USA,** a cross-country journey set in the present requires planning, money and resource management, and expands geographic awareness.

■ The Complete National Geographic

(Mindscape $199) Featuring 7,500 articles (and all the photos) from more than 1,200 issues of National Geographic, this package has the added benefit of a powerful search engine for research. PLATINUM AWARD '98. 12 & up. Win/Mac. (415) 897-9900. *Buyer Beware:* National Geographic's atlas set is difficult to use because the maps are too big to be read well on a screen and too cumbersome to print. This collection should have been reworked for multimedia.

■ Encarta Africana 🄯2000 PLATINUM AWARD

(Microsoft $69.95) This extraordinary multimedia title tells of the history, geography and culture of Black people. It should be a must-have title in any home, as it casts a light on ignorance—revealing the depth and profundity of African culture on our world. *PREVIEW 2000:* A second edition is slated for this year. 10 & up. Win. (800) 426-9400.

Typing

We are going to have to keep typing to our computers until voice recognition software becomes a lot more reliable. A child who can't type will have a much harder time producing reports and surfing the web. Here are two titles that can help.

■ JumpStart Typing

(Knowledge Adventure $19.95) This program uses a good mix of games to encourage keyboard familiarity. 7–10. Win/Mac. (800) 457-8357.

■ Mavis Beacon Teaches Typing

(Mindscape $40) Similar to a high-school course in typing, this program has a business-like feel. 13 & up. Win. (800) 973-5111.

Thought-Provoking Programs

Simulations and games develop thinking skills and often expose children to information they might be resistant to spending time with in more "traditional" settings. Most of these games are for children in late elementary school or older, though depending on your child's reading and reasoning skills (and patience), some could be enjoyed by younger children as well.

Trivia Games

■ MegaMunchers BLUE CHIP

(Learning Company $39.95) **Math Munchers,** the classic rapid-fire math drill game, has been bundled with a language skills and general knowledge trivia game at a price that is less than what just one of the disks cost last year. The game doesn't get in the way of the drill. 8–12. Win/Mac. (617) 761-3000. *PREVIEW 2000*: More multiple choice trivia games from IBM (**Brain Quest**) and Broderbund (**Carmen Sandiego Quick Challenge**) are slated, but will kids find them fun enough to stick with after mom and dad bring them home? Stay tuned.

Computer Puzzlers and Games

■ I Spy

(Scholastic $29) We weren't sure that screen resolutions were good enough to bring these books to life digitally, but amazingly, these puzzles are actually better on the computer. Visual discrimination, logic, and memory are all put to the test in these gorgeous brainteasers. PLATINUM AWARD '98. 5–9. Win/Mac. (800) SCHOLASTIC. *PREVIEW 2000*: A new **I Spy Jr.** title will be released with more brain-teasing puzzles.

■ Thinkin' Things Series *2000*

(Edmark $29.95 each) This BLUE CHIP series of logic games and puzzles has been expanded and revised this year. **All Around FrippleTown** (4–8) has four activities that explore following directions, listening skills, logic and analysis. Best of all, these are fun activities that let kids drive a car, create flags, make cookies, and go ice skating! **Toony the Loon's Lagoon** (4–8) is a revamped version of earlier Thinkin' Things 1 titles with a great 3-D updated look. Also recommended, **Galactic Brain Benders** and **Sky Island Mysteries.** Win/Mac. (800) 691-2985.

Simulations

■ Star Wars Episode 1: The Gungan Frontier 2000

(Lucas Learning $29.95) This program is essentially SimPark in outer space. Playing as either Queen Amadala or ObiWan, kids help JarJar Binks colonize one of his planet's moons. The game teaches about ecosystems and the interdependence of all living things while it develops logic and thinking skills. 10 & up. Win. **PREVIEW 2000**: Two more "learning" games based on Episode 1 will be released.

■ SimSafari

(Maxis $30) Kids have to balance a budget and an ecosystem in this challenging game that puts them in charge of an African game preserve. This game requires non-linear thinking and the ability to solve multiple problems simultaneously. 8 & up. Win. (800) 245-4525.

■ SimCity 3000 2000

(Maxis $49.95) The latest, greatest upgrade to the king of all sims, which places players in the role of urban planner. 10 & up. Win/Mac. (800) 245-4525.

■ RollerCoaster Tycoon 2000 PLATINUM AWARD

(Hasbro Interactive $30) RollerCoaster Tycoon puts you in charge of every aspect of an amusement park, from rollercoaster design to how much to charge for the cotton candy. Though the subject matter seems "light," the game is a learn-by-doing school on subjects as diverse as physics and economics. (800) 400-1352. **PREVIEW 2000: Lego Land** (Lego $29.95) will explore the same subject matter aimed at a younger audience.

■ Railroad Tycoon 2000

(Gathering of Developers $49.95) Becoming a transportation multimillionaire is the object of this transportation and stock market game set between 1004 and the present. 10 & up. (877) 463-4763

Adventures

Kids' adventure games are generally interactive cartoons in which kids solve visual logic problems to further a story. For example, they may have to solve a puzzle to open a locked door. Kid testers repeatedly tell us they enjoy them—primarily, we think, because of the "cute" protagonists. Among the better titles are: **Mia: The Search for Grandma's Remedy** (Kutoka $34.95, 5–8, (877) 858-8652) with delightful 3D rendered characters; **Blue's Clues Adventure** (Humongous $29.95, 3–5, (800) 499-8386) which lets kids virtually jump into the Blue's Clues universe. Also recommended from Humongous: **Spy Fox 2,** and **Freddy the Fish** titles. *PREVIEW 2000*: Hasbro's **Clue Chronicles** will be a single-player game for 10 & up, using the cast of characters from Clue, the mystery game of deduction, in 3D off-the-gameboard adventure. (800) 400-1352.

Classic Games

Computer versions of board and word games provide a way for kids to hone their strategy skills and solve the problem of how to play when there's no one to play with. They are also valuable resources for physically challenged kids who can operate a computer, but have trouble with the dexterity required to manipulate the pieces of a game set.

Board Games
■ Hasbro Classic Board Games *2000*

(Hasbro Interactive $29.95 each) Hasbro's series of classic games continues to improve. The line goes from early childhood's **Candy Land** (and the forthcoming **Chutes & Ladders**) to games more appropriate for 10 & up, such as **Clue, Risk,** & **Scrabble.** *PREVIEW 2000:* **Guess Who,** the twenty-questions style game of deduction, looks like fun for elementary school-age kids. The flagship of the line, **Monopoly,** will get a full facelift and will allow users to customize their own boards with the places where they live! Also this year, one of the greatest board games of all time, **Diplomacy,** a game of negotiation and strategy set in WWI, will get the Hasbro multimedia treatment. Most of these games feature Internet capability, so you can play with friends and relatives all over the country. Ages vary from 4 to adult. Win. (800) 400-1352.

■ Hoyle Board Games

(Sierra $29.95) Fourteen classic board games (reversi, Chinese checkers, dominoes, to name a few) are wonderfully brought to life with on- and off-line play. 8 & up. Win/Mac. (800) 457-8357.

■ Complete Chess 2000

(Knowledge Adventure $39.95) This 3-disk set includes PLATINUM AWARD-winning **Maurice Ashley Teaches Chess.** Directions such as: "Hit the king with the double barrel lasers of the bishops" make the game come to life. Tutorials on pivotal aspects of the game are reinforced with challenging puzzlers. Checkmate! PLATINUM AWARD '97. 10 & up. Win. (800) 457-8357.

Chessmaster 6000 2000

(Mindscape $39.95) Players looking for a stronger game of chess should look no further than Chessmaster 6000, with a library of over 300,000 games, audio commentary, over 40 computerized opponents, and free on-line play. *PREVIEW 2000:* Playstation and Gameboy Chessmaster products will also be available this year. Win/Mac.

Sports

Some of the most fun games to play with your child on the computer are sports titles. The computer levels the playing field, and might even give a slight advantage to kids.

Among our favorite titles for kids under 10 are **Backyard Baseball** and **Backyard Soccer** (Humongous Entertainment $40 each) and **Tonka Raceway** (Hasbro Interactive $29.95). *PREVIEW 2000*: Promising titles include: **Hot Wheels** by Electronic Arts, **Lego Racers,** and **Humongous Backyard Football.**

Electronic Arts has developed the best sports titles for the 10 & up set: **FIFA Soccer 2000, Triple Play Baseball, Madden Football, NBA Live,** and the **Need for Speed** series are all outstanding.

Creativity Software

Word Processors

■ Creative Writer 2 BLUE CHIP

(Microsoft $34.95) This is the best word processor for late elementary school kids. Children can make the program their own by selecting custom thematic borders and sound effects. More than a word processor, Creative Writer 2 sparks the imagination with evocative clip art, and activity projects such as cards, banners, and even Web page building. 8 & up. Win. (800) 426-9400.

■ Writing Blaster

(Knowledge Adventure $30) This word processor for kids comes with over 100 templates for easy-to-publish projects from greeting cards to journals, e-mail, and storybooks. While there is overlap with the Creative Writer audience, this program is designed for younger kids. 6–9. Win/Mac. (800) 457-8357.

■ WordPerfect Office 2000 Voice-Powered Edition 2000

(Wordperfect $149 upgrade) When your child is ready to move up to a full-fledged word processor, this is our recommendation. Microsoft's Word 2000 is bloated with features you don't need designed to implement the corporation's web strategy. In contrast, WP2000 is powerful, yet intuitive. Best of all, it comes with Dragon System's voice recognition software which—unlike any of the others we've tried—makes typing-by-talking a working reality. (800) 772-6735.

Arts & Crafts Software: Playing with Dolls

■ Barbie Cool Looks Fashion Designer

(Mattel $44.99) This follow-up to the fashion designer features more dolls and more fashions. This no-needle approach to making clothing for Barbie is spectacular, as is watching Barbie and company model the outfits you've created in 3D. 6 & up. Win. (310) 252-2000. **PREVIEW 2000: Barbie Gotta-Groove** lets girls design dance routines that on-screen dolls can perform, and teach to real-world friends.

■ American Girl Dress Designer PREVIEW 2000

(Learning Company) Unlike the Barbie Fashion Designer, this program does not produce full outfits. Instead, kids can design paper doll and clothing cut-outs with a historical flavor based upon the American Girl Dolls. Win/Mac. (800) 716-8503. Pass on The American Girls Premiere (The Learning Company $34.99) We were disappointed with the difficulty of getting the results we wanted from this movie-making package based on the popular historical dolls.

Painting on the Computer
■ KidPix Studio Deluxe BLUE CHIP

(Broderbund $29.99) No program makes doodling on the computer more fun! Truly fun for all ages, we've seen toddlers through adults delighted with its creative toolkit. 3 & up. Win/Mac. (800) 716-8503.

PREVIEW 2000: Kidpix 3rd Edition, the first major rewrite of this favorite program in years, will add new animation tools plus integrated e-mail. One of the coolest features will be "paint-by-sound," where the paintbrush will respond to the child's voice! A similar drawing engine will be used in other programs in the Mattel line using licenses from American Girl and Sesame Street.

■ SketchBoard Featuring Disney's Magic Artist 2000

(kidBoard, inc., $99.00 for PC version, $119 for Mac) This software/hardware bundle combines a great drawing program with an excellent piece of hardware: a drawing tablet with a computerized "pen." The tablet allows greater precision and a more "familiar" drawing interface than a traditional mouse. 6 & up. Win. (800) 926-3066. This excellent tablet has been updated and bundled with **Disney's Magic Artist 2** 2000 PLATINUM AWARD.

Imaging Products

Scanners
■ Slimscan C3 USB

(Microtek $79.95) Computer crafts have gotten much more fun and sophisticated with the introduction of low-cost, easy-to-use color scanners. Your child can bring photos, art, and text into the computer using this flat-bed scanner at a super price. The USB version makes setup extremely easy. (800) 654-4160.

Cameras

Many digital cameras are available, but most have been too expensive to give to a child. Here are two that attempt to bring cutting-edge technology to kids:

■ JamCam Version 2 *2000* PLATINUM AWARD

Last year's kid-camera of choice has been replaced by a much higher (640x480) resolution portable camera that can hold 24 images. While still not as sharp as grown-up cameras, it is plenty for most kid-craft projects. It comes bundled with Microsoft **Picture It! 99,** a very impressive photo project editor. 10 & up or younger with adult software assistance. Win/Mac. (800) 926-3066.

■ Quickcam Home *2000*

(Logitech $99) This tethered camera plugs into the USB port of your computer and can grab moving and still images. (800) 231-7717.

Reference Titles

Suite
■ Encarta Reference Suite

(Microsoft $129.99) The undisputed champion of home reference titles! On one DVD you get **Virtual Globe, Encarta Deluxe Encyclopedia, Encarta World Dictionary** (and supporting reference titles), and the best report organizer on the market at a remarkable price. The new version has voice recognition, a consistent, interface between applications, and a futuristic, snappier look that invites users to browse. Also available on CD. PLATINUM AWARD '99. (800) 426-9400.

Encyclopedia
■ World Book Millennium 2000 Series *2000*

(World Book $69.95 for the Deluxe Edition) World Book has long been one of our favorite reference titles because of the excellent quality of its writing. It contains every article from the 24-volume World Book print edition, plus videos, maps, simulations, animations, 360-degree panoramas, photos, and sound. New this year are simulated web-sites for each century that give a "you are there" view of the world as it was. World Book offers two other options worth noting: for an additional $20 the encyclopedia is bundled with reference titles including a world atlas, three **Information Please** almanacs, and the **Merriam-Webster's Reference Library.** This year World Book is also launching an entirely on-line encyclopedia ($49.95 per year) at www.worldbook.com.

On-Line Reference Sources

We continue to be concerned over the safety of the Internet for kids (and teens). We suggest that you invest the time and money needed to set up **CyberPatrol** (The Learning Company $39.95, (617) 761-3000) which filters out most offensive sites before you permit your child to surf. Discuss Internet safety and privacy with your kids. A good introduction can be found at www.safekids.com/child_safety.htm.

The first two places kids should turn to when doing homework on the web are **Yahooligans** (www.yahooligans.com) and **Ask Jeeves for Kids** (www.ajkids.com). Both of these are search engines designed for kids that return results they deem appropriate for kids.

A big problem with doing research on-line is that many sites (even the so-called educational ones) can be a waste of time—particularly sites where kids answer other kids' academic questions. One site that is worth investing in is **eLibrary** (http://www.elibrary.com), a subscription-based reference compendium of thousands of titles selected for relevance to students. A free trial subscription is available. You should also be aware that the full text to over 9,000 public domain books is available at http://www.cs.cmu.edu/books.html.

Software for the Whole Family

Must-Have Utilities

Improve the performance and reliability of your system by

investing in these utilities:

KidDesk—Limits kids to programs which you approve.

CyberPatrol—The best internet-filtering software, it helps keep your kids safe on-line.

Norton System Works — Get this for the virus protection and emergency services.

Inforian Infoquest—The best Internet search software.

NetCaptor—Your Internet Explorer browsing will be less cluttered and more organized with this free add-in.

Family Software You Should Invest In

Here is our short list of titles that fit the lifestyles of many homes:

Quicken—best home finance software; **Microsoft Graphics Studio Home Publishing Suite**—most versatile home desktop publishing/photo editing kit; **Sierra's MasterCook Suite Featuring Betty Crocker 5**—includes recipes, nutritional guides, and more; **Generation's Family Tree**—one of the best genealogy packages; **Sierra's Complete LandDesigner**—design and maintain the perfect garden.

Computer Add-ins

■ Plastic Meets Software

Hasbro, Mattel and a new player, Zowie, will be introducing toy-like hardware that controls software. Zowie's playsets look like a dollhouse and a boat, and plug into the serial port. Hasbro and Mattel's sets attach to the keyboard and essentially act as alternate keyboards. There will be sets that look like a kitchen, cash register, big rigs, and power tools. The test will not be the plastic, but the software—which was not available as we went to press.

Keyboards

■ Microsoft Natural Keyboard 2000

Although it takes a while to get used to the unconventional design of this keyboard, our own experience indicates that it actually reduces typing strain that might lead to carpal tunnel syndrome.

■ Cordless Desktop 2000

(Logitech $99) This wireless keyboard/mouse combo really works. They look and feel just like standard components, but without the clutter. (800) 231-7717.

Mice

■ Marble Mouse 2000

(Logitech $39.95) This pointer fits your hand like a mouse, but works like a trackball. Its giant red ball gave precise control and a touch of futuristic whimsy that was appealing to adults and kids alike. (800) 231-7717.

■ Microsoft Force Feedback Mouse
Logitech Gaming Mouse *PREVIEW 2000*

These two force-feedback-enabled mice are primarily designed for gamers who play shoot-em-ups, as they shake and vibrate in reaction to play.

Joysticks and Game Controllers

■ Top Gun Joystick

(Thrustmaster $24.95) We kid-test most games with this inexpensive stick because it is smaller, more kid-sized, than other joysticks. The new low price makes it an even better buy. (503) 615-3200.

■ Sidewinder Precision Pro Joystick 2000

(Microsoft $74.95) For larger hands, this joystick provides built-in throttle and rudder control. The original model now comes in a USB version to make hooking it up and swapping it with other game controllers even easier. (800) 426-9400.

■ CH Yoke LE *PREVIEW 2000*

(CH $109) Jet fighters use joystick-like controllers. Commercial and private planes tend to use yokes, like this 14-button, three-axis controller, perfect for Sierra's **ProPilot,** Looking Glass Studio's **Flight Unlimited III,** or **Microsoft Flight Simulator.** (760) 598-2518.

Steering Wheels and Driving Controllers

■ NASCAR Sprint *2000*

(Thrustmaster $69.95) This wheel and pedal set deliver great realism at an affordable price. You'll never go back to a joystick for racing games again. (503) 615-3200.

■ Wingman Formula Force Wheel *2000*

(Logitech $129) This is our steering wheel of choice, even in games that are not force feedback enabled. On the games that are (and most driving titles today use the force), this wheel delivers unbelievable realism and control. (800) 231-7717.

Sound and Video Cards

Computer add-ins are updated so often that the fastest, greatest card of the moment is often quickly eclipsed before a review's ink is dry. Getting the card is only the first step in improving system performance, you need to keep your drivers current—so you need a company that frequently posts updates. Check with the manufacturers for current pricing and models. Most of these companies prefer that you contact them on the web. Prices range around $200–$250.

3D Video Card Manufacturers

■ Creative Labs *2000*

TNT2 Riva Ultra is one of the hottest, fastest cards on the market. (www.creativelabs.com)

■ 3dFX *2000*

Voodoo2 was the gaming standard last year, and it continues to be popular. However, part of its success was based on many companies licensing the standard. Now, with 3dFX buying STB and making Voodoo3 a proprietary standard, it remains to be seen whether this company will continue to dominate the gaming industry. The Voodoo3 3500TV has super graphics, plus tv and FM tuning, video capture, and DVD support. (www.3dfx.com).

■ Matrox *2000*

The highest praise we give to the Matrox card was that universally, game tech-support people called it a great card. We never had trouble finding drivers and getting games to work. The new **Millennium G400** comes with 32 mg of RAM and can support two monitors at once! (www.matrox.com)

Sound Card Manufacturers

■ Creative Labs 2000

The Soundblaster series has been at the forefront of PC sound from the beginning. The new Live card gives multi-channel surround sound and excellent fidelity. (www.creativelabs.com)

■ Diamond Multimedia 2000

Our card of choice has been the MonsterSound MX300 because of its painless setup and solid game support. The way it creates 3D sound with only two speakers is simply uncanny. (www.diamondmm.com)

The Game Machines: Sony, Nintendo, & Sega Dreamcast

Gameboy

Gameboy and Gameboy Color continue to be unbelievably popular, fueled largely by the **Pokemon** craze. While we are concerned when a child plugs into a game system to the exclusion of other kinds of play, the pervasiveness of Gameboy has made it a fixture in the landscape of the early 21st century, and the signs are it is only going to get more popular. This year the Pokemon franchise will expand with **Pokemon Pinball** 2000 **Platinum Award** and a new yellow cartridge. Moreover, Pokemon will cross over to PC and N64, bringing in new players. The icons of childhood play (**Barbie, Sesame Street** and others) are also migrating to Gameboy this year. Among the coolest gifts for kids who are already invested in Gameboy are the accessories from Interact: their Gameshark cartridge unlocks hidden levels, and their HandyPak magnifies and lights the screen.

Playstation

Next year's introduction of the next generation of Playstation promises awesome computer power plus DVD coupled with incredible graphics. In the meantime, Playstation has great sports software (**3xtreme Sports, MLB 2000, Coolboarders 3**), some edutainment software (**Elmo's Letter Journey**) and can double as a CD player. Interact's **DexDrive** ($39.95) lets kids trade game solutions via computer (a Nintendo version is also available), and their **V3**

Steering Wheel ($59.95) makes race games much more involving and easier to control.

Nintendo 64

As we go to press the Nintendo 64 still has the best graphics and most memory of any system on the market—however, that will change with the introduction of the Sega Dreamcast. What it will have for at least the next year is the most kid-friendly game software. **Mario Party** and **Mario Racer** are just examples of Nintendo's commitment to lower-violence titles for kids. Also, sport titles for N64 (**Triple Play 2000, Madden Football, 1080 Snowboarding**) play excellently on this fast machine. The lack of a CD player limits the versatility of this platform

Sega DreamCast

(Sega $199) This unit has graphics that beat out all the other game platforms and most home computers. Most of the software in the first group of games is designed for the 14 & up set. We were appalled that the newest incarnation of **Sonic** (the most kid-friendly staple in the Sega line) starts with the annihilation of a city, something totally inappropriate for kids. The sports titles look great, but the software coming out at launch is not primarily designed for children.

This chapter was written byte-by-byte by Technology Editor **James Oppenheim.** *James is a computer consultant, attorney, and father of two avid school-aged computer users.*

VI • Using Ordinary Toys for Kids with Special Needs

In recent years, there has been new interest in promoting toys for kids with special needs. Unfortunately, many lists are little more than catalogs, with no explanation of why a product is especially suited for kids with disabilities; nor do they suggest adaptations or activities. Our continuing goal is to suggest products that are entertaining and to provide useful tips for getting the most play and learning value. We also know that children enjoy playing with products that are like their siblings', cousins', or neighbors'. By adapting ordinary toys, we can help put their play lives into the mainstream.

Most toys have more than one use and will provide various kinds of feedback for children with different kinds of disabilities. Although we have used headings for infants, toddlers, and preschoolers, age guidelines are blurred, since conventional age labels will be less meaningful for children with significant developmental delays. For children with visual or hearing impairments, learning to make effective use of other senses is essential. Similarly, those with motor impairment need products that respond and motivate active exploration.

Many toys are chosen because they are especially easy to activate, physically, and provide interesting sensory feedback.

While all of the new products here are highly recommended, the most outstanding products selected for these pages have received our Special Needs Adaptable Product (SNAP) Award for 2000. It's our hope that bringing attention to the products will serve kids and motivate manufacturers and publishers to become more aware of children with disabilities, who, like all children, need quality products.

Infants and Toddlers

All the toys in this section were selected because they provide plenty of sensory feedback. Some of the best toys for infants and toddlers need little or no adapting.

Note: Reviews of top-rated basics are in the Infants and Toddlers chapters and will also be of interest. Here we have focused on products that are adaptable, easy to activate, or loaded with sound, light, texture, or motion.

BASIC GEAR CHECKLIST FOR INFANTS AND TODDLERS

✓Mobile	✓Fabric blocks	✓Teethers
✓Musical toys	✓Soft huggables	✓Floor toys
✓Crib mirror	✓Manipulatives	✓Balls
✓Fabric rattles	✓Bath toys	✓Infant seat

■ Colorfun Grabbies 2000

(Gund $5) Soft rattles are a safer choice for babies that still can't control their hand motions. These small velour, easy-to-grasp and shake chick and frog rattles have stitched features. **Activity Tip:** Use for tracking by moving the rattle from side to side in baby's line of vision.

(732) 248-1500.

■ Deluxe Gymini 3-D Activity Gym

(Tiny Love $44.95-$54.95) Larger than the original, this primary color play mat with criss-cross arches and dangly toys is ideal for gazing and batting for visual stimulation. Because of dangly toys, use with supervision only. Basic gear for babies. (800) 843-6292.

■ Kick Start Gym 2000 SNAP AWARD

(Playskool $34.99) Baby can activate music, sounds and motion with a swipe of a hand at the dangling toys or by kicking the foot pad. Accidental hits will do for starters. If the sound startles baby, turn it off. Spinners above will still be activated. An innovative gym that's more stable than most, but should still be used only with adult supervision. (800) 752-9755.

■ Earlyears Soft Busy Blocks 2000

(International Playthings $12) These blocks have more give than most so baby can easily grasp them. One has a gentle rattle safely inside, another crinkles when touched, and the other squeaks. **Activity:** "Which block has the jingle? Is it this one?" Pick up one block and shake it. "Not this one." Continue until you find the one the jingles. Mix the blocks up and play the game again. Knowing the one with a jingle takes looking and listening. (800) 445-8347. Still top-rated, **Lamaze Clutch Cube** (Learning Curve $12.99) comes with four handles for easier grasping. (800) 704-8697.

■ Infant Carrier PlayCenter 2000

(Summer Infant $9.99) This activity bar attaches to any infant carrier seat and invites baby to reach out and touch. We love this one because it is uncomplicated with a smiley little figure that's easy to spin. Comes in primary colors or black, white and red. (800) 268-6237.

■ Tolo Musical Activity T.V.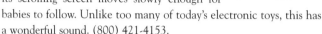

(Small World $20) This is a musical toy that starts out on the crib rail and becomes a great take-along/floor toy. We love the old-fashioned quality it has when it plays "It's A Small, Small World." Much like old Fisher-Price versions that many of us grew up with, its scrolling screen moves slowly enough for babies to follow. Unlike too many of today's electronic toys, this has a wonderful sound. (800) 421-4153.

■ Puppet Play Mates

(Tiny Love $11.95) Puppets are ideal for tracking and peek-a-boo games with your child. This innovative glove puppet has four inter-changeable heads that Velcro on. (800) 843-6292. Still recommended: **Lamaze's Peek-a-Boo Puppet** (Learning Curve $15). (800) 704-8697.

■ Slumbertime Soother

(Fisher-Price $34.99) There are traditional musical toys in the infant chapter that we recommend for all babies. This particular musical crib toy, however, has lights that change with the music (and soothing nature sounds) that provide added stimulation. With an innovative remote control, music can be restarted from 20 feet away. New for 2000, **Lights 'n' Sound Aquarium** ($29.99) has two fish that swim about in an "aquarium." Plays either music or sea sounds for auditory stimulation (happily with volume control). Looked promising, but was not ready for testing. (800) 432-5437.

■ Wimmer-Ferguson My First Photo Album

(Manhattan Toy $12) The bold graphics of this fabric book will attract and stimulate the youngest "readers". Nice for lap time sharing, focusing and talking. **Activity:** Add photos to the vinyl pockets and play a peek-a-boo game. "Where's Grandma?" Change photos often for new interest. See the infant chapter for this company's other high contract gazing toys. (800) 747-2454. Still top-rated: Sassy's **Visual Cards** ($6.99) that come with high contrast images and licks of primary colors. Flip them for a change of visual interest from time to time as they stand on the changing table or in the crib. (800) 323-6336.

Making Things Happen

■ Tomy Chuckling Charlie *2000*

(International Playthings $8.50) It's easy to push Charlie about on floor or tabletop. He giggles as he goes. **Activity:** On a large piece of poster board, draw a roadway that leads to either different shapes or colors. Make a batch of cards with corresponding colors or shapes. Each player draws a card and must move Charlie to the matching place on the board. First player to get a card with each color or shape is the winner. Can be played cooperatively. For an even easier to activate toy, the **Balancing Elephant** ($13) is a playful, but noisier twist on a chime ball. A swipe of the hand starts the music. Designed to roll around, but if you leave the ball attached to the stand it can be enjoyed on a table top. (800) 445-8347.

■ Enchanted Garden Sock Toys

(Manhattan Baby $10) Slip these bright velour mitts on hands or feet for warmth as well as visual and auditory stimulation. (800) 747-2454.

■ Scoop, Pour'n'Squirt *2000*

(Sassy $8) A child-friendly fish with a handle is ideal for filling and pouring water. Comes with two fish squirters that develop hand power as kids squeeze them. Also recommended, **Turtle Tower** ($8)—one of best tub toys ever. Three turtles stack on a center post base that attaches to the side of the tub. The best part is the funnel in the center post that spins as water runs through it! (800) 323-6336.

■ Tolo Activity Cube & Gripper Ball *2000*

(Small World $10 each) To develop two handed play, kids need a variety of manipulatives with interesting payoffs. An **Activity Cube** for little fingers to activate has a mirror, squeaker, roller and spinning ball. The **Gripper Ball** has four easy-to-grab rounded handles and a see-through hourglass in the middle with beads that roll from side to side. (800) 421-4153.

Balls & Rolling Toys

■ Colorfun Ball

(Gund $7–$12) Few toys are more basic than a ball to roll back and forth for early social games and to motivate kids to crawl. A brightly colored ball done in soft velour, that jingles and is easy to grasp, toss, and roll. New soccer and basketball are also fun. (732) 248-1500. Or look for **Jingle Ball** (The First Years $2.99), a colorful softball-sized ball, covered in washable parachute nylon with a quiet jingle inside. (800) 533-6708.

■ Nesting Action Vehicles *2000*

(Fisher-Price $8.99) A versatile set of four chunky vehicles can be stacked in a tower, rolled along the floor, lined up, or nested inside each other for peek-a-boo surprises! Our tester just liked rolling them. **Activity:** Using two cars at first, hide the littlest red car under one car. Ask "where's the red car?" Add more cars to the game. (800) 432-5437.

■ Sesame Street Pop & Go Vehicles *2000*

(Fisher-Price $4.99 each) We found these inexpensive vehicles great for motivating kids to move about. With popping beads safely enclosed in a see-through top they also have pull-back action so they really take off. (800) 432-5437.

Manipulatives

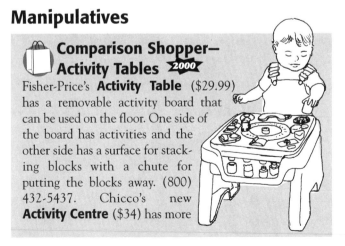

Comparison Shopper— Activity Tables *2000*

Fisher-Price's **Activity Table** ($29.99) has a removable activity board that can be used on the floor. One side of the board has activities and the other side has a surface for stacking blocks with a chute for putting the blocks away. (800) 432-5437. Chicco's new **Activity Centre** ($34) has more whistles and bells with a train that moves on a set track by pulling a lever. There is also a removable building block side but no fun chutes for the blocks. Both have their advantages- a toss up. (877) 424-4226.

■ Dunk & Clunk Circus Rings

(Sassy $8.50) Multi-textured rings and rattles slip into special slots in the lid of this see-through container. Beginners will like tasting, tossing, and dropping pieces into the plastic box, but will eventually use this innovative shape sorter for developing fine-tuning of wrist and finger action. Also top-rated, **Fascination Station** (great high-chair toy). (800) 323-6336.

■ Lamaze My First Fish Bowl 2000

(Learning Curve $19.99) For kids with visual disabilities the textures and varying sounds of each shape provide tactile cues. Babies explore the interesting textures and sounds of a rattling star fish, a crinkly crab, a jingly fish, and a squeaky crab. All come in a fabric fish bowl with clear vinyl sides for filling and dumping. (800) 704-8697.

■ Ambi Teddy Bear Carousel 2000

(Learning Curve $17.99) Push down on the big yellow knob and the yellow and red teddy bears inside the dome will spin quietly. A flat-bottomed top that's easy enough to learn to activate with independence. (800) 704-8697. Also interesting, the **Smile Go Round** (Brio $21), a flat-bottomed spinner with a second button that stops the spinning for double lesson in cause and effect. (888) 274-6869.

■ Bear City Activity Center 2000

(Chicco $34) A super combo toy that includes shapes to sort and hammer, bears to role play, doors to open, buttons to push and a plunger that makes two cars spin. Lots of plastic, but lots to do! (877) 424-4226.

■ Circus Rings

(Sassy $6.99) Classic size-order post and ring toys are so hard to do that kids with or without disabilities can't do them. Happily, there are more forgiving choices. Sassy's plastic single-sized stacking rings have interesting patterns, colors, and textures and fit in any order. (800) 323-6336. **Lamaze Stacking Rings** (Learning Curve $19.99) are larger than Sassy's and all fabric. Each ring has a different pattern and sound, and stacks in any order. (800) 704-8697.

Big Muscle Play

■ Easy Store Activity Zoo

(Little Tikes $49.99) With safely attached toys to spin and move, this open-air activity center is a good choice for motivating exploration and movement. Looked promising but was not available for testing. **Peek-a-Boo Activity Tunnel** BLUE CHIP (Little Tikes $45) This plastic tunnel is a playful invitation for crawlers to go through. **Activity ideas:** Try rolling a ball or small cars down ramp for child to catch. (800) 321-0183.

■ Soft Rockin' Tigger Rocker
2000 SNAP AWARD

(Little Tikes $39.99) Fabric covered and low to the ground, this huggable, easy-to-straddle rocker is especially kid-friendly and has a soothing action. (800) 321-0183.

■ Bigger Family Shuttle Bus Ride-On 2000

(Step 2 $29.99) Our tester not only loves riding this straddle-and-drive vehicle, he loves loading the chunky play figures on and off-he even takes them to bed! **Activity:** Encourage your child to make special pretend deliveries (pizza, ice cream!). (800) 347-8372.

Preschool and Early School Years

As children grow, they need a rich variety of playthings to match their expanding interests and abilities.

☼ **BASIC GEAR CHECKLIST**
FOR PRESCHOOL AND EARLY SCHOOL YEARS

✓ Construction toys   ✓ Art materials
✓ Sand and water toys   ✓ Big-muscle toys
✓ Musical toys   ✓ Electronic toys
✓ Toys for pretend   ✓ Puzzles, games,
   (dolls, trucks, puppets)   and manipulatives
✓ Tape player and tapes

Age ranges are purposely broad; products need to be selected on the basis of your child's particular needs. Many basic toys reviewed in the Preschool and Early School Years chapters will be of interest and need no special adaptation. Here we have focused on products that lend themselves to adaptation.

Sounds and Sights Toys

■ **Barney Song Magic Bongos** *2000*

(Playskool $29.99) Last year we raved about the **Song Magic Banjo** which used a light motion detector to activate the stringless banjo. The new **Bongos** set has its own magic. Hit either of the drum heads and it plays one of 11 songs; hit the instrument button and it plays one of five instruments. The speed with which you hit the drums directly affects the pace of the music you hear. It takes time to learn how to play at the right speed. **Activity:** Play a "Freeze!" game. Players clap or dance until the music stops and then eveybody must freeze! A fun game for developing listening skills. (800) 752-9755.

■ **Kids' TomTom Drum**

(Remo/Woodstock Percussion $40) For a more tradition drum, this can be played with beaters or hands. There is no right or wrong way to play a drum and beating out the rhythms of different kinds of

music sharpens children's listening abilities in a fun-filled way.
Activity: One person hits the drum and the other person must change positions with every beat. When you are moving, use exaggerated goofy motions and freeze into funny poses. Switch roles—kids love the power of making you move. (800) 422-4463.

■ Music Blocks *2000* SNAP AWARD

(Neurosmith $69.95) Want a rewarding tool for developing matching skills? Color concepts? Cause and effect? It's all here! If only all toys had the sound quality of this innovative product. With a touch of fingertips players activate a phrase of music or rhythm (depending on the cartridge). Shapes on the blocks determine what instrument you'll hear. Part of the fun is mixing up the shapes on the blocks for a variety of sounds. Kids with visual disabilities can "read" raised symbols on the blocks. We suggest also buying the percussion and orchestral cartridges. Pricey but one of the most innovative toys we've found for kids with or without disabilities. (562) 434-9856.

Manipulatives, Puzzles, and Tracking Games

■ Fruit, Farm, & Pets Puzzibilities *2000* SNAP AWARD

(Small World $8) Kids will have fun fitting these giant pegged whole-piece puzzles together. Lift the fish and there's a matching fish below. Each has three distinct pieces to know, name and match. (800) 421-4153.

■ Geometric Puzzle Board *2000*

(Guidecraft $15) Five big geometric shapes with stout, easy-to-grasp handles fit into the color matching spaces of the puzzle board. This classic styled puzzle is perfect for knowing and naming familiar shapes and colors. **Activity:** Put three or four chips under the puzzle pieces. Mark a die or make a spinner with each of the shapes. Players roll and take a chip from under the shape they roll. Winner is first to collect 10 chips. (800) 544-6526.

■ Plan Toys Form & Shape Boards
2000

(Small World $15 & up) These handsome wooden sorting boards develop matching skills, shape recognition and dexterity. The **Form Board,** with 9 solid pieces to lift and match, is easier than the 19 piece **Shape Matching Board** with each shape divided in two. (800) 421-4153.

■ I Can Spell! Alphabet Puzzle

(Tag Toys $40) Kids can explore letters with their eyes and hands with this large wooden puzzle. Word picture cards are used to match letters and to form familiar words. **Adaptation:** Add knobs to letters for easy grasping. Make enlarged word cards the same size as the letters. Encourage child to trace letters with fingers. (800) 488-4824.

■ Magic Sound Animal Blocks *2000*

(Small World $10) When you connect these animal picture blocks, the animals moo, baa, bark, or meow. A playful way to work with putting two parts together to make a whole, and get an auditory payoff. (800) 421-4153.

Comparison Shopper— Lacing Toys *2000*

One of the favorite ways to develop fun motor skills is with lacing toys. Learning Curve's **Kid Classics Threading Cheese** or **Apple** ($11.99 each) are the best place to start because there's no right or wrong way to thread the lace through the objects. (800) 704-8697. **Lauri's Lacing & Tracing Dinosaurs** *2000*

SNAP AWARD (Lauri $6.95) are slightly more challenging, with punched holes on sturdy chip board that kids "sew" with colorful laces. (800) 704- 8697.

■ Tomy Ball Party Connecting Bridge
2000 SNAP AWARD

(International Playthings $29) Hands down one of the best toys on the market. Two towers and multiple bridges (with ridges) become a runway for ten oversized (and safe) plastic balls that go bumpity-bumpity bump down the ramps. Can be configured (by parents) in multiple ways and combined with **Roll Around Tower** ($24.99). (800) 445-8347.

■ Beads on Wire Toys

(Educo $12 & up) These great tracking toys have colorful beads that can be turned, pushed, and counted. (800) 661-4142.

Games

Matching, Memory & Language Games

Games are entertaining ways for kids to develop social skills, and counting, matching, and color concepts. You'll find other good choices in Preschool, Early School and Computer chapters.

■ Maisy Memory Game **2000**

(Briarpatch $19.95) Features popular storybook character, Maisy with easy-to-identify objects to know and name. Still top-rated, **Goodnight Moon Game** ($19.95) a simple matching game for 2½ & up or more challenging, **I SPY Preschool Game** ($14.95) a terrific getting-ready-to-read game. (800) 232-7427.

■ Theodore Tugboat Rootin' Tootin' Card Game **2000**

(International Playthings $15) Players turn their cards one at a time at the same moment and if they see a match the first player to hit the special "tooting" bell takes all the cards that have been turned so far.

Requires looking at details and rapid reflexes! For a more traditional Lotto game, see **Picture Pairs** with clear photo images from DK (800) 445-8347.

■ Mr. Potato Head Electronic Game ⭐ 2000

(Playskool $7.99) Here's an entertaining way to know & name body parts. Players dress Mr. Potato Head with a push of his buttons and must follow through by pushing the enter button as well. So there are sequencing and listening skills here without the need for much dexterity. We just wish he didn't say- "You're doing good!" (800) 752-9755.

■ Barnyard Boogie Woogie ⭐ 2000

(International Playthings $20) Most of the action happens "off the board" as players must move and sound like the animal they land on before they can collect a playing piece. First to collect five animals wins. (800) 445-8347.

■ Little Linguist ⭐ 2000 SNAP AWARD

(Neurosmith $69.95) Fifteen play figures fit one by one on the player. Push buttons to hear name or sound figure makes. It comes with English and Spanish cartridges (French & Japanese available). For kids with language delays three-dimensional objects offer a more memorable association. Excellent sound quality! **Activity:** Put several objects in sight. Ask: Which animal roars? Child selects and self-corrects by using the toy. (562) 434-9856.

■ Simon Jr. ⭐ 2000

(Tiger $9.99) This classic electronic light and sound memory game has been shrunk to a hand-held size. Players can start at a slower beginner level but watch out the pace does pick up! Volume can be turned off. (847) 913-8100.

"Name That Shape" Games

Games that develop sense of touch are especially important for kids with visual disabilities. These products are similar but offer alternative ways of providing sensory feedback. Most come with more pieces than kids can handle, so start with a few and gradually add more.

■ Touch-N-Tell 2000

(Plan Toys $15) Distinctive textures on the wooden playing pieces match those on the board. **Activity:** Give child a chance to handle the blocks and talk about how each feel. Have child "find the block that feels smooth, rough, bumpy," etc. Introduce them to the board and try to find the slots in the board that match. (800) 421-4153.

■ Feel & Find 2000

(Simplex/ Battat $15) 22 sets of shapes and cards with the corresponding image are fun to play with in several ways. **Activities:** (1) Take only three cards and shapes for your child to match up to develop the ability to recognize images in both two and three dimensions. (2) Put some of the shapes in the bag and have child feel and name it. Pull it out of the bag to see if she's right. **Adaptation:** For kids with visual impairment, cut out and glue sandpaper to shapes and cards. (800) 247-6144.

■ Touch'n'Play Lotto

(Guidecraft $32) Four wooden playing boards and matching Lotto pieces have raised, textured shapes for sensory feedback through the fingertips. (800) 544-6526.

ABCs & 1, 2, 3s

Most kids learn to read with a mix of approaches; these products give kids playful practice with sounds and letters and things to count.

■ Dice With Holes & Cones

(Let's Learn $12.50 & $19.95) These big fabric dice come in 4" or 8" cubes and have holes that children can poke a finger into as they count. You can one use or two for counting or adding games or for any game that calls for dice. **Activity:** Play a game of odds & evens: Player 1 is odds, Player 2 is evens. Players take turns rolling die or dice. Player 1 must roll an odd number to get a point; Player 2 must roll and even number; play a 20-point game (800) 675-0090.

■ Magic Walls & Foam Magic Letters & Numerals 2000

(Dowling $25) Post this oversized magnetic board (2'x 3') to the wall and now kids can use the raised foam magnetic letters, shapes, and numerals ($12.95 a set) to play word and math games. (800) 624-6381. Kids may find these thick **Jumbo Letters & Numbers** (Learning Resources $8.95 per set) easier to grasp than the usual size. Available in upper and lower case letters and numerals. (800) 222-3909.

■ Wooden Alphabet & Math Blocks with Braille

(Uncle Goose $30) These wooden blocks look like classic alphabet blocks, but with one wonderful difference! Two faces of each cube have a letter impression and raised Braille cell for that letter. . New for 2000 a **Braille math set** ($17) includes 0–9 and plus and minus sign. (888) 774-2046

■ Letter Detective 2000

(Ravensburger $18) A special box that kids can put their hands into is used for feeling and identifying alphabet letters by touch. There are several games suggested that testers enjoyed. **Adaptation:** You can also use this well-made box for other feel-and-say games. (800) 886-1236.

■ Hug'n'Learn Little Leap 2000

(Leap Frog $39.99) This huggable frog plays games with letters and sounds. Unlike other quiz machines, this does not limit answers to what comes before or after a letter to one letter. It cues kids to see multiple answers. Kids with limited gripping power may have trouble activating Frog's hands, so test before you buy. New for 2000, and easier to activate, **Fun & Learn Phonics Bus** ($34.99) sings "The Wheels on the Bus" and says letters or sounds when pushed. Has quiz mode for finding letters, but it's mighty loud! (800) 701-5327.

■ Phonics Writing Desk 2000
SNAP AWARD

(Leap Frog $34.99) One of the most amazing phonics toys we've ever tested! It provides, visual, auditory and tactile feedback in a playful way. Kids get to practice

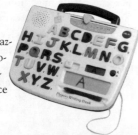

writing letters with a stylus on a magic-slate-like surface below an electronic window that beeps as it demonstrates how to shape each letter. It switches from upper to lower case letters. Still top-rated, **Create-a-Word Supermat** ($34.99) Kids push letters printed on the giant (39" x 28") talking mat and it says letters or sounds. (800) 701-5327.

■ Number Express

(Lauri $13.95) Learning number sequence from 1–5, and the shapes of numerals, is fun with a five-piece train that links together like a puzzle. For counting, big easy-to-grasp pegs fit onto each car and colorful pegs can be stacked. Also, **Tall Stacker Peg & Pegboard Set** ($13.95). Not for kids who still mouth their toys. **Activity ideas:** Explore the materials in a playful way. Challenge child to discover how tall a stack of pegs they can make before they fall. Are there more red pegs or yellow? Make patterns with a few pegs like yellow, green, yellow—what comes next? (800) 451-0520.

Construction Toys

Building invites creative thinking and decision making. Color, counting, and size concepts are built in (we couldn't resist). Best of all, blocks offer a win-win opportunity because there is no right or wrong way for them to be used. Kids with visual challenges can learn their shapes by rubbing the textured blocks on cheeks or hands. For shopping info about classic and new blocks sets, see the Preschool and Early School Years sections.

How to adapt blocks:

Add strips of sticky-backed Velcro tape to standard wooden unit blocks or Mega Blocks for a more stable base for building. To increase two-handed skills, have child play at pulling blocks apart and putting them together.

Use colorful plastic Lego Primo, Duplo, and standard Lego building blocks for color-matching, counting, and size discrimination concepts for a child with learning disabilities. **Activities:** Provide containers and play size, shape, or color sorting games to reinforce concepts. Put the toys away by playing a singing color game: To the tune of "Where is

Thumbkin?" sing, "Where is red? Where is red? Here it is! Here it is!"

Pretend Play

Pretend play is not just great fun. It's the way kids develop imagination and creative thinking skills and try out being big and powerful. Pretending also brings the world down to the child's size and understanding. It's a way to develop communication skills and an outlet for expressing feelings and fears.

■ Create a Clown or Princess *2000*

(Creative Education of Canada $25) Any of these costumes are great for pretend, language and even dexterity because kids help design their costumes with Velcro-backed decorations that range from bells, feathers, pom-poms, gems and badges. New for *2000*, The **Clown** and **Princess's** sets. We still prefer the action drama of **Create-a-Fireman, Dress-a-Police,** and our favorite (especially for birthdays!), **Create-a-Crown** ($12). (800) 982-2642.

Housekeeping Equipment

Playing with replicas of real household equipment is a safe way for kids to step into new roles. Add real ingredients to play kitchens like water for pouring, play-dough, dry cereal, etc. Kids love the messiness of it all, which motivates ample touching and exploration that strengthens fingers and hands as well as language and curiosity. For descriptions of toy kitchens, plates, and other pretend props like phones and mowers, see reviews in the Toddlers & Preschool sections.

■ Pretend & Play Teaching Telephone
2000 SNAP Award

(Learning Resources $39.95) For learning functional use of a phone, important numbers and the concept of 911, this is a gem! Even the concept of taking messages is built into the play. You can program in any phone number and leave a message. When your child calls that number she hears your message. (888) 222-3909.

■ **Fruit Play Set** *2000*

(Plan Toys/Small World $15) Like a real knife, there's a right and wrong side of the wooden "knife" that kids use to cut apart Velcroed halves of three wooden fruits. Veggies set also available. (800) 421-4153.

> **ACTIVITY TIP:** For sniffing, tasting, and touching, present real fruits in parts or wholes. Put pieces in a bag. Child must name fruit without visual cues.

Transportation Toys

■ Bigger Family Van

(Step 2 $15) Four big play figures—a mom, dad, brother and sister—are fun to load and unload in the big family van that's scaled for easy roll-about games. Also in the same line, a jaunty jet with two play figures, a school bus, and easy-to-activate "merry-go-round." **Activity idea:** Dropping passengers off or picking them up can make a fun sequencing game. (800) 347-8372.

■ Happy Crane Construction *2000*

(Fisher-Price $19.99) There's so much to make happen on this small pretend crane-shaped setting (that smiles a la Thomas the Tank. Comes with a dump truck (that beeps) and "boulders" to place down three easy to activate chutes. Also consider, **Little People Fun Sounds Garage** ($30) that has been updated with electronic sounds of the garage (horns, keys, cash register, telephone, and hammer). (800) 432-5437.

■Little People Adventure Airlines 2000

(Fisher-Price $14.99) This jumbo plane has a handle to lift it off the ground, propellers that spin, wheels that click, and two little people to load and unload.

Also clever, the **Little People School Bus** ($14.99) an updated classic. Four Little People bounce up and down as this jaunty yellow bus with googly eyes rolls along. It has a wheelchair ramp and is slightly larger than the old model. Fun for loading and unloading. **Activities:** Play "Who Got Off?" Have child look at the four Little People. "It" closes her eyes and you remove one passenger. Can she tell who got off the bus? Also: For language, use figures to act out "The Wheels On the Bus Go Round & Round." (800) 432-5437.

■ Tolo Baby Driver Steering Wheel 2000

(Small World $10) Attach this suction-cup toy to high chair or any table for miles of action. Adjustable yellow steering wheel with a moving gear shift, beeping horn, and ratcheting sounds! (800) 421-4153. For more bells and whistles, older kids will enjoy the sounds and lights of V-Tech's classic **Little Smart Tiny Tot Driver** ($22) an electronic dashboard and steering wheel. (800) 521-2010.

Remote-Control Vehicles

(Little Tikes/Tyco/Mattel/Playskool) For kids with physical challenges, remote-control toys are often favorites. We generally look for a single button to start, stop, and turn, rather than complex vehicles. There are good choices this year in all price ranges. See Preschool and Early School Chapters for our top picks.

■ X-V Racers Scorcher Chamber Stunt Set 2000

(Mattel $24) This is the newest in the line of X-V Racer track sets and is even more fun because the vehicles now light up as they travel. Use the power charger to rev up the specially motorized X-V racer and watch it zoom. These cars ($10 each) can be used on or off track. To get them going, the car must be placed on the charger as kids count to ten, so there's a bit of math built in. Put them on the floor or a track and watch them go! A good choice for learning to sequence of steps needed to rev them up. **Activity:** Use a long empty box or an extra large mailing tube to create a tunnel that cars can zoom through. (800) 524-8697.

■ Wild Wrecker Motorized Gears Building Set 🏆2000

(Learning Resources $37) By far the best gear sets this year come from Learning Resources. Testers loved both the **Wild Wrecker** that builds motorized trucks and the zany **Oogly Googly** ($37) kit for making alien-like creatures. Directions for both sets were less than great, but still got great reviews. 7 & up. Both are great solo toys that develop problem solving skills as kids make moving "machines." Still top-rated: **Gears! Gears! Gears!,** the original and simpler set with one size gear ($20/$40). (800) 222-3909.

Trains

See Preschool chapter for latest wooden train sets. For kids who can't fit tracks together, adapt by mounting to a play board. A tabletop makes this toy accessible to a child in a wheelchair.

Puppets

Few toys provide a better way to get kids to express their feelings. Without the need to move themselves, kids in wheelchairs or beds can take on pleasingly active roles through the puppets. For top-rated puppets and stages, see the Preschool and Early School Years sections.

How to Adapt a Puppet

Fill the puppet with a Styrofoam cone. Push a wooden dowel into the cone and your puppet is ready for action!

Place puppets over big plastic soda bottles that can be moved around like dolls.

Attach a magnet to stuffed finger puppets or Little People-type figures and use them on a metal cookie sheet.

For a kid who can't grasp a rod, attach the puppet to the child's arm with Velcro straps. His hand may not go inside the puppet, but the child can activate the whole puppet by moving his arm.

Velcro puppets with changeable features have wonderful play value. **Pick a Puppet** (Creative Education of Canada $13). (800) 982-2642.

Morphing Marty (Manhattan Toy $15) **2000** **SNAP AWARD** is a green talking head that comes with 22 features that attch with Velcro. (800) 747-2454.

Medical Pretend Props & Games

For kids with chronic medical needs, pretend props can help prepare for treatments or work through feelings and fears. See Preschool Chapter for the best Doctor's & Vet's Kits.

VIDEO TIP: The Doctor, Your Friend (CBS Fox $9.95) With his usual calm approach, Mister Rogers takes young viewers for a well-child check-up explaining what the doctor is doing as she goes along. Closed captioned. Video Stores.

Dolls & Dollhouses

Many wonderful dolls and soft animals are described in the Toddlers, Preschool, and Early School Years sections.

Mail Order Dolls

The dolls below will be especially interesting for children with special needs since they are available with adaptive equipment such as walkers, wheelchairs, and braces. All collections include boy and girl dolls and are also available in multiethnic variations. We suggest requesting catalogs from several before you buy:

• **Lakeshore** ($30) 16" vinyl dolls & various equipment. (800) 421-5354.

- **Pleasant Company** ($82 doll / $28 wheelchair only). (800) 845-0005.

- **Constructive Playthings** ($20) 15" fabric dolls with a younger look than vinyl dolls. Easier to bend to fit into a wheelchair. Various equipment. (800) 832-0572.

Comparison Shopper— Potty-Going Dolls

Hard to believe there are so many choices in this department! This year there were lots of dolls that talk and giggle while they tinkle—we found all that chatting a distraction. We prefer the pricey (but tubbable) anatomically correct **Fan-Fan** boy or girl drink-and-wet dolls ($80) from Corolle. A smaller, newer, and less expensive boy doll with potty seat ($44) looked promising but was not ready for testing. (800) 628-3655.

Notable Mass Market Dolls

■ Decky Doll 🏆

(Mattel $23) Barbie has a new pal, a fashion doll in a two-toned wheelchair. This year Becky is the school photographer. (800) 524-8697.

■ ActiMates Barney

(Microsoft $99) It's like having a playdate with a real live Barney! Relatively lightweight and soft to the touch, Barney's arms and head move, but that's not all! Barney keeps engaging the player with songs and games, and encourages child to continue. Games encourage child to play & sing along. Almost magical as a stand-alone toy, Barney also hooks up to the VCR or computer (see Computer chapter for review).Takes 6 AA batteries. '98 SNAP AWARD (800) 426-9400. Also top-rated, **Playtime Big Bird** (Tyco $30), who says "peek-a-boo," "patty cake," and "This Little Piggy." (800) 488-8697.

■ Teletubbies 2000

(Playskool & Microsoft) We agree with critics who say that Teletubbies do little to develop language, and that their non-verbal sounds mirror rather than expand children's verbal skills. That said, kid testers enjoyed hugging the dolls that say a few phrases. Kids also liked the new Actimate version with color and light shows that are activated by squeezing the dolls' hands. We wish they didn't light up with alphabet letters that they don't say. Playskool (800) 752-9755 / Microsoft (800) 426-9400.

Dollhouses and Equipment 2000

🛍 Comparison Shopper— Dollhouses

Little People Home Sweet Home (Fisher-Price $29.99) is portable, smaller and less detailed than your typical dollhouse. It closes to store all the pieces. Fisher-Price's new **Loving Family Dollhouse** ($49.99) designed with greater detail has all the amenities of home but is very, very pink (did we mention how pink?). (800) 432-5437. Plan Toys' **Wooden Doll Houses** ($99 & $139) have a modern-looking A-frame design with open roofs for easy access. The pricier one has sliding doors and wallpaper. Wooden furnishings for each room are beautifully crafted. ($20 per room). (800) 421-4153. **Activity:** Play a little memory game of "Who's at the door?" Have child cover eyes. Put one of the play people outside. Child opens eyes and tries to guess who is missing. Child opens dollhouse door to see.

■ Playmobil System X 2000

(Playmobil $99 & up) We like many of the accessory sets for this system almost as much as the structure itself which has a police headquarters, hospital and heliport. Adults will need to assemble the building. There's a lot of little pieces of plastic detailing here, so this is for older kids. (800) 752-9662.

Magnetic, Felt, & Fabric Dolls & Playsets

Many magnetic and fabric play sets are good for dramatic play, language, storytelling and concept development. Here are our top-rated choices:

■ FELTKids Playhouse 🏆*2000* SNAP AWARD

(Learning Curve $14.99) This felt Playhouse Playmat unfolds into four colorful rooms that kids can decorate with characters and play scenes furnishings ($9.95 per room). **Activity:** Use the cut outs to reinforce position words like upstairs, downstairs, under, next to, etc. as they arrange the rooms. Play an "I Spy" game using position words: "I spy something upstairs that's red." (800) 704-8697.

Q **Adaptation for fabric toys:** Make your own play board by gluing colored felt on the lid and sides of a sturdy box. Use board for sticking on cut-out shapes, letters, and animals. Box can be used to store pieces.

■ Magic Cloth Paper Dolls & Play Board 🏆*2000*

(Schylling $12) These magnetic cutouts come in a variety of familiar characters (such as Arthur, Rugrats, and Blue's Clues. A newly designed 13" x 12" board with handle and pockets for storing playing pieces. Also new, **Barbie Boutique** with Barbie clothes which, unlike the 3D variety, need little dexterity to handle. (800) 541-2929.

■ Magnetic Fun Board 🏆*2000*

(Small World $10) Characters from Thomas the Tank Engine are easily moved around this handsome magnetic board. Playing pieces that look like chunky puzzle pieces are easier to grasp and slide about than many magnetized play sets. (800) 421-4153.

■ Woodkins 2000

(Pamela Drake $11.95) For kids who don't have the dexterity to sew, cut, or paste, this wooden doll frame has fabric choices that stay in place with a "frame" that closes over the edges of the doll. Pippy has four faces for changing moods. Available as boy or girl, and several ethnic variations (800) 966-3762.

> **Q** **Adaptation idea for magnetic toys:** Put pieces on a cookie sheet so that players can see the choices and reach for a change easily.

Art Supplies

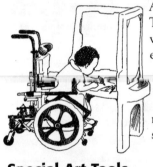

Art materials are more than fun. They provide a great way to motivate kids to develop dexterity and express feelings without words, and they give tons of sensory feedback. Creative exploration, without lots of rights, wrongs, or rules, also gives kids a wonderful sense of "can do" power.

Special Art Tools

❋ **Chubby Colored Pencils** (Alex $10) These pencils have thicker "lead," an easier-to-grasp hexagonal shape, and are especially wonderful for kids who cannot grasp traditional pencils. (800) 666-2539.

❋ **Beginner Paintbrushes** (Alex 3 for $6) These extra-large brushes with handles shaped like bulbs help kids with fine motor difficulties to paint. Also, **Sponge Painters.** (800) 666-2539.

❋ **Chunkie Markers** (Bluepath $10 & up) Bypass brushes altogether! Washable paint in easy-to-grasp bottles with sponge applicators. Bluepath (800) 463-2388.

Stamp Kits and Stencil Kits. Although we like kids to create their own pictures, stampers and stencils can be extremely satisfying for older kids who want realistic results. To adapt stampers for kids with fine motor difficulties, glue a dowel handle to the back of each stamp.

Play-Doh (Hasbro $2 & up) Ideal for pounding, poking, and molding. A rolling pin is great for pretend. For kids who are reluctant to get their fingers into the action, wrap the ball of dough around a small surprise. (800) 327-8264.

Crayola Model Magic (Crayola $5) Older kids will like this soft, white, pliable compound that air dries in 24 hours and can be painted. (800) 272-9652.

Tutti Frutti Play Putty (International Playthings $5 & up) Putty comes in such scents as mint, banana, and even bubble gum. Scented feedback makes it especially appealing as a playful learning tool for kids with visual challenges. (800) 445-8347.

> **ADAPTATION IDEA: Adapting Crayons, Markers, Glue Sticks, and Brushes:** For an easier grip, use a foam hair curler over the drawing tool. Or wrap a crayon with a small piece of Velcro and then have the child wear a mitten. The Velcro will stick to the mitten, allowing the child to color without dropping the tool.

As always, we look for craft kits that are quick and easy, and create satisfying results. Here are our favorites:

■ **Tug Boat Craft Kit** *2000*

(Creativity for Kids $14) Easy to assemble, the pieces of the jaunty wooden tugboat need little sanding—except for the fun of sanding. With some easy pasting and painting, kids create a real floatable tugboat and barge for floor or tub play. (800) 311-8684.

■ Paint the Wild Kits *2000*

(Balitono $7.50 & up) Beautifully crafted wood carvings that kids can paint and display or use as play figures. New for *2000* : A 3-drawer treasure chest, cats, or bugs. (609) 936-8807.

■ Hand Painted Ceramic Treat Jar *2000*

(Creativity for Kids $18) After it's painted this ceramic treat jar makes a perfect container for treats. Comes with acrylic paints that need to dry 24 hours and then pop it into the oven for a final finish. Adult supervision. Still top-rated, **Ceramic Piggy Bank** ($12). (800) 311-8684.

■ Musical Jewelry Box Activity Kit
2000 SNAP AWARD

(Alex $15) A small ballerina pops up when you open this lavender music box that plays "When You Wish Upon a Star." Our tester couldn't wait to decorate her "treasure" box with jewels, stickers and glitter glue. A perfect gift kids can make and use. (800) 666-2539.

■ Scratch-Art Fabulous Frame & Key Chains *2000*

(Scratch-Art $10 & up) Scratch the black surface of the special paper with a wooden drawing tool to reveal bright colors. Our favorite kits created frames and key chains. Very quick. Comes with stencils but free form is fine. (800) 377-9003.

■ Crayola Wipe-Off Play Mat *2000*

(Crayola $10 & up) Crayola's improved White Board (11" x14") can be used with special wipe-off markers. **Adaptation:** Add Velcro strips to convert this into a triangular stand-up slanted board. Also available, a smaller version that zips closed. (800) 272-9652.

■ Polaroid Cameras *2000*

(Polaroid $24.99 & up) Our testers enjoyed the novelty of the new **Polaroid Taz** (you know, as in manian) and **Barbie** cameras that can be used with special film that frames the picture with Looney Tunes or Barbie-styled flowers. Great for special occasions! Older testers also raved about the new **I-Zone Instant Pocket Camera** that is ultra-compact and comes with flash and focus-free lens. It takes 12 sharp but

extra tiny color photos (1" x 1½"). Film $5.99/$6.99 with sticker backing for decorating notebooks or cards. (800) 343-5000.

ACTIVITY TIPS: Smelly Art: Add a few drops of scented oil or spices to homemade dough for extra sensory stimulation. Play a "smelling matching" game: Make pairs of matching balls of putty in paper cups and cover with foil. Punch small holes in foil for sniffing. Players take turns smelling cups to make matching pairs. Add more pairs as child develops the ability to make matches.

Dab-a-Dab-a-Do Sponge Art: Sponges are easy to grab and motivate artistic and messy art explorations. Cut your own sponges or buy a premade set.

Marble Painting: Place a piece of paper in a shallow box. Dip a spoonful of marbles in tempera paint and place them in the box. Tip box to produce a marvelous marble masterpiece. Great for kids with limited motor control.

Make a Slanted Play Board: For kids who need a slanted surface to work on, cut the sides of a cardboard box at a slant and it's all ready for coloring and other projects or see **Crayola Wipeoff Play Mat** above.

■ Magna Doodle *2000*

(Fisher-Price $10 & up) Kids draw directly on the no-mess board with stylus or magnetic shapes. The new version has shapes that stay in place better. **Adaptation:** Add tall grips to the magnetic shapes for kids who cannot grasp the small "pegs." Glue wooden dowels or sponge cut-outs in the same shape as the magnet. New for *2000* , **Barbie Magna Doodle** allows kids to "dress Barbie" with magnetic forms. The new Baby Magna Doodle did not test well. (800) 432-5437.

Easels

There are a number of great stand-alone or table-top easels on the market. See Preschool chapter.

Big Muscles/Physical Play

Toys that challenge children to use their big muscles help them develop gross motor coordination, a sense of their own place in space, independence, and self-esteem.

■ Air Cushion Hockey
2000 SNAP AWARD

(Hedstrom $67) Without requiring a huge investment, air hockey is a fun family game. With adjustable legs and a fan (not too loud). Our testers gave this table high ratings. Works well for kids in wheelchair or not. (800) 233-3271.

■ Laser Tennis   **2000 SNAP AWARD**

(Tiger $39.99) You can play this game sitting down. So it may not use big, big muscles, but it's a racket sport—sort of. Testers were amazed that the "tennis ball" is really an LED light that moves across the playing board when hit with a special reflector racket. It won't replace Ping Pong, but it takes less space, there's no ball to pick up, and can be played solo against the computer. (847) 913-8100.

■ Metal Detector   **2000**

(Wild Planet $13) Young sleuths will hunt up hidden metal treasures with this full-size metal detector that lights up and beeps when you find metal. **Activity:** Stage a metal treasure hunt that can motivate kids to explore. Long handle makes this wheelchair-friendly. (800) 247-6570.

■ Easy Score Basketball Set

(Little Tikes $35) This looks like a big kid's hoop, but it's designed for young slam dunkers, adjusting from 2½' to 4'. Unlike most, the hoop has an extra-wide back and a big backboard to make scoring easier. For larger sets, see Preschool Chapter. (800) 321-0183.

■ 3-in-1 Baseball Trainer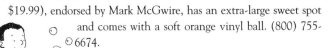

(Little Tikes $29.99) Tee balls are the way to go for beginning sluggers who do not have the eye-hand coordination to hit a pitched ball. This new set also has a pop-up pitching machine for more advanced hitting. Comes with five balls and user-friendly flat-sided bat. (800) 321-0183. The oversized **Vortex Power Bat** (OddzOn $19.99), endorsed by Mark McGwire, has an extra-large sweet spot and comes with a soft orange vinyl ball. (800) 755-6674.

■ Tonka Bubble Fire Truck

(OddzOn $19.99) Push the red fire truck and tons of little bubbles emerge. The faster you push, the more bubbles you get! Makes bubbles more easily than the classic Fisher-Price **Bubble Lawn Mower** that requires more speed to produce the bubbles. (800) 755-6674.

■ Koosh Loop Darts

(OddzOn $16.99) Satisfies the desire for an older "cooler" toy that is still kid-safe. Played with loopy Koosh balls that cling to a special dart board. Beginners will find hitting the target a challenge while more advanced players may like the math built into the scoring process. **Adaptation:** Simplify the scorekeeping math by giving a 1/5/10 value to the colors on the score board. (800) 755-6674.

🛍️ Comparison Shopper— Playhouses

Patio & **Victorian Playhouses** (Little Tikes $250 & up) have one wall that swings out, making them especially accessible for wheelchair or walker. Opening wall provides a larger play area. Both have a table for two, built-in doll seat, as well as a complete kitchen with stove, sink, storage, and big windows. These are big pieces of equipment for children of mixed ages, with many years of play value built in. (800) 321-0183.

Push Toys

See Toddler Chapter.

🛍️ Comparison Shopper— Pedal-Free Easy Riders 2000

For a first ride-on, your best bet is the new but less maneuverable **Push & Ride Racer** or **Semi Truck** (Little Tikes $20). Little Tikes' classic **Cozy Coupe II** ($44.99) has been updated for 2000 with a neat electronic key and horn. (800) 321-0183. For firefighters in training, Step 2's **Fire Engine for Two** ($90) is a fun choice. (800) 347-8372. Both run on foot power (no pedals) so kids need to use big muscles for physical play. We like the gender-free colors of both.

> 🛍️ **SHOPPING TIP:** Battery-operated ride-in cars that can be activated with a touch of a button may be a good choice for kids who are unable to pedal. Such toys, however, require constant supervision, regular battery recharges, and a hefty investment.

Trikes and Bikes

Your child may be able to ride a trike or bike with few or no adaptations. You'll find our guidelines for buying and descriptions of top-rated wheeled toys in the Preschool and Early School Years sections.

How to Adapt a Wheel Toy

Adapting a bike may involve adding an easily made belt of Velcro. Other kids may need a trunk-support seating system, foot harnesses, or a hand-driven trike. Two companies that specialize in adapted riding toys and supplies are J. A.

Preston Corp. (800) 631-7277 and Flaghouse Inc. (800) 221-5185.

Balls

Large balls invite gross motor and social play. Five notable sets with added sensory feedback: **Scent Balls** (Hedstrom $1.99) Kids loved the orange, bubble gum, and peanut butter smell of these 6" balls. (800) 233-3271. **Gertie Balls** (Small World $3.99 & up) are soft and slightly sticky to the touch, making them easier to hold on to. (800) 421-4153.

■ Turbo Hoops

(Hedstrom $89.99) Who needs the arcade? Now kids can play hoops at home! This hoops game has an electronic scorer, comes with three balls, and folds against the wall when not in use. Fabric and net act as a catcher for the balls, and the height seems right for a kid in a wheelchair. Fun way to build upper-body strength. Takes patience to assemble and 4 AA batteries. (800) 765-9665.

Sand Fun

For kids who can't get down on the ground to play in the sandbox, why not bring the sand up to them? Put a small sandbox on a picnic table and, voilà! child in a wheelchair can now dig in.

Books

For years, children with special needs were essentially invisible in picturebooks. Today publishers are issuing more books that reflect feelings of, and issues faced by, children who are physically or mentally challenged.

Friends and Family

■ What Happens Next?

(by Cheryl Christian/photos by Laura Dwight, Star Bright Books $3.95) Here's a baby on the left page and a tub on facing page. What happens next? Open the sturdy flap page and see the baby taking a bath. A series of sequencing events are caught in photos with the "answer" in the fold out. Photos include a child with Down syndrome. Also see, **Where's the Puppy?** (800) 788-4439.

■ Be Good to Eddie Lee

(by Virginia Fleming/illus. by Floyd Cooper, Philomel $14.95) Jim Bud does not want to be bothered with "that dummy" Eddie Lee when he and Christy go hunting for frog eggs. Eddie Lee, a neighbor with Down syndrome, follows them and ends up showing Christy who is really a dummy. 5–9.

■ Where's Chimpy?

(by Bernice Rabe/photos by Diane Schmidt, Whitman $13.95) Misty, a little girl with Down syndrome, does not want to go to bed without her toy monkey, Chimpy. With help from Dad, she solves the mystery of the lost monkey by recalling the events of the day. 3 & up.

NOTABLE PREVIOUS WINNERS: My Buddy (by Audrey Osofsky/illus. by Ted Rand, Holt $14.95) about a boy with muscular dystrophy and his dog; **Leo the Late Bloomer** (by Robert Kraus/ illus. by Jose Aruego, Harper new board book edition $6.96); **Patrick and Emma Lou** (by Nan Holcomb, Turtle $6.95) about a boy with CP and his walker, and his friend with spina bifida.

Siblings

■ Big Brother Dustin

(by Alden R. Carter/photos by Dan Young with Carol Carter, Whitman $14.95) Dustin, a boy with Down Syndrome, prepares with his parents and grandparents for the arrival of his baby sister. Beautifully told and marvelously illustrated with photos that capture the ups, downs, and wonder of expectant-hood——across generations. 3 & up.

■ Bird Boy 2000

(by Elizabeth Starr Hill/illus. by Lesley Liu, Farrar Straus $15) Chang has never been able to speak with words, but he is able to communicate with his father's fishing birds and dreams of raising one of his own. Hill gives young readers an unusual glimpse into life on the Li River with a touching story about a boy who doesn't let an untrustworthy friend or his disability keep him from his dreams.

■ Ian's Walk: A Story about Autism

(by Laurie Lears/illus. by Karen Ritz, Whitman $14.95) Ian, who has autism, hears, tastes, and sees things differently from his two sisters. So a simple walk to the park to feed the ducks is anything but simple. Told in the first person by his sister, this tender tale captures the ambivalent feelings that siblings must deal with as they also deal with their brother's special ways of experiencing the world. A reassuring tale for siblings. 5 & up.

■ Little Louie the Baby Bloomer

(by Robert Kraus/illus. by Jose Aruego & Ariane Dewey, HarperCollins $15.95) Little Louie is late in learning how to throw a ball, pull a wagon, rattle his rattle, and talk. But Leo, his big brother and the original late bloomer, takes the time to teach him and in Little Louie's own good time—he blooms. A continuation of a tender and reassuring classic about a family of patient tigers. Not to be missed! 3 & up.

■ Way To Go, Alex! 2000

(by Robin Pulver/ illus. by Elizabeth Wolf, Albert Whitman $14.95) When Carly helps her brother (who has mental retardation) train for the Special Olympics she forgets to prepare him for running through the blue ribbon at the finish line! This tender story reflects much of the ache along with the pride and affection siblings have for their sibs with disabilities. 6–8.

PREVIOUSLY RECOMMENDED BOOKS ABOUT DOWN SYNDROME: Veronica's First Year (by Jean S. Rheingrover/illus. by Kay Life, Whitman $12.95) When Nathan's sister is born with Down Syndrome, his parents help him understand that she will do many things on a different time schedule from his. **Thumbs Up, Rico!** (by Maria Testa/illus. by Diane Paterson, Whitman $11.95) Rico, a boy with Down syndrome, is the star of this chapter book in which he makes a new friend and finds a place on the basketball court. 7 & up.

Kids Coping in Mainstream Classrooms and the World

■ The Gym Day Winner

(by Grace Maccarone/illus. by Betsy Lewin, Scholastic, $3.50) Sam is not the fastest player in 1st grade, but team work helps him to score anyway. Pam, a girl in a wheelchair, is just one of the winning team members—not the one who needs help. A refreshing twist.

■ Seeing Things My Way

(by Alden R. Carter/photos by Carol S. Carter, Whitman $14.95) Amanda goes to a mainstream class, but gets a lot of extra help with her schooling with special equipment and teachers. This first-hand account tells how the world looks to Amanda and other kids with severe visual impairments and optimistic and determined outlooks. 6–9.

Inspirational Books

■ Waiting for Mr. Goose *2000*

(by Laurie Lears/illus. by Karen Ritz, Whitman $14.95) Stephen has AD/HD and is always being told to slow down and pay attention. When he finds a goose that needs his help, he discovers that can be extremely resourceful and patient!

■ Howie Helps Himself

(by Joan Fassler/illus. by Joe Lasker, Whitman $13.95) Howie, a boy with cerebral palsy, wants to be able to move his wheelchair on his own. A book that reinforces a positive sense of "can do." 4–8.

■ Let's Dance!

(by George Ancona, Morrow $16) A celebration of dance that looks at many types of dance from different cultures, as well as dancers in wheelchairs. 5 & up.

PREVIOUSLY RECOMMENDED INSPIRATIONAL BOOKS: **Brave Irene** (by William Steig, Farrar, Straus); **Harry's Pony** (by Barbara Ann Porte/illus. by Yossi Abolafia, Greenwillow $15).

For the Visually Challenged

■ Rugby & Rosie

(by Nan Parson Rossiter, Dutton $14.99) Rugby is a Labrador retriever who is less than thrilled when his family bring home Rosie, a lab pup. A bond grows between the dogs and the boy who cares for them. Readers get a sense of the love and work needed to raise a guide dog. 5 & up.

■ Listen For the Bus

(by Patricia McMahon/photos by John Godt, Boyds Mills $15.95) A photo essay about David, who used to go to a school for the blind, but is now going to public school and learning his way around. 5 & up.

> **SHOPPING TIP:** A neat novelty for a child learning to read Braille is a plastic placemat with the Braille alphabet imprinted on it. From Straight Edge.

Coping with Hearing Impairments and Introducing Sign Language

Every day more than 500,000 Americans use American Sign Language to communicate. Few other subjects have so caught the imagination of artists and publishers. You'll find great choices here for kids of every age.

■ Opposites & Happy Birthday!

(by Angela Bednarczyk & Janet Weinstock, Star Bright Books $4.95 each) These two Beginner's Books of Signs are handsomely done in sturdy cardboard. Opposites are shown with photos plus drawings of a child signing each word. **Happy Birthday!** has signs for words like gifts, candles, cake, and happy birthday greeting! (800) 772-4220.

■ The Handmade Counting Book

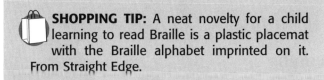

(by Laura Rankin, Dial $15.99) Painterly images of toys, seashells and flowers help readers learn to sign numbers from 1–20, 25, 50, 75, & 100 in American Sign Language. All ages. Also: **The Handmade Alphabet** .

PREVIOUSLY RECOMMENDED SIGNING BOOKS:
Handsigns (by Kathleen Fain, Chronicle) All ages; **HANDTALK ZOO** (by George Ancona & Mary Beth, Aladdin) **More Simple Signs** (by Cindy Wheeler, Viking).

■ Dad and Me in the Morning

(by Patricia Lakin/illus. by Robert Steele, Whitman $11.95) Before dawn, a special alarm clock wakes a young boy who is deaf. Quietly, he and his father and go down to the seaside to greet the rising sun. 4–8.

■ Hello! Good-bye!

(by Aliki, Greenwillow $15) With multiple pictures to examine, Aliki takes the concept of hellos and good-byes and explores the many ways we greet each other with and without words. A charming concept book that speaks to the idea that simple words can express a wide range of feelings. Includes child with wheelchair. 4–7.

Videos

■ Playing From the Heart ⭐*2000*

(Globalstage/BBC $27) This is the story of Evelyn Glennie, the world famous percussionist and her determination to become a professional musician despite the fact that she lost her hearing at eight. In a stylish performance by the Polka Children's Theatre in England, this is not your typical TV dramatization. An inspiring story about a young woman with dreams and the family that supported her. Followed with a delightful interview with Ms. Glennie. (98 mins.) Closed captioned. 8 & up. (888) 324-5623.

■ Silent Lotus

(Reading Rainbow $23.95) How people who are deaf communicate is the main thrust of this excellent video from the PBS show "Reading Rainbow." The storybook *Silent Lotus* is about a girl who cannot hear or talk but learns to communicate through dance. Also includes a section on signing. Closed-captioned. (800) 228-4630.

Audios & Equipment

■ Alex, Ben & Co.

(Kid'n Together $9.98 tape/$14.98 CD) Inspired to sing songs to help his son Matthew (who has Down syndrome) learn concepts like naming body parts, the ABCs, counting, and more, Alex Meisel and his brother created this collection of classics and original music with dollops of humor and upbeat flavor. (800) KID-NFUN.

■ Ella Jenkins' Nursery Rhymes

(Smithsonian Folkways $9.50) A good choice for working on memory and language skills. Jenkins sings familiar rhymes and cues kids to repeat and join in. (800) 443-4727.

■ Lynn Kleiner Rhythm Sets *2000* SNAP Award

(Remo $24.95 & up) Many instruments for young kids make noise instead of music and are basically unsafe. Strike up the rhythm band with these kits that are well crafted with sound and safety in mind. **Babies Make Music** includes jingle shaker, wrist jingle and a small drum and scarf (safe enough for toddlers who still mouth their toys). 2 & up. **Kids Make Music** includes a 7" tambourine, triangle, wrist bell (with big jingles) rhythm sticks, and one maraca; **Kids Make Music, Too** has an 8" drum, scarf, finger cymbals, woodblock with mallet, and one egg shaker. 3 & up. (800) 397-9378.

■ Talk Blaster

(Long Hall/Nickelodeon $49.96) This amusing multiringer phone rings with a choice of a moo, honk, bell, laugh, or Nick theme. For kids with hearing disabilities the Talk Blaster gives a visual cue—a power rod that lights up with incoming calls—and has a high/low ringer volume. This touch-tone phone is also hearing-aid compatible. Takes 3 C batteries. (516) 293-6900.

■ 28 Instant Songames *2000* SNAP Award

(Belle Curve $20) Along with this excellent tape of songames (75 min.), there's a 28-page booklet full of playful ideas. Written by two occupational therapists, these games inspire body awareness, self expression, and imagination. (888) 357-5867.

For other electronic equipment, see Audio Chapter.

Resources

Books: Most bookstores will order any books listed here from major publishers. Here are the phone numbers for several smaller publishers they may not regularly deal with: **Turtle Press** (814) 696-2920; **Albert Whitman** (800) 255-7675; **Woodbine House** (800) 843-7323.

Videos: Many of the titles in the Video chapter will be

enjoyed by all children. In fact, many are closed-captioned. **Descriptive Video Service** (DVS), for visually impaired audiences, adds between-the-scenes narrations to TV and videos. For information about DVS television or videos, write to DVS, WGBH, 125 Western Ave., Boston, MA 02134. DVS video titles include "The Lion King" and "Anne of Green Gables."

Additional resources: A number of useful catalogs are targeted directly for the special needs market. Many contain useful adaptation devices. Browsing the catalogs below can help you find some great products as well as ideas for adapting more widely available toys.

- **Achievement Products** (800) 373-4699
- **Lighthouse, Inc.** (800) 829-0500
- **Communication Aids** (414) 352-5678
- **Constructive Playthings** (800) 832-0572
- **Enabling Devices** (800) 832-8697
- **Environments** (800) 342-4453
- **Flaghouse** (800) 221-5185
- **Funtastic Learning Catalog** (800) 722-7375
- **Jesana Ltd.** (800) 443-4728
- **Kapable Kids** (800) 356-1564
- **Lakeshore** (800) 421-5354
- **Toys for Special Children** (800) 832-8697

Online sites of interest
- **www.disabilityresources.org**
- **www.familyvillage.wisc.edu**
- **www.autism-resources.com**
- **www.geocities.com/heartland/plains/8950**
- **www.nichcy.org**
- **www.cec.sped.org/ericec.htm**

Other Publications of Interest

- **Exceptional Parent** magazine is dedicated to parents and caregivers of children with special needs. Published nine times a year. (877) 832-8697.

- **The Oppenheim Toy Portfolio** newsletter includes a feature in every issue on adapting toys, as well as new books and videos of special interest. Published quarterly. Visit our website at www.toyportfolio.com.

Two national organizations provide toy lending-library services and play-centered programs for children with special needs and their families. To locate the center nearest you, contact:

- **National Lekotek Center,** 2100 Ridge Avenue, Evanston, IL 60201, or call (800) 366-PLAY.

- **USA Toy Library Association,** 2530 Crawford Avenue, Suite 111, Evanston, IL 60201, or call (847) 920-9030.

Top-Rated Mail-Order Catalogs/On-Line Sites

For busy families, mail-order catalogs and on-line services are a time-saving way to shop. This list includes companies that feature many of the products we recommend.

Children's Catalogs

These catalogs offer a variety of toys, puzzles, games and outdoor equipment. Some also have selected books, videos and audios.

Back to Basics Toys	(800) 356-5360
Childcraft	(309) 689-3873
Constructive Playthings	(800) 832-0572
FAO Schwarz	(800) 426-8097
Gifts for Grandkids	(888) 472-6354
Grand River Toy Co.	(800) 567-5600
Grandparent's Toy Connection	(800) 472-6312
Hand in Hand	(800) 872-9745
HearthSong	(800) 325-2502
Right Start Catalog	(800) 548-8531
Sensational Beginnings	(800) 444-2147

School Catalogs of Interest

Community Playthings	(800) 777-4244
Environments	(800) 342-4453
Learning Resources	(800) 222-3909

Specialty Catalogs

Chinaberry (books)	(800) 776-2242
Educational Insights	(800) 933-3277
Lego Shop at Home	(860) 763-4011
My Twinn (dolls)	(800) 469-8946
National Geographic	(800) 638-4077
Nature Company	(800) 227-1114
Pleasant Company (dolls)	(800) 845-0005
T.C. Timbers (wooden toys)	(800) 468-6873

Audio, Video, & Music Catalogs

Anyone Can Whistle	(914) 331-7728
Big Kids	(800) 477-7811
Family Planet Music	(800) 985-8894
Music for Little People	(800) 409-2457
Signals WGBH Educational Foundation	(800) 669-9696
Wireless	(800) 669-5959

On-Line Sites

eToys.com
babycenter.com
barnesandnoble.com
rightstart.com
brainplay.com
cdnow.com
kidflix.com
backtobasics.com
musicblvd.com
redrocket.com
amazon.com
smarterkid.com

Safety Guidelines

Many people assume that before toys reach the marketplace they are subjected to the same kind of governmental scrutiny as food and drugs. The fact is that although the government sets specific safety standards, there is no agency like the FDA that pretests and approves or disapproves products.

The toy industry is charged with the responsibility to comply with federal safety standards, but they are self-regulating, which means it's not until there are complaints or reports of accidents that the Consumer Product Safety Commission (CPSC) enters into the picture. The CPSC is the federal government agency charged with policing the toy industry—but not until the products are already on the shelf!

What does all this mean to you as a consumer? Basically it means "Let the buyer beware!" Both small and large manufacturers have run into problems with small parts, lead paint, strangulation hazards and projectile parts.

The CPSC releases useful recall warnings that are posted in most major toy stores, and manufacturers are required to release recalls to the wire services. The CPSC has a hotline if you want further information about a recalled product or want to report one that perhaps should be recalled; you can call (800) 638-CPSC. The CPSC also publishes a safety handbook that you can request.

To protect your child, here is a safety checklist to keep in mind when you're shopping for playthings:

For infants and toddlers:

- **Dolls and stuffed animals.** Select velour, terry or non-fuzzy fabrics. Remove any and all bows, bells and doo-dads that can be swallowed. Stick to dolls with stitched-on features rather than buttons and plastic parts that may be bitten or pulled off.

- **Crib toys.** Toys should never be attached to an infant's crib with any kind of ribbon, string or elastic. Babies and their clothing have been known to get entangled and strangled by such toys.

- **Soft but safe.** Be sure that soft toys such as rattles, squeakers and small dolls are not small enough to be compressed and possibly jammed into a baby's mouth.

- **Heirlooms.** Antique rattles and other treasures often do not meet today's safety standards and can be a choking hazard.

- **Wall hangings and mobiles.** Decorative hangings near or on the crib are interesting for newborns to gaze at but pose a safety hazard once a child can reach out and touch. They need to be removed when an infant is able to touch them.

- **Foam toys.** Avoid foam toys that can be chewed on and swallowed and present a choking hazard.

- **Push-and-straddle toys.** If you're looking for your child's first push toy, make sure it's stable and your child can touch the ground when sitting on the toy.

- **Toy chests.** Old toy chests with lids that can fall do not meet today's safety standards. They can severely injure and even entrap small children. New chests have removable lids or safety latches. We recommend open shelves and containers for safe and easy access instead of the jumble of a deep toy chest.

- **Age labels and small parts.** When you see a toy labeled "Not for children under 3," that's a warning signal! It usually means there are small parts. Such products are unsafe for toddlers—no matter how smart they may be! They are also unsafe for some threes and fours who frequently put things in their mouths.

- **Batteries.** Toys that run on batteries should be designed so that kids cannot get to the batteries.

- **Quality control.** Run your fingers around edges of toys to be sure there are no rough, sharp or splintery, hidden thorns. Check for products that can entrap or pinch little fingers.

For older children:

- **Eye and ear injuries.** Avoid toys with flying projectiles. Many action figures come with a number of small projectile parts that can pose a safety hazard if pointed in the wrong direction and that certainly pose a danger if there are younger children in the house.

- **High-power water guns.** Doctors report many emergency room visits from children with eye and ear abrasions caused by the trendy high-powered water guns.

- **Burns.** Avoid toys that heat up when used. Many of the toy ovens and baking toys become hot enough to cause burns.

- **Safety limits.** Establish clear rules with kids for sports equipment, wheel toys, and chemistry sets.

- **Adult supervision.** Avoid toys labeled "Adult supervision required" if you don't have the time or patience to be there.

For mixed ages:

Families with children of mixed ages need to establish and maintain safety rules about toys with small parts.

- Older children need a place where they can work on projects that younger sibs can't get hurt by or destroy.

- Establishing a work space for the older sib gives your big child the privilege of privacy along with a sense of responsibility.

- Old toys need to be checked from time to time for broken parts, sharp edges, or open seams. Occasionally clearing out the clutter can foster heightened interest in playtime. It also brings old gems to the surface that may have been forgotten.

New Safety Standard for Bike Helmets

We applaud the new federal safety standard that all bike helmets will need to meet by February 1999. Do little kids really need helmets? Look at the data and you decide:

About 900 people, including more than 200 children, are

killed annually in bicycle-related incidents; about 60% of these deaths involve a head injury. Data shows that very young bike riders incur a higher proportion of head injuries! More than 500,000 people are treated annually in U.S. emergency rooms for bicycle-related injuries. Research indicates that a helmet can reduce the risk of head injury by up to 85%!

New helmets must adequately protect the head, and have chin straps strong enough to prevent the helmet from coming off in a crash, collision, or fall. Helmets for children up to age five will cover more of the head to provide added protection to the more fragile areas of a young child's skull. New helmets will carry a label stating that they meet CPSC's new standards, to eliminate confusion about which certification mark to look for on helmets.

CPSC offers the following tips on how to wear a helmet correctly:

- Wear the helmet flat atop your head, not tilted back at an angle.

- Make sure the helmet fits snugly and does not obstruct your field of vision.

- Make sure the chin strap fits securely and that the buckle stays fastened.

Noisy Toys

In addition to all the above criteria, we have always considered the noise level of products. Loud toys are more than just annoying—they can actually pose a risk to your child's hearing. This year, with the generous assistance of Nancy Nadler of the League for the Hard of Hearing, we tested the sound level of many new toys. In doing so, we discovered that many ordinary rattles and squeakers produce sounds measured at 110 to 130 decibels. Yet experts say that sustained exposure, over time, to noise above 85 decibels will cause hearing damage. Because current regulations allow manufacturers to make toys which produce sounds up to 138 decibels at a distance of 25cm, parents must be informed consumers. We suggest that you:

- consider noise levels of toys before purchasing them.

- remember that musical toys, such as electric guitars, drums, and horns, emit sounds as loud as 120 decibels.

- stop and listen before purchasing a toy that makes a noise. If it sounds too loud for your ears, it probably is! Don't buy it.

- be very careful with toys designed to go next to the ear (such as toy phones and toys with headsets).

- remember that noisy floor toys are best listened to at a distance... teach your child not to place his ears on the speaker of the toy.

These guidelines have been prepared in conjunction with the League for the Hard of Hearing.

Subject Index

Brand Name and Title Index

NOTE: Toys and equipment are listed under manufacturer or distributor. The following codes are used for titles of works: (A) = Audio tape; (B) = Book; (C) = Computer software/CD-ROM; (M) = Magazine; (V) = Video.

335